Johann Joseph Ignaz von Döllinger, Margaret Warre

Addresses On Historical And Literary Subjects

In Continuation Of Studies in European History

Johann Joseph Ignaz von Döllinger, Margaret Warre

Addresses On Historical And Literary Subjects
In Continuation Of Studies in European History

ISBN/EAN: 9783744653299

Printed in Europe, USA, Canada, Australia, Japan

Cover: Foto ©ninafisch / pixelio.de

More available books at **www.hansebooks.com**

ADDRESSES
ON
HISTORICAL AND LITERARY SUBJECTS

[*IN CONTINUATION OF 'STUDIES IN EUROPEAN HISTORY'*]

BY

JOHN IGNATIUS von DÖLLINGER, D.D.

LATE PROFESSOR OF ECCLESIASTICAL HISTORY
IN THE UNIVERSITY OF MUNICH

TRANSLATED BY

MARGARET WARRE

TRANSLATOR OF 'STUDIES IN EUROPEAN HISTORY' BY THE SAME AUTHOR

LONDON
JOHN MURRAY, ALBEMARLE STREET
1894

TRANSLATOR'S PREFACE

THE FAVOURABLE RECEPTION given by English readers to the first volume of a translation of Doctor IGNATIUS VON DÖLLINGER's Academical Addresses, a work originally undertaken at the request of the venerable Author, has led the Translator to offer another volume of his Lectures to the English public.

One of these Lectures—'Universities Past and Present'—occurs in the second volume of Addresses published in Germany in 1889; the remaining seven are selected from a volume edited, after the Author's death, by Doctor Max Lossen, and published by C. H. Beck, of Munich, 1891.

In this, as in the previous volume, the Translator is greatly indebted to the kindness of those who have assisted her by careful revision of the translation. More especially she would wish to acknowledge with gratitude the aid freely given amidst other pressing work by the Rev. Dr. Plummer, of Durham University. To Miss Murray also she would wish to express her thanks for her most valuable and ungrudging help in the correction both of the MS. and the proofs.

In the absence of the Translator on the Continent, the task of seeing the work through the press has been entrusted to her brother, the Rev. Dr. Warre, Headmaster of Eton.

The extract in the following pages from the German Editor's Preface, as far as it relates to the last seven Lectures published in this volume, will be read with interest.

EXTRACT FROM THE PREFACE
BY THE
GERMAN EDITOR.

OF the essays which form the third and last volume of the Academical Lectures of Ignatius von Döllinger, only one, on 'The Empire of Charles the Great and his Successors,' has hitherto been printed, in the *Münchner historisches Jahrbuch* for 1865. As this journal has for many years past been out of print, and Dr. Döllinger's treatise, which was expanded from an academical lecture, is much used and quoted at the present day, and has reached an almost classical importance, I do not hesitate to reprint it here.

The rest, which have not been printed before, are taken from the Author's MSS.

Dr. Döllinger did not give the last touches for publication to any of these essays. Only a few of them were completed to the same extent as were the MSS. which he gave me for Vols. 1 and 2 of his Academical Lectures, published in his lifetime. I was, therefore, obliged to supply the deficiencies in them, and must crave the reader's indulgence, especially in Historical matters, in which I do not claim to be an authority, for errors that have been overlooked, or new discoveries that have not been noticed.

Of the Lectures delivered by him on 'The Anniversaries of the Academy,' that on 'Founders of Religions' is the first, and was originally intended to have been included in the first volume of his Academical Studies. But Dr. Döllinger withdrew it, probably on account of criticisms received from different quarters to the effect that an address on the Founders of Religion that left out of consideration the Founder of the Christian Religion was faulty in its conception.

While admitting the justice of this criticism, it seems to me that the Lecture contains such fine and just observations, as, for instance, those on Oliver Cromwell and on the lighter side of the divisions of Christendom, that it ought not to be set aside.

Only a few fragments are extant on the subject of the French Revolution. Their publication will, however, serve to recall a subject which was for many years a favourite one with Dr. Döllinger in his lectures to the University.

The last lecture, on the Literature of the United States of America, bears traces of being a hasty composition written for a particular occasion; but it shows most clearly how Dr. Döllinger, in the midst of his deeper studies of the past, had an intelligent regard for the questions of the day out of which History is being made (*die werdende Geschichte*).

The two Lectures on 'Religious Freedom' and on the 'Destruction of the Templars' had been destined by the Author for the third volume of his Academical Lectures. He hoped to live and labour long enough to collect further material for them, and after the delivery of the lectures he carried his study of the subjects still further, as he often did with much that he has published.

With regard to the 'History of Religious Freedom,' he once said, when I pressed him to allow his lecture in the meantime to be printed in the *Allgemeine Zeitung*, that it was only after the delivery of the lecture that he became fully aware of the difficulty and complexity of the question. He thought at that time of expanding the lecture into a small volume, but only went so far as to make a collection of short fragmentary notices, quotations, and references to sources not available to others. A few of the most complete of these I have put as an Appendix to the lectures. I have handled with reverent care the last work of his life, his address on the 'Destruction of the Order of the Temple.' The subject had occupied his attention for many years—according to his own statement, since the year 1841. In the year 1864 (March 18) he had given a lecture on it to the Historical class of the Academy, and, as it appears, had got it nearly ready for the printers. But he had again put it aside, or partly destroyed it, so that of his older MS. only a few leaves remain. When, on November 15, 1889, he was about to deliver the public lecture on the Templars which had been already announced, his new studies were only partly ready. Those who heard this last address of Dr. Döllinger's observed that he spoke unusually slowly. Professor Cornelius, and, indeed, most of the audience attributed this to bodily fatigue. But from the MS. it appears that his slow delivery was not due to the debility of old age, but that Dr. Döllinger was partly speaking extempore. I mention this as some proof of the vigour of his mind up to the time of his last illness. After his speech he again resumed his work on the subject. A number of fragments remain, and are appended to the lecture which has been compiled from stenographic notes taken at the time of its delivery and compared with his MS. memoranda.

How warm an interest Döllinger took in this his last work may be gathered from the Recollections which a lady, an intimate acquaintance, has lately published. 'If the Lecture,' he said, ' has made so much impression upon you, what will you feel when you come to know the Minutes of the Trial, which I faithfully give word for word. You will shed tears, for I also, in reading them, was profoundly affected.'[1]

MAX LOSSEN.

[1] [To an English friend he once remarked, with regard to his long study of the case against the Templars, 'It is very pleasant work clearing the memory of innocent men from foul and unjust charges.']

CONTENTS

LECTURE	PAGE
I. UNIVERSITIES, PAST AND PRESENT	1
II. FOUNDERS OF RELIGIONS	50
III. THE EMPIRE OF CHARLES THE GREAT AND HIS SUCCESSORS	73
IV. ANAGNI	181
V. THE SUPPRESSION OF THE KNIGHTS TEMPLARS	202
VI. THE HISTORY OF RELIGIOUS FREEDOM	229
VII. VARIOUS ESTIMATES OF THE FRENCH REVOLUTION	255
VIII. THE PART TAKEN BY NORTH AMERICA IN LITERATURE	269
INDEX	295

ACADEMICAL ADDRESSES

I

UNIVERSITIES, PAST AND PRESENT[1]

As the flattering task has devolved upon me of delivering an address in the presence of two princes of our royal family, an assembly of my esteemed colleagues, and a select number of the younger students of our Academy, I have chosen as a fitting subject for my discourse the welfare and growth of the Institution to which we all belong, and the interests by which we are united. I must be allowed to take you to a standpoint high enough to give us a comprehensive survey of nations and of centuries, so that, when we return to the present time and its needs, we may see more clearly the conditions upon which the prosperity of our schools depends, and the laws by which their fate in the future will be determined.

Universities took their rise out of independent institutions formed by eminent teachers and their zealous pupils, without, however, at first being universities in the modern sense of the word. The oldest was the Medical School at Salerno, which was already of some repute in the eleventh century. Next came the School of Law at Bologna, which flourished from the middle of the twelfth century; later, in the thirteenth, that of Padua was an offshoot from Bologna. The University of Naples in 1224 was the first to be founded under royal patronage, and it enjoyed a

[1] An address delivered as Rector of the University of Munich, December 22, 1866.

monopoly, for the inhabitants of the Sicilian kingdom were forbidden to frequent other schools. The law schools of Italy, more particularly that of Bologna, consisted of several independent colleges, separated from one another either by difference in nationality, or in the subjects professed, such as Law, or 'Arts.'

Except at Salerno, it was the study of law, Roman and canonical, which principally prevailed in the schools of Italy. These legal studies were not pursued on a scientific method, or for scientific ends, but solely for practical purposes and for securing tangible results, such as gain, ecclesiastical preferment, or state employment. It was by means of law, ecclesiastical and civil, as then constituted in Bologna, that Italy at that time ruled the world and made all the kingdoms of Europe at once her servants and her debtors. But in these Italian schools it was impossible either then or afterwards for the study of theology, philosophy, or general science, to flourish side by side with that of law. Dante early lamented this, saying that no one would study anything but the Decretals. How gloomy and hopeless, too, sounds the description given by the only real and deep scholar of the day, Roger Bacon! 'The civil law of Italy,' he cries, 'has for forty years been destructive not only to the study of wisdom'—he means philosophy, natural science, and theology—'but even to the Church of God and to all kingdoms.'[2] His ideal was the attainment of widespread comprehensive knowledge, Divine and human, physical and metaphysical, guided and superintended by the Church and fostered by the clergy. But this, he found, was not what men looked for in his time, for the clergy would study nothing but jurisprudence, in order to rise by this ladder to the paradise of high dignities and rich benefices. Hence were it not, Bacon thought, for the two new monastic orders (the Minorites and the Dominicans), who were almost alone in applying themselves to true

[2] *Rogeri Bacon Opera quædam hactenus inedita*, ed. Brewer, Lond. 1859, p. 418.

learning, all would be lost. In Bacon's time, in the year 1262, Bologna counted twenty thousand students, amongst whom were thousands of mature manhood, almost all aiming at nothing else but proficiency in the law—a host, indeed, which united under one banner might have conquered and governed the world.

On this side of the Alps things were very different. From the opening of the thirteenth century, the High School of Paris, called at first '*Studium Generale*,' afterwards '*Universitas*,' protected and favoured originally by the popes, and later by the kings, grew up to be the most powerful and distinguished of all such institutions. Resting upon the permanent foundation of numerous colleges, it was nevertheless poor, not even possessing a house, yet scarcely needing one, since the colleges in which both scholars and teachers lodged increased so much in numbers that at length they contained almost the whole university. Law for a long while, owing to a special papal prohibition, was not taught in Paris. Philosophical and theological studies threw all others into the shade, and a man, after fifteen or sixteen years' study of theology, would, at thirty or forty years of age, be still a student. The most learned scholars in foreign countries, even in their old age, reckoned it an advantage to have belonged, at least for a time, to the University of Paris. Nearly half the great town was transformed into a school. Oxford of to-day may give an approximate idea, although only in local and architectural features, of the ancient High School of Paris. The statement of a Venetian ambassador at the end of the sixteenth century, subsequent therefore to the troubles of the religious wars, that Paris reckoned more students than all the Italian High Schools put together, viz., nearly thirty thousand, appears hardly credible ; but the Procurator-General, Arnauld, also speaks of twenty to thirty thousand, and some estimate may thus be formed of what this body must have been in its palmy days.

But Paris was not a University in the full sense of the term, as now understood in Germany. Throughout the whole of the Middle Ages it had, properly speaking, no Faculty of Law. Notwithstanding this deficiency, the other High Schools of France never succeeded, even remotely, in emulating that of Paris; they never rose, indeed, above the character and secondary importance of 'Special Schools:' Orleans, for instance, Bourges, Cahors, and Angers for the study of law; Montpellier for that of medicine.

In Germany two centuries elapsed before there was even a thought of putting an end to the intellectual inferiority of the nation to the Italians and French by starting a German High School. Every German who desired high culture had to seek it in Paris, Bologna, or Padua. The English had made better provision for their own intellectual needs, for Oxford and Cambridge, which are still the intellectual eyes of the British Empire, were already in great repute from the middle of the thirteenth century. In Germany, however, no electoral prince or emperor cared to put his hand to a work so urgently needed. Neither was there any voice raised among the people to demand it. The century following the death of Frederick II. was full of disturbances, disputes for the throne, and internal wars, and so was decidedly unfavourable to such works of peace. Besides, the spirit of disunion, the principle 'each one for himself,' had already become dominant in Germany. As in the German Church united action was no longer thought of, so in the matter of higher education no strong centre was desired. People were satisfied with the idea that gifts were differently distributed amongst the principal nations of Europe. The *Imperium* had fallen to the share of the Germans; the French had the monopoly of learning. The priesthood had its seat in Rome. By the disposition of Providence, learning had found its home in Paris, and Christendom needed no more than one foundation for each.[3]

[3] Thus in the *Chronica M. Jordanis de Imperio*, p. 306 (in the Syntagma of Schardius): *studio unus locus, videlicet Parisius, sufficit.* The author

Nobody imagined that for Germany to preserve her Empire and its basis—national unity—she ought to possess her own national seat of learning.

At length, in the year 1348, the Emperor Charles IV. founded the High School of Prague, modelled on that of Paris. Even then no unanimous impulse or demand springing from the heart of the nation called into existence this firstling of German education, but rather the mere accidental circumstance that the Emperor Charles had himself studied in Paris, and, in remembrance of his student life in the *Rue du Fouarre*, desired to have a copy of the High School of Paris in his own hereditary kingdom of Bohemia. But the University of Prague, remote from the heart of Germany and divided between Slavs and Germans, was from the first drawn into the storms and vicissitudes of the Hussite controversy, and lost its German element. The University of Vienna, founded in 1365, might have become more important and beneficial to Germany; but scholarship was already on the decline : the right material was wanting for a faculty of Arts, the faculty of Law was so sterile that for a considerable time civil law was not even taught in Vienna, the faculty of Medicine barely existed, and the interest taken by Germany in the university was very slight.

In Germany it was not until the end of the fourteenth and during the course of the fifteenth century that schools of law were founded in the universities. Even then it was foreign, that is to say Roman law, which was imported from Bologna and Padua, for German law was not as yet developed into a national system, and in the new High Schools it was neither represented nor respected. How different

was a Canon of Osnabrück in the time of Rudolf of Habsburg. One sees how in former days theory had to be accommodated to prejudice, even in face of contradictory circumstances. Oxford, whither Germans were not in the habit of going, is ignored, whilst for the sake of palliating the slothful backwardness of the Germans in not possessing a High School of their own, a fundamental principle is assumed, by which only one Studium ought to exist, belonging of right to the French.

would have been the history and condition of Germany if at the time when her first law-books, 'The Mirror of Swabia' and 'The Mirror of Saxony,' appeared, she had possessed even two or three law schools of her own, and had attempted a more complete and systematic digest of law! Then a German code of law, or at least the beginnings of one, might have arisen; and Roman law, in its least attractive and most incomplete form of a mere glossary of the Pandects and Institutes, would not for so long have usurped and maintained the sole authority in the schools. How great might have been the consequent changes in diplomacy, in criminal law, in politics, and in ecclesiastical affairs! Take, for instance, the general use of torture founded on Roman law and the *dicta* of Italian jurists; consider the Roman theory of the arbitrary legislative power of the monarch; the doctrine that every territorial lord was to be regarded in his own country as a Roman emperor; the privileges of the Roman *Fiscus*; the terribly severe laws against high treason, and the Draconian penalties attached to them; finally, the legal axiom that the prince is above the law.

German law itself knew nothing of all these things, and we may say its tendency was antagonistic to them. They were the fruits of Roman jurisprudence, matured in the heads of Italian lawyers of the later Middle Ages—the *later* Middle Ages, be it remarked—for the older and better law schools of Italy were extinct, and corruption had come in with the school of Bartolus and Baldus some time before the study of law was transplanted over the Alps into the German High Schools.

German Universities long retained the character of artificial institutions imported from foreign lands. They exercised no educational influence upon the mind of the nation. Their theologians and canonists had indeed the opportunity of putting themselves forward and of expressing their views at the great reforming Councils of the fifteenth century. The fact that learned men, gathered from all the capitals of Europe to these councils, were thus associated for years together, and consequently interchanging ideas and information, inevitably reacted upon and infused fresh vigour into the High Schools. Yet, owing to the preponderance of the theological faculty upon the northern side of the Alps, the prosperity of the schools depended upon the condition of the church; and as that was at that time in a deplorable state of confusion, the defeat which the councils suffered when abandoned by the princes was a defeat for the High Schools as well, and was felt by their members as such. With few exceptions, the names of the German professors of the fifteenth century have sunk into oblivion; no service of permanent value, and no book of national importance, can be attributed to them. The only German philosopher, Nicholas of Cusa, the only teacher of political law, Peter of Andlau, and all the historians of the time, were strangers to the universities. Only Geiler of Kaisersberg and Sebastian Brand belonged for a short time to a High School.

Yet, after the fourteenth century a rivalry in the founding of Universities had sprung up. To the five that existed at the beginning of the fifteenth century, nine had been added by the year 1500, most of them with restricted means and scanty endowments. Even separate towns like Erfurt wanted to possess their own university. Not one of the fourteen rose even to the low standard of the science of that day. Thus Tübingen and Leipzic had first only two professors of medicine, of whom, in Tübingen, one had a salary of one hundred, and the other of sixty, gulden. In those days the endowment of a university was facilitated by the ease with which the gift of some of the prebendal stalls attached to the numerous and generally well endowed ecclesiastical institutions could be bestowed upon the professors. As almost all these educational bodies were formed upon the pattern of Prague, and so of Paris, theology, in its scholastic form, preponderated, and the faculty of Arts, also allied to scholasticism, was usually subordinate to the theological faculty. As a rule, the chancellor of the university was a church dignitary, yet these schools were never looked upon as purely ecclesiastical institutions, nor did the graduate tutors require a licence from the State to teach what they pleased. These institutions were free States within the State. Libraries or museums scarcely existed. Migrations of entire universities, in consequence of war, sickness, or internal disagreements, were as easy as they were frequent.

One observation here occurs.

How plainly the character of the three great nations and their consequent development are reflected by this history of their universities! France—which for centuries has consistently and irresistibly progressed towards a more rigid and narrow system of centralisation; a nation of thirty-six millions, with only a single city in which an educated Frenchman would wish to live, a city which as the centre of attraction absorbs all national life—France has never possessed more than one university, and that in Paris. The others were only ' Special Schools.' And France, unable since the Revolution to endure any independence in her public bodies, whether municipal or educational, has demolished her ancient university, and has set up in its stead a complex machinery of administration, embracing and directing the whole scheme of instruction for the country, with officials who have no right of independent action, but are tools in the hands of the government of the day. The French university has now nothing in common with German and English universities but the name.

England, on the contrary, keeping in view throughout her whole history the double aim of practical excellence and political freedom, and averse to all centralisation, has possessed from the outset two great Universities, two learned bodies, which have preserved their republican constitution and independence to the present day. One, by itself enjoying a monopoly, would have become too exclusive, and have ended by falling asleep upon the pillow of its privileges and ancient honours. As it is, each has served to criticise and incite the other, while each has followed one of the two characteristic tendencies of the English mind; thus it is that Oxford has devoted herself to theology and classical learning, and Cambridge to mathematics and the more practical objects of study.

Germany—where, towards the close of the Middle Ages, individualism had superseded or absorbed every other tendency, and where the two great institutions and centres of unity, the empire and the church, had gradually relaxed their hold—became the mother of numerous universities; but many of them were but sickly and stunted children. Each town of second or third rank, each little territory smaller than an English county, must needs possess its own little school, a pocket edition of a university in duodecimo form for private use, the result being that the two universities, Erfurt and Duisburg, had in 1805 only twenty-one students each, and at Erfurt there were twice as many professors as students. Foundations on a larger scale arose later, after larger States had been formed.

With the sixteenth century a new order of things began, and the German universities rose to unexpected power and importance. The humanists, or philologists, and teachers of the ancient classics began to make way, and wherever they were not worsted in the conflict which at once arose between them and the representatives of scholasticism, they inevitably broke down the barriers and bulwarks behind which the two faculties of Arts—viz., grammar and philosophy — sheltered their incapacity and poverty of thought. Then, whilst here and there, and with variable results, the universities were still engaged in these little wars, there burst forth that memorable religious strife which, kindled by the youngest of the schools, increased into an overwhelming storm and swept everything before it. From the Northern Sea to the Alps the German nation was troubled to its innermost depths by this as by no other movement before or since, and finally was cleft for centuries into two almost equal halves. It was inevitable that the new movement should lay hold of the German universities, and that they should be convulsed, and in the end transformed, by it. They were the arsenals where weapons were forged for the strife; often, also, the battlefields where the victory or defeat of one or the other doctrine was decided. And as theological questions and ecclesiastical interests were destined for a long time to supersede and overpower everything else, the prosperity of the High Schools now more than ever depended upon the character and quality of the theological faculties. But the reputation and prominence of these were dearly bought; for the result was that the German universities became for the first time *instrumenta dominationis*, and princes at once assumed the right to appoint and eject at their pleasure first the theological, and then other professors. The ease with which the religion of a whole country could be changed by the appointment or removal of three or four professors was the origin of the territorial system, which had for its fundamental principle the axiom that the prince had the right to decide the religion of the country. Reformation and counter-reformation followed, and the combined operation of the two giant forces, the principles of Roman law and the religious supremacy of princes, had disastrous effects on the German Empire, on the freedom of the nation, and on the authority of the old feudal estates, both Catholic and Protestant. The picture is one far too painful to paint here, and fortunately not necessary to my subject.

In quarters where the Reformation triumphed new schools quickly arose, such as those of Marburg, Königsberg, Jena, Helmstädt, Altorf, destined to become hotbeds of Protestant theology and those principles of Roman law which are most favourable to princely despotism. Thus it is reported of Helmstädt that the States of the country regarded the ducal university as nothing more than a body of men paid to advocate princely claims, and hated it accordingly.[1] As Church and State were united in the person of the prince, the legal and political object of a High School did not interfere with its ecclesiastical character. In the Wittenberg statutes of 1595 it was enacted that the faculty of Philosophy must belong to the church. Convocations for disputation and for conferring degrees in all faculties were held in the churches even after the beginning of the eighteenth century, and it was customary for all professors and doctors to take the oath on the sacred books.

It was fortunate for Germany that in the seventeenth century, the gloomiest of her history, her schools did not perish, but survived the Thirty Years' War.

Yet so unsatisfactory was their condition in respect both of morals and learning, particularly during the first decades of the century, that Germans willingly went abroad in search of better intellectual training, or to escape the tyranny of the fagging system, which amongst the wild students had become intolerable. Lawyers turned to the law schools of France, medical students to Italy—for Italy, owing to her schools of Padua and Pisa, and to the influence of men like Telesio, Baglivi, Fabrizio, Cardano, and Galileo, had become once again, though only for a short period, the instructress of Europe in philosophy and natural science.

At the close of the great war, in the year of the peace of Westphalia (1648), Valentine Andrea penned these sad words, which read almost like an epitaph on the intellect of Germany: 'I have long known, by my own experience, that there is nothing more profane than our religion, nothing more unwholesome than our medicine, nothing more unjust than our justice.'[5]

The latter days of the century exhibit a picture equally sad. When Germany was deeply sunk in political weakness and shame, when foreign arrogance and foreign

[1] Henke, *Georg Calixtus und seine Zeit*, i. p. 48.
[5] From a letter in Moser's *Patriotisches Archiv*, vi. 348.

avarice had gradually dismembered the feeble and paralysed body of the empire, when the Palatinate had been laid waste, and Heidelberg destroyed by fire, a death-like calm settled down upon our universities. Not a note of patriotic indignation was heard; not a voice was raised to wake the nation from its lethargy. Professors and students alike seemed wholly resigned and ready to submit to anything with dull indifference. The Catholic foundations—many of which, as consisting only of one or two faculties, did not deserve even the name of 'university'—vegetated rather than possessed conscious life upon the meagre diet and in the scanty breathing space allotted to them. The Protestant educational bodies were overpowered by theological interests and controversies, and their history is almost exclusively a history of the strife between Lutheran orthodoxy on the one side, and Calvinism, eclecticism, and pietism on the other. Helmstädt formed a solitary exception. There classical learning was always promoted, and there laboured Hermann Conring, a man unrivalled in his day for diversity of talent—a professor of medicine, but at the same time eminent as a law student, a theologian, and an historian. His application of the historical method to German law and politics marks him as the prophet and pioneer of a scientific system of teaching, for the brilliant results of which, in later days, the German schools were indebted to him.

Until nearly the end of the seventeenth century, lectures in all faculties were delivered in Latin; German was excluded from the lecture rooms, although, according to Leibnitz, it is better suited than any other to be the language of philosophy and learning, since it 'takes nothing for granted and allows no room for groundless fancies.' Thus we Germans had taken centuries to deliberate before actually founding a university of our own, and even then had imported jurisprudence, philosophy, and natural science from Italy. Hence teachers in Germany were neither able nor willing to impart to others in any language but Latin what they themselves had learnt in that tongue. At length Thomasius at Halle, and Budæous at Jena, began almost simultaneously to make use of the German language in their colleges. Yet the custom of lecturing in Latin was upheld with extraordinary tenacity, and a very long time elapsed before German came into general use. For nothing is easier or more welcome to inferior and narrow-minded teachers, who can work only in a groove, than the use of a dead language like the Latin. Under the cloak of the old idioms, even in their impoverished modern form, confusion of ideas and absence of thought are easily concealed; platitudes which would be insufferable in German sound more respectable in Latin.

But no one can think except in his mother-tongue, and a dead language must always be foreign to our innermost thoughts and feelings: thus the double task was laid upon our youth of mentally turning the Latin into German, and then of understanding the translation. And this exercise was all the more futile, because in the case of abstract ideas German and Latin are not equivalent, and the most significant German words can with difficulty, and only by a paraphrase, be rendered into Latin. It is thus quite easy to understand that so long as this supremacy of Latin and its exclusive use in teaching continued in the High Schools, learning would inevitably first stagnate and then begin to retrograde, through being out of touch with the national life and all outside movement.

At the end of the seventeenth, and far into the following century, German universities in general were held in little esteem, and the princes were often the first to set the example of contempt for them. It is hardly possible for any public body to be made to suffer more acutely from scornful and contemptuous treatment than did Frankfort-on-the-Oder from the behaviour of King Frederick William I., or Halle from that of his son.[6] They were looked upon

---

[6] Comp. Stenzel's *Geschichte von Preussen*, iii. 504, and Tholuck's *Vermischte Schriften*, ii. 36.

and treated as the worn-out, though still indispensable, survivals of an earlier time, refuges of intellectual narrowness and literary pedantry quite useless for all practical purposes. Whilst the upper classes tended more and more to become French in customs and language—so that a prince, like the Landgrave Ernest of Hessen Rheinfels, and a scholar, such as Leibnitz, actually corresponded with each other for years in French—Thomasius, who had the restoration of the mother-tongue to its rights very near at heart, found it necessary to set his pupils in Halle exercises in German composition. Most of them, he says, could not even write a short German sentence or letter correctly. 'Whoever tries to restore the use of German is looked upon as a lunatic,' wrote Gabriel Wagner a few years earlier; the exclusive employment of foreign languages, especially for philosophical subjects, appeared to him an insufferable evil. It is significant of the utter disrepute into which the universities had fallen that Leibnitz, the greatest German scholar of his day, in his plans and proposals for the promotion of learning, made no allusion to the universities; he seems to have thought that they had sunk so low as to make any reformation hopeless.

From 1690 until about 1730 Halle took the lead amongst German High Schools, and could boast of teachers in all the faculties whose names are connected with the remembrance of real intellectual progress. In theology, philosophy, and legal science, thoughts and aims discouraged and suppressed in other schools here found refuge and free development; the institutions of Franke attracted the sympathetic attention of all Germany.

This freedom was crippled when the philosopher Wolf was expelled and Spangenberg banished, after which time the reputation and influence of Halle sank; and about 1734 the wealthier school of Göttingen came to the front, under the favour of British patronage and the guidance of a prudent statesman. Göttingen was the first school founded with the definite purpose of promoting intellectual reform in Germany. The names of Mosheim, Böhmer, Gessner, Haller, and after them of Pütter, Schlözer, Michaelis, Heyne, Lichtenberg, the freedom in teaching, the absence of censorship, the increasing number of educational books compiled by her professors and introduced into other universities, combined to secure to Göttingen, for about half a century, the first rank among the High Schools of Germany.

In one department especially, that of history, the influence exercised by Göttingen on the German mind was of great importance. From the middle of the sixteenth century historical lectures had, it is true, been delivered in other German universities, at least in the north; but they had taken the form of historical tales, selected for their application to particular purposes, rather than of history strictly so called, and the teacher was rightly called *professor historiarum*. Profane history served only as a background and illustration of church history; and church history was freely employed in the sectarian controversies which at the time were matters of the greatest importance in the eyes of Germans. Such parts of German and Italian history as dealt with questions of public and constitutional law were used as a storehouse or arsenal by political teachers; but before the beginning of the nineteenth century there was no tolerable textbook of universal history—the first was by Cellarius in Halle—nor before Köhler and Struve was there any readable history of Germany. Besides Mascov of Leipzic it is to such scholars of Göttingen as Pütter, Gatterer, Schlözer, and Spittler that we owe the dawn of a new era in German historical research. Looking back after the perusal of such a work as Spittler's 'History of the European States,' which appeared in 1794, to works produced before 1750, it must be acknowledged that great progress had been made in those forty years; and it is a hopeful sign for the future of our German schools that such rich fruits of German research and German ingenuity were matured by them.

Suddenly, and quite unexpectedly, during the last decades of the century, Königsberg, the most remote of German schools, became a centre of attraction to all Germany as the possessor of a single scholar, Kant, the great reformer of philosophy. Soon there was scarcely a university where the doctrines of the great thinker of Königsberg were not taught by one of his pupils or admirers. Scarcely had Kant passed away when Jena, long known as the school of able and strictly dogmatic orthodox theologians, became, under Fichte and Schelling, the seat of that philosophic movement which absorbed for a time the best powers of German intellect, and forced all other studies into the background. This so-called natural philosophy, the outcome of the earlier system of Schelling, was a premature attempt to formulate, by the help of universal logical conceptions translated into terms of physical science which was just then in a transitional state, a complete system of the science and course of Nature, such as Fichte had constructed for history; and the favour with which it was received by the universities threatened for the time to imperil the progress of sober empirical research. But the unexpected discoveries made in physics and chemistry by foreign students of natural science, who refused to shelter themselves within an edifice so hastily raised and of such frail materials, exposed the untrustworthiness of the system, and the attempt to account for natural phenomena by such a method had to be abandoned—an example of the innate power of science to correct her own mistakes in the course of time.

The eighteenth century ended and the new century began with political storms, revolutions, and changes of frontier, one consequence of which, amongst others, was the disappearance of a considerable number of German universities—Helmstädt, Rinteln, Frankfort-on-the-Oder, Duisburg, Wittenberg, Erfurt, Mayence, Bamberg, Cologne, Paderborn, Munster, Dillingen, Salzburg—all perished; some in the course of nature, as the result of a long process of decay, some by summary suppression, averted in some cases by amalgamation with other schools. These institutions were, upon the whole, neither missed nor regretted. Most of them had for a long time dragged on a miserable shadowy existence, with only two or three faculties, and without a single scholar of general repute to boast of. At many of them life was restricted to such a modest routine of work that their existence had scarcely been heard of beyond the walls of their own town. The destruction of the school at Mayence, founded by the elector a few years previously and reckoning six hundred students in the year 1787, was the only case which was felt to be a calamity.

An institution, however, destined from its infancy to outshine all others, and to exemplify to the fullest extent all the best capabilities of Germany in the matter of higher education, was at that very time on the eve of being founded. Immediately after the peace of Tilsit, when Prussia had suffered the loss of half her population as well as of half her revenue, and had been reduced to a third-rate power, the king and his counsellors had resolved to found a university in the capital. It was to be combined with the already existing Academy of Science. The regeneration of Prussia could not fail, it was believed; it began from the foundation of this magnificent institution. At first it was almost decided to break with old university traditions; even the distinction of the faculties was to be abandoned, and a school of higher scientific learning organized upon totally new lines. It is remarkable that such a man as Fichte, of a thoroughly German cast of mind and thoroughly imbued by French revolutionary ideas, should have advised the total overthrow of the old, and the organization of a new, institution, planned upon the Platonic conception of a State governed by philosophers, his scheme involving the entire suppression of individuality and freedom both in teachers and taught, and the establishment of a kind of literary monasticism of a thoroughly despotic form.[7]

But at this juncture William v. Humboldt, statesman and scholar, took the matter in hand, and stamped the infant foundation with the impress of his own powerful and versatile mind. It was not his aim to form a centre of Prussian patriotism; indeed, had all the appeals made to other lands been successful, two-thirds at least of the teachers would have been foreigners. This was the first instance since the Reformation of a High School founded in Germany on purely unsectarian principles, simply with a view to the spread of secular education and sound learning. Each of the eminent men under whose guidance the school was started—Frederick Augustus Wolf, Fichte, Savigny, Schleiermacher, Reil—represented only the school of thought or teaching created or developed by himself. The result surpassed all expectation. In 1815, the fifth year after its foundation, the University of Berlin reckoned 56 teachers; in the year 1860 there were altogether 170, i.e. 97 professors, 66 private tutors, and 7 lecturers. Thus within forty-five years the strength of the tutorial staff had been tripled. In the year 1835 the number of students was 2,000; it is now 2,180.

The result of this growth, as then seen in Prussia, would hardly have been possible in any country outside Germany. The vast superiority of the metropolitan school and the precedence naturally granted to it by the Government, far from repressing the growth of others in the country, or sapping their vitality, exercised a beneficial and invigorating influence upon them. Halle rose to fresh eminence, and became the favourite school of theological students, numbering at one time eight hundred. The theological faculty in that place was the best specimen, upon the whole, of Protestant theology at that time, and it still continues to be more influential and popular than any

[7] For details see Köpke, *Die Gründung der Universität zu Berlin*, 1860, p. 47 ff.

other in Germany. Breslau, since the time of its fusion with Frankfort-on-the-Oder, although possessing amongst its professors no stars of the first magnitude, has maintained its position in the front rank of such institutions, and has sent forth many able scholars into the world. Bonn, founded in the year 1818, has always had a high reputation, and owes its continued prosperity as well to its favourable situation on the banks of the Rhine, as to its excellent school of philology and the influence of Niebuhr's great reputation.

You will not expect me on this occasion to expatiate upon the services and advantages of our own great High School, which has now been dominant here for forty years. Thanks to the prudent foresight of the kings whose names it bears, Ludwig and Maximilian II., it has grown during these four decades into a stately tree, fast rooted in the soil of the fatherland, whose spreading boughs are laden with fruit. May it have power to defy all coming storms!

The venerable University of Vienna, the first, in point of age, of all German schools, has been at last regenerated by long-needed reforms that have widened and deepened its aims, and relieved it from oppressive burdens. About the middle of the last century this university attained in Germany, and even in Europe, to a reputation that it had never before enjoyed, chiefly on account of the rare excellence of its medical school. The names of Van Swieten, de Haen, and Stoll, who were attracted thither from foreign countries, were held in the highest esteem. But the successors of these men did not equal them in ability; the other faculties were weak and scantily represented, and owing to these causes, combined with severe censorship and a mass of coercive and restrictive regulations, the University of Vienna and all her Austrian sisters were brought into a most miserable condition by the first half of the present century. 'The universities of Austria,' I am quoting from the work of an Austrian scholar, 'sank to the level of special schools for Government officials and for lawyers and medical men. True learning was cultivated only exceptionally, and found little support from the teachers.' Under the enlightened guidance of Count Thun a work of revival has now been successfully carried out; able men have been invited from other countries, of whom Munich has furnished her contingent, and the public schools (*Gymnasien*), which had fallen very low in Austria, have also been greatly improved. The University of Vienna at the present day may be regarded as the worthy centre and principal representative of scholarship in the empire. Her reputation and usefulness would doubtless be enhanced if political dangers and difficulties, and a constant sense of standing upon hollow and insecure ground, did not act as a hindrance to intellectual progress.

On comparing the present with the past, it is easy to see how great has been the advance made by Germany in the matter of university education. In the seventeenth and beginning of the eighteenth centuries our schools fell far short of the needs of the nation. Consequently their reputation and influence were but slight; some people, indeed, regarded them as a passing, although for the time a necessary, evil. The different branches of study were disconnected, and still trammelled by traditional scholastic forms; men were contented with the training required for the ordinary purposes of trade, or at best with the education indispensable for the useful professions. Learning was looked upon as something to be achieved by many years of mechanical, ant-like industry in collecting and mastering facts, and the measure of scholarship was the amount of knowledge amassed in this way. Such literary work as went beyond the narrow sphere of the specialist, and might have appealed to public interest and been valued by the nation, was not produced by the professors. Almost every university was converted into an arena for the contests of various parties—contests carried on very seldom to the advantage of learning, and frequently with other than intellectual weapons. Professional quarrels had become proverbial. Speaking of one faculty—viz., that of law—Niebuhr remarked that it was only the rise of philology that rescued it from two centuries of barbarism.[8] We might be tempted to speak also of two centuries of barbarism in connexion with medicine, philosophy, physics, and chemistry.

Turning now to consider the honourable position held at the present day by our German universities, we may well affirm that they are centres of growth and guidance for all the better and higher instincts of German intellectual life. If we recall the shortness of the period—about fifty years—during which this transformation has been accomplished, and such wonderful fertility in all departments of knowledge has been developed, we are bound to acknowledge that a parallel to it could hardly be found in history.

All great and lasting additions to our knowledge have been won by men who combined in themselves proficiency in a variety of study. I will instance three names belonging to different periods: Scaliger, Leibnitz, Haller. The last of these names reminds us that the bearer of it, like a second Aristotle, was master of all the learning of his time. Leibnitz, with a versatility since unrivalled, was the first scholar in whom the spirit and clear insight of antiquity were combined with the expansiveness and wider knowledge of modern times, and in whom boldness and originality in research were united in a remarkable degree. Finally, the distinguished name of Scaliger marked a new era, because such was the comprehensiveness of his mind that he acquired an equally thorough knowledge of theology and history, of grammar and the exact sciences, of the Bible and the classics. In our own days the study of both theology and law has been purified, widened, and deepened through being combined with that of philology and history, whilst our knowledge of medicine has been extended by pressing into its service every branch of physical science, so as to

Letter to v. Schuckmann, given by Köpke, p. 229.

comprise the study of mankind—of man as a whole, and of his environment in nature, organic and inorganic. Thus these sciences have gained as much in richness of material as in certainty of method, and therefore in truth. They have become torches, illuminating the world with a brighter and purer flame. It is now easier to eliminate unsound elements, to discover and to get rid of errors, than it used to be. Yet since the cultivation of each science is connected by a thousand links with the development and prosperity of the rest, and since each is organically connected with the others, it follows that if one member suffers, all must suffer; and however paradoxical it may sound to many ears, it is none the less true that if one science— physics or chemistry, for example—falls into decay, theology and legal science must also decline. The same holds good of national life. If but a single branch of the tree of knowledge is blighted, the whole is affected.

It is here that the true worth of the German universities, and of their unique and inimitable characteristics, becomes evident. In them every branch of learning and of science is cultivated to the best advantage. But this can only be done by the exclusion of unsystematic, fragmentary knowledge and pointless methods of disconnected study. Otherwise the internal necessity, the casual connexion of isolated facts or theories, and their position as members of one organic whole, cannot be made clear.

In a university, the faculties and sciences ought to watch over and supplement one another. This is, so to speak, automatic, where the teachers continually keep sight of the mutual interdependence of all departments of knowledge, and do not forget that each science has a pressing interest in making use of the rest, and that it cannot escape from their influence, or afford to disregard their opposition; for each is bound to recognise its membership in the great body of culture and knowledge. The teacher should endeavour to place clearly before his pupil the connexion of each subject with all the rest, of each part in a subject with the whole, and of each fact with those before and after it, so that as each point in the subject is brought forward, it may be understood in all its bearings. The teacher will attain this object if he goes to work not merely by set rules, but by the historical method, and tracing the gradual growth of his subject through various epochs of development up to its present stage.

The intellectual bond which unites the members of a university consists not merely in a community of aims and interests, but in the interchange of benefits, and in the incitement to constantly renewed activity and ever-extended advancing research, which the individual receives from the whole body. And not only the living, but those also who have passed away, contribute, by the remembrance of their labours, their merits and their writings, towards the emulation thus kindled. For such an association as a university draws life and nutriment from its past—happy, indeed, if the sins and follies of former times, as yet perchance not fully recognised or overcome, do not disturb and confuse the present, and thus embitter the minds of the rising generation.

Among the advantages derived by scholars from intercourse in an academical community, I do not hesitate to place the modesty that shows itself in a correct estimate of their own work, and in a moderating self-restriction. For the isolated scholar, carrying on his researches independently and in silent seclusion, is far too prone to overrate the value of his own department of study, whether the subject be of universal interest or confined to the innermost life of the mental microcosm. He easily yields to the temptation to substitute the subordinate for the dominant, to consider his special subject the centre of all other knowledge, with the double result, first, that he is incapable of constructing and developing his particular science with due regard to its appropriate relation to the whole, and, by failing to recognise its correct position, is led into serious errors as to its bounds and powers; secondly, that as the priest of his own idol, he miscalculates his personal merits and importance, grows confirmed in one-sided views, and imagines himself to be misunderstood and neglected. Now against such a misfortune our universities are a most excellent preservative. Every one finds his proper level, and is constantly reminded that he is but one member of a great body, and, at the best, can grasp but a fragment of truth, and furnish but a small contribution towards the solution of the great problems of science.

It may be well to inquire here into the causes that have made Germany in the present day the classic land of universities, although she had been the last of the great Powers to found them and the slowest to profit by them, and what it is that has enabled her to bring them to such scientific completeness and excellence, so that she not only far surpasses other countries, but stands almost alone in having realised the true ideal of a university.

In *France*, which in the Middle Ages possessed the most complete university, the model for all others, the institution is now utterly extinct. It has been truly remarked that had not the first Napoleon conceived the idea of establishing his imperial university—that is to say, his great educational machine—the very name of 'university' would long since have perished in France.[9] In France there are now only special schools—viz. eight of law, five of medicine, eight schools or faculties *des sciences*, *i.e.* of the exact sciences (mathematics and natural sciences), and four faculties *des lettres* (philosophy, philology, history, and literature). In two cities, Paris and Strasburg, all the faculties are represented, but they are quite independent and disconnected. The first and most distinguished learned foundation in France at the present day is the 'Collège de France,' founded by Francis I., which in 1789 possessed nineteen professorships for languages, literature,

[9] Cournot, *Des Institutions d'Instruction Publique en France.* Paris, 1864, p. 296.

mathematics, natural science and medicine, canonical and common law, and a chair, besides, for the combined study of history and morals. Since the Revolution this number has been increased to thirty, and it is worthy of notice that amongst the additions is included a professorship of the Slav languages and literature—one seldom found in Germany, but which ought certainly not to be omitted in a High School of the first rank. The one chair of history and morals still remains in its undefined generality, and when we see that medicine is represented at the Collège de France by only one professorship, while the neighbouring independent medical school has twenty-six and the Sorbonne can boast of a similar number, it must be admitted that the organization and co-ordination of the higher schools of Paris have been ruled by accident and personal influence, rather than by any fixed system.

The two *English* universities have, on the contrary, entirely preserved their original character as great, influential, and independent self-governing bodies. But they differ widely from universities, as we understand the term. I should describe them as continuations of the public schools (*Gymnasien*) combined with clerical colleges and the study of theology. Even the foundation of new professorships, a few years ago, has made no essential alteration in their hereditary characteristics. The progressive method of instruction adopted in Germany, by which the entire range of a subject is gone through in a series of daily lectures, has hitherto found no place in England. Six to ten lectures in the course of the whole year, suited to the capacities of a mixed audience, are considered by the professors as a sufficient fulfilment of their task. They do not, like German teachers, begin at the central point of a subject, and then work it out to its full extent, so as to master it as a whole, but content themselves with taking a bird's-eye, superficial view, and throwing a vivid light upon some particular parts of it.[1]

[1] As, for example, Thomas Arnold, whose loss was so much regretted in

The English universities are not adapted for the training of public servants, lawyers, doctors, or professors of natural science; their office is, by the study of classics and mathematics, with that of logic and moral philosophy, and by a college training, to turn out for the benefit of the State and of society the cultivated and independent *gentleman*, and to replenish the ranks of the clergy of the Established Church with men who have received a classical and literary, rather than a theological, education.[2]

In saying this it is not my intention to depreciate the English universities. I believe them to be excellent of their kind, and well fitted to do the work required of them by the nation. I only wish to point out that they are something quite different from institutions bearing the same name in Germany, that they stand in closer relation to the universities of the Middle Ages, and have retained more of their character. The German universities correspond far better than the English to the ideal of what ought to be aimed at and realised in the nineteenth century. At the same time I do not hesitate to acknowledge, as the result of my observations on the spot, that the colleges of Oxford and of Cambridge, now renovated and reformed, and taking the place of the old collegiate halls (*Bursen*) which in Germany have unfortunately ceased to exist, aroused in me, in many respects, a sensation of longing and envy. I could see clearly how in them instruction grew into conviction, and how the result showed itself not merely in the advancement of learning, but in elevation of mind and strengthening of character. Indeed, I have often asked myself why we Germans have so entirely neglected a

England, completed at Oxford a course on modern history in nine lectures.

[2] I cannot venture to place the theological learning acquired at an English university higher than I do in these words, and I call to witness Voigt's opinion that an English theological student who has gone through the regular course at Oxford or Cambridge does not fundamentally differ from the Prussian student of philology.—*Mittheilungen über das Unterrichtswesen Englands und Schottlands*, 1857, p. 55.

system recommended equally by reason and experience, which preserves thousands of parents from sleepless nights of sorrow and anxiety, and saves countless young men from ruin or from lifelong remorse. Thanks to our own large-hearted and philanthropic King, Maximilian II., this want has been recognised in Bavaria, and an example has been set of what ought to be done in this direction.

The four *Scotch* universities of Edinburgh, St. Andrews, Glasgow, and Aberdeen, stand upon a lower level than those of England. As a matter of fact, nothing else could be expected in a country where, by the confession of her own scholars, the pursuit of learning for its own sake, rather than for practical purposes, is treated as ridiculous. We are told by Professor Blackie, of Edinburgh, that ' in the Scotch universities learning at the present moment is at the lowest possible ebb.'[3] History, for instance, is virtually unknown. Edinburgh possesses, indeed, a medical school famous in the British Isles, but Scotchmen whose names have attained to eminence in literature have seldom had any connection with the universities.

In the *United States of America*, also, universities, in the true sense of the word, in its historical development, are not to be found. The institutions which bear the name, and which even pretend to the right of creating Doctors of Law and of Theology, hold a position midway between the German *gymnasium* and the philosophical faculties of a

---

[3] Blackie, *On the Advancement of Learning in Scotland.* Edinburgh, 1855, p. 10. ' I make the broad assertion, that Scotland at the present moment is in no sense of the word a learned country; specially that in our universities learning is at the lowest possible ebb.' As Blackie had compared the productions of Scotland with those of Germany entirely to the disadvantage of the former, Kelland, the Professor of Mathematics, remarked, in a speech directed against Blackie, that the Scotch confined themselves to studies in immediate connection with life, whereas for the Germans the subterranean vaults of a dead language, or the sources of the moss-grown avenues of conflicting history—studies often as barren as the shadow of the upas tree—possessed an endless charm. Meanwhile an Association for the extension of Scottish universities has been formed, but we have no report of its proceedings.

German university. It is well known that there does not exist, either in England or America, a scientific code of law; and theology adapts itself to the doctrinal notions of any one of the thirty or forty sects which combine to support the school.

The one-and-twenty universities of *Italy* resemble German ones at least superficially, except that in general they have no theological faculties, as in Italy the clergy are educated exclusively in episcopal seminaries, and are consequently separated by a wide gulf from the educated classes, and estranged from their modes of thought. Thus it happens that in comparing the higher schools of America with those of Italy, a curious contrast presents itself. In the country which is historically the youngest, and whose foundations are things of yesterday, theology enjoys such high consideration that these schools were founded especially for its sake and for the training of Christian preachers, and hence the majority of them were originated by the great religious bodies, not by the towns and provinces. In that land, on the contrary, which is the ancient home of civilisation and education, and was the teacher at one time of all cultured nations, the science of theology is so despised as not to be even nominally represented at most of the universities. The clergy—more numerous, in comparison with the population, than in any other European country—are perfectly content with the elementary instruction received in the 217 seminaries, and, with few exceptions, have no aspirations after higher knowledge. Moreover, this condition of things has existed not merely for the last twenty years, but for a long time past. If, in the seventeenth century, such a man as Noris had not taught for a time at the University of Pisa, it would be difficult to name a single really distinguished and learned theologian belonging to an Italian university. Recent events in Italy, caused chiefly by the general hatred and contempt of the upper and middle class laity for the clergy, must be incomprehensible to any one who ignores this state of things.[4]

The corrupt state of the Italian universities, far too numerous for the needs of the country, and the urgent necessity for thorough reorganization, have lately been candidly acknowledged by their own Professor Bonghi, who writes with full knowledge of the subject. Reform, meanwhile, is rendered all the more difficult by the pitiable condition of the public schools.

The universities of *Spain* fell long ago, like so many elsewhere, into a state of the deepest corruption. A century ago they were already regarded by statesmen and scholars as strongholds of every kind of abuse. Their revenues have been squandered in revolutions and civil wars; their buildings are in ruins. The students still form, according to the account of a German eye-witness, the class from which servants are chosen, and the same writer adds[5] that the old evils still remain, concealed under a French dress, much as everything in Spain at the present day is entirely under the influence of French ideas and customs.

The history of the *Czechs* and the *Poles* sufficiently proves that the Slav nations and states are dependent upon German assistance for the foundation and preservation of their universities.

Russia has a thoroughly German school at Dorpat, and the other six universities of the Russian Empire, the most recent of which was founded at Odessa in 1865, are organized upon German models and have a large pro-

[4] Note the forcible declaration recently made by Massimo d'Azeglio, the man above all others who far surpassed his contemporaries and fellow-countrymen in his correct, impartial, and far-sighted appreciation of the present situation in Italy. In his *Questioni Urgenti*, 1861, at p. 53 he notices '*Quell' intimo motore piantato in cuore della maggior parte degli Italiani, il gusto di far dispetto ai preti.*' It is only in France that similar causes have produced similar effects, not to mention that in the latter country the position of the lower classes is different, and that amongst the upper classes there exists a more favourable feeling towards the clergy than in Italy.

[5] Dr. Heine in *Janus*, 1846, ii. 513.

portion of Germans on their teaching staff. Yet, as the Government organs complain, competent professors of law are not to be found in Russia.

In *Switzerland* the contrast between the Latin and Teutonic elements is strikingly evident in the universities. German Switzerland possesses no fewer than three great High Schools, and even the little town of Basle has not suffered its university to perish since the division of the district, but has found means, on the contrary, to secure the services of several most able scholars. French Switzerland, on the other hand, although by no means destitute of intellectual power, has not even attempted to found a university.

Holland, our nearest neighbour and next-of-kin, gives evidence of this relationship in her three advanced schools, but, according to German ideas, they are furnished with a very insufficient teaching staff. *Belgium* unmistakably shows the influence of the two races in her four universities, which are organized partly on French and partly on German lines, but none of the four comes up to our German intellectual standard of a complete and genuine university.

In the kingdom of *Denmark*, as it formerly existed, the German University of Kiel attained to greater scholarly renown than the purely Danish University of Copenhagen, and the reason of this may principally be found in the scantiness of the population of Denmark acting as a hindrance to the development of national literature. This accounts for the facts that the school of Copenhagen, organized entirely upon the German model, can only boast in recent times (besides the great philologists Rask and Madvig) of a few distinguished theologians, such as Münter, Grundtwig, and Martensen ; and that Germans, who are in the habit of translating all foreign works into their own language, have made but few translations from the Danish.

The organization of the two *Swedish* Universities of Upsala and Lund differs entirely from that of ours in Germany. Many of their characteristics are survivals from the Middle Ages, as, for instance, the rule that every student must be assigned to one of the 'nations.' Of these 'nations,' each of which has its own hostel and library, there are now thirteen in Upsala. But the difference between the Swedish and the German standard of University education is apparent in the fact that two professors of law and five of medicine are considered sufficient; yet it must not be forgotten that Linnæus and, more recently, Berzelius and Geijer, taught in these schools.

Thus we are led to the conclusion that German universities, with all their advantages and all their defects, partly remediable, partly incurable, are the most adequate form in which the German character can find expression, and German intellect satisfaction. The charm and advantage of university life are to be found in the mixture of freedom and dependence, of corporate discipline and personal spontaneity, existing both among teachers and taught; in that mutual intercourse in which the master freely imparts the most precious and hardly won results of his scholarship and the pupil receives them with grateful comprehension; once more, in the teacher's solicitude for his own line of thought and argument, and the scholar's helpful and indispensable response; and in these things is also to be found the reason why such universities are peculiar to Germany. The learned and educational side of the German character has embodied itself in this form, and wherever German life is in the ascendant, something resembling our universities is sure to be established.

The Germans, there is no doubt, are the most adaptable of all nations; in them a genuinely cosmopolitan spirit is more fully exhibited than in any other people. This enables them to feel heartily in sympathy with the best qualities of every other great nation, to be disinclined to take offence at foreign peculiarities. While many a nation carries its peculiarities with it all over the world, as a snail carries its shell, and is continually thrusting forward the most unattractive side of its nationality, the German temperament is on the surface less rugged and harsh than that of other races. The German is ever ready to give way to others, and even allows a foreign language to displace his own. If, owing to this, he is sometimes open to the reproach of instability and of easily allowing himself (as experience shows on our frontiers and among our emigrants) to be absorbed by more unyielding foreign nations, this is because the nature of the German is many-sided and flexible, and he has the power of recognising the advantages of others, of sympathizing with their characteristic qualities, and even of appropriating them and carrying them to perfection. It is this gift that makes our people emphatically the central people of mankind. In a series of literary works our colleague Riehl has brought to light the wealth of characteristic traits and customs, and of local and national peculiarities, that exist in Germany, though hidden from the general eye. To depict the nation as a whole, taking into account the chief aspects of its life and work, would be a task for which the devotion and research of a lifetime would hardly suffice, and it has never been undertaken. The incomprehensibility of the nation, our national spirit, has deterred every one from the attempt. Although, for instance, English literature is rich in works on France, Italy, and other nations, no Englishman has yet ventured to write anything like a complete work on Germany. What the French have written on the subject only proves that Frenchmen have still less insight into German character than Britons.

But Germans have the gift of understanding the thoughts and aims of other nations, whether by personal observation or by the study of foreign literature and history. This readiness to appreciate and value the superior qualities or national peculiarities of foreigners, this power of self-adaptation to them, might be described as a high sense of justice. But I should rather call this power, as displayed in science and literature, the *historic sense* of the Germans, and I venture to assert that they possess this sense in a more eminent degree than any other people. The power and inclination so far to break through the clouds of habit, to pierce through the thick atmosphere of the present and the mists of sense and prejudice, as to gain a clear insight into the mind and character of remote times and of foreign peoples, is without doubt among the highest and noblest endowments given to man by God. But it is only bestowed upon those who at the same time possess the indefatigable desire to watch and search for truth and who are courageous and steadfast enough to give the highest price for what is most precious, and to forego the joys and gratifications of life for its sake; who, not contented with superficial observation, or with profiting by other men's labours, press onward to discover for themselves the foundation of things. I might, employing an expression of Goethe's, define the German intellectual eye as 'radiant.' The Frenchman asserts that his country's mission is to illuminate the earth (either as the sun, or as a volcano). Far be it from us to question the high qualities of his nation, or to dispute the primacy which France still enjoys as the possessor and the parent of world-famed literature. The intellectual influence which she exercises throughout, and even beyond, the limits of the civilised world is direct and immediate, whilst our own is indirect. Through the universality of her language France is, so to speak, present everywhere ; she consciously accepts the task of converting into current coin, sometimes into very small coin, and of putting into circulation, the gold that Germany has brought out of the mines of science. We cannot pretend to this kind of success. For, to begin with, the German language is so difficult to master perfectly that it can never become a universal language like French or English ; and, besides, we have not the art of expressing our thoughts with that perspicuity, elegance, and precision of form which insure for the best works of our neighbours a ready acceptance in the widest literary circles, and commend them to the taste of all nations.

It is not only in the works of Frenchmen that this superiority of form and excellence of style are to be found, satisfying the taste of every cultivated mind and comparable to the best classic models of antiquity. Macaulay the Englishman, Geijer the Swede, Colletta the Neapolitan, Lelewel the Pole, and Karamsin the Russian are severally models of finished style, and I earnestly recommend our younger authors to study, though not to copy, them, although the bent of their minds, and their views and treatment of history, may differ widely from ours, and they cannot be compared with our best German historians in thoroughness and breadth of research, or in the sifting of their materials.

That we are not unduly exalting ourselves in claiming the historic gift with its responsibilities, in the sense we have explained, as a special attribute of our nation, can be proved by evidence convincing even to foreigners. Books on the condition, history, and literature of a nation written by foreigners are usually despised and thrown aside as unsatisfactory attempts by the reading public of the country in question. It is supposed, and for the most part with justice, that they are not likely to contain anything really new or instructive to the sons of the land. De Tocqueville's work on North America, Guizot's History of the English Revolution, the writings of the Americans Ticknor and Prescott upon Spain are, indeed, exceptions to this rule. But now compare with these the multitude of important works in which German scholars have set before us in a manner new and satisfactory, even to the people of the countries concerned, the history, the literature, and the institutions of foreign nations.

Of B. A. Huber's *Geschichte der englischen Universitäten,* Mr. Gladstone, then Chancellor of the Exchequer, said to me, when I saw it lying upon his table, that to him it was an indispensable work, and better than anything that had been written in England on the subject. The writings of Gneist upon the English Law and the English Constitution, and the two great historical works of Lappenberg (completed by Pauli) and Ranke, which supplement one another, are so admirable, and contain so much that is new and remarkable, that even German literary men cannot help availing themselves of them. The same may be said of Ranke's 'History of France.' The only complete history of Portugal is by Schäfer; the only satisfactory history of Russia during the last two centuries is the work of Herrmann. No educated Dane would be likely to prefer the works of Suhm and of other Danes to the history of his country by Dahlmann.

Hegel's 'History of the Constitution of the Cities of Italy' still continues unrivalled by Italian writers, notwithstanding their frequent and diligent researches into the municipal history of their country. Again, the history of the law schools of Italy, by Savigny, was welcomed as a work which no native scholar would have been capable of producing, and has been twice translated into Italian. The history of French law has been written by Schäffner and Stein, and Schäffner has also so exhaustively treated the history of modern social movements in France that it would be impossible to give the preference to French works on these subjects. Every Russian in quest of full information as to the internal condition of his great empire would be compelled to turn for it to the investigations of Herr von Haxthausen, which contain an amount of detail that no Russian work could furnish.

Von Schack's history of the Spanish drama has well supplied a want felt even on the other side of the Pyrenees. Any one comparing German with English commentaries on Shakespeare will not hesitate to concede the preference to the former, as by far the most comprehensive and thoughtful. An almost inconceivable mass of literature has for some time past been accumulating among all cultivated nations on the subject of the great poet who is the glory and pride of Italy. Yet if we compare the writings of Witte and Wegele, and the King of Saxony's Commentary, with Italian works on Dante, it must be acknowledged that the palm must here also be given to the Germans. Even before the appearance of the King's work, Count Cesare Balbo exhorted his countrymen to bestir themselves to bring out a commentary worthy of the great poem, lest, he said, they should be forestalled even in this by those wonderful and conscientious workers, the Germans, who are gradually making themselves masters of all those branches of learning which belong of right to Italians."

These blossoms and fruits of learning have for the most part been nurtured and matured in the garden of our universities, and sufficiently prove that they, and they only, are true nurseries of all branches of knowledge and research. It is only at the universities that forces exist strong enough to cope with the enormous mass of fresh material that calls for scientific investigation. The German universities in their present form are products of the *historic sense* of the nation, and they, in their turn, foster this sense, preserve it from corruption, and guide it aright. This characteristic is seen in the fact that the universities have continually enjoyed the favour and support of the national government and the learned professions, and that, as a whole, they have grown and developed into their present form by virtue of germs of life within themselves, without break of continuity, or pressure from without. This historic sense shows itself in the desire for continuity, and in sympathy therewith it never seeks to destroy or demolish for the sake of raising a new edifice upon the ground levelled, but preserves and

---

" *Vita di Dante.* Napoli, 1840, p. 155. *Sarà fatto un dì o l'altro da uno di quei meravigliosi e coscienziosi Tedeschi che poco a poco usurpano a sè tutte le erudizioni nostre.* He adds to this the good advice that his countrymen should not reject the productions of Germany with idle contempt, but should accept them with thankfulness, and profit by them. The historian Cantù has lately repeated this advice to the Italians with reference to German works upon Italian history.

adds to the old, from time to time eliminating and replacing what has become harmful. A great deal has been accomplished in this way. Co-operation between Catholics and Protestants at the universities was looked upon in former times as a difficulty bordering upon impossibility, even when the course of German history and the state of learning had made it an inevitable necessity. When attempted for a time at Erfurt and Heidelberg it had signally failed, and Erfurt was ruined in consequence. It has now become more and more a matter of course, and even in places where each party has its own theological faculty at work, as is the case at Tübingen and at Bonn, it cannot be denied that the association has been to the advantage of both. The fagging system, the bane of German universities for two centuries, has disappeared, and although much room still remains for improvement in the moral condition of the young men at many, perhaps at most, of our High Schools, yet even in this respect substantial progress has been made, and the number of really studious and thoughtful young men, living temperate and moral lives, is now, as we know, greater than it was at any time between 1550 and 1750.

Our universities have attained in the present day to a position enabling them to fulfil a fourfold purpose, creditably on the whole, and without hindrance or prejudice to one another. First, they are institutions which provide a general education of the best type; secondly, they are the schools in which our young men are trained and fitted for the public professions; thirdly, they are nurseries for future teachers; fourthly and finally, they are learned bodies devoted to the extension of knowledge by means of practical research and literary activity. The German universities give practical proof that these purposes, frequently declared to be incompatible even by professors, can not only very well exist side by side, but are of advantage one to the other. The scholar, for instance, who is distinguished as an investigator and skilful worker, usually has the best success as a teacher. For just as no man can preserve knowledge who is not in a position to add to it, so no man is capable of teaching in a truly scientific manner save him who continues his researches, and is not satisfied with merely collecting or digesting materials supplied by others.

> Wer in der Weltgeschichte lebt,
> Wer in die Zeiten schaut und strebt,
> Nur der ist werth, zu sprechen und zu dichten.

Does not this saying of Goethe's mean that it is by the historic sense that a man is set apart to be a priest of learning and a teacher of youth? In order to make my idea properly intelligible, I give the names of four Germans belonging to recent times who, in my estimation, are the heroes and representatives of the historic sense These are *Niebuhr*, *Alexander von Humboldt*, *Jacob Grimm*, and *Karl Ritter*.

Niebuhr's brilliant power of combination, historic acuteness, and creative fancy, enabled him to penetrate through the veil that Livy had thrown over Roman history, and to reconstruct it, thus opening up a way for the future use of that gift of just insight which has since produced such great results, and has made it possible to distinguish accurately between events as they are reflected in the troubled mind of the historian and as they really were.

Again, I class *Humboldt* among the typical examples of the German historic sense, not only on account of his successful historical researches, but because he carried the same method that he employed in history into his treatment of natural science, namely, the acute observation of facts; the collection and classification of all discoverable details in order to focus them upon the subject; the investigation of the moral or physical laws which connect them; the recognition of unity amid diversity, and of diversity in unity. Thus in Humboldt the consideration of history was always joined with the observation of nature, and the one was assisted by the other.

By a similar combination of qualities *Ritter* became the creator of geographical science. It was he who first pointed out the intimate relations between geography, ethnography, and history, hitherto treated as parallel but separate studies. This he effected by investigating and proving the influence exercised upon mankind and the history of nations by physical environment.

Finally, we admire in *Jacob Grimm* the historic sense carried to the highest perfection in the power of grasping the most hidden springs of German character as shown in language, customs, legends, myths, and history, and of sparing no pains in order to set the character before us in its objective reality.

But the creative power of our German historic sense (that mighty impulse to master every subject, and to account for all things by learning the inherent laws of their nature) is better seen in the condition of the various sciences as now taught in our schools, and by our literature, than in single characters.

In the first place, the German historic sense finds abundant scope in *Theology*, which, for the very reason that Christianity is a fact, and an historical fact, bears a pre-eminently historical character and requires to be investigated and interpreted accordingly. Germany has consequently become the classic land of Theology, and out of her stores other nations, such as England and America, draw authority and materials for their theological researches and controversies.

In the *Science of Law*, the historic school founded by Hugo and Savigny has evoked the sense we speak of, and has led to the establishment of the principle that law is not a product of legislative despotism, but is a side of national life, the outcome of the innate tendencies of a people and of its past history. Moreover, the comprehension of law without a knowledge of the actual conditions out of which it has grown, or to which it refers, is an impossibility. Just as the Roman school, in opposition to the old dogmatism, established the fashion of treating Roman law as the outcome of a long period of historical development, so, thanks to the same historic sense, there arose in the Teutonic historical school a justifiable reaction against the absolute and exclusive supremacy of Roman law, with the result that, after three centuries of neglect and contempt, German law, with its increased respect for personality and for real freedom, and its more Christian views of life, once more rose into deserved esteem, in spite of many discrepancies, due to difference of race. The two schools have in course of time been reconciled, on the ground that certain parts of Roman law have passed by common consent into German law, and that the real law of the German nation consists in a combination and revision of the two elements Roman and Teutonic. Out of this reconciliation comparative jurisprudence has sprung, the science of comparative international law, which elucidates for each nation its own national law by the study of that of foreign countries, and shows that each is a member of one comprehensive organic system. If the beautiful definition given of law by the Romans—viz., that it is 'the science of right and wrong, the knowledge of things divine and human '—is borne in mind, it will be more and more clearly recognised that all human law is primarily founded upon Divine justice, and that, as it is thus connected by close sisterly ties with theology and moral philosophy, it cannot afford to dispense with their help.

In the region of *Political Science*, a complete faculty has sprung up in our own day, and lays claim to equal importance with that of civil law, whilst in certain branches, notably those concerned with the rights of government and of the people, they run together. This combination of politics, statistics, constitutional law, criminal law, and political economy in one complex whole, only to be described by the generic name of 'political science,' has appeared to foreigners in the light of a strange and emphatically German peculiarity,[7] just because here again we see a triumph of our historic sense, which aims at accounting for the constitution of the State, not by *a priori* reasons, but in accordance with the historic and economic conditions peculiar to each people, and with this view insists that every condition and manifestation of political life is a legitimate subject for scientific treatment. Hence political science will come more and more to be treated in our schools as the philosophy of political history, which draws general conclusions from the sum of historical events and phenomena, and from a mass of historical examples, while it never loses sight of the wide diversity both between nations and times. It is through the historic method as applied by German professors like Roscher, Knies, and Kautz to political economy that that science also is in process of being freed from the dominion of one-sided systems, and from mistaken endeavours to set up conclusions drawn from philosophical premises, or from an insufficient observation of facts, as general truths. That such an erudite work as Roscher's, teeming with historical references, invariably to the point, and never introduced for the sake of mere ostentation, should be the result of labours carried on at a German university, a work that could be written neither in England nor in France, but only in Germany, is a fact which redounds to the honour of our schools.

In *Medicine* also we owe it to German professors that the need of historical research has been thoroughly recognised. The work of Kurt Sprengel was a new departure, and an early result of the new method. Since its appearance, the history of medical science has been elaborated in many works, and the sequence and internal connexion of different systems and methods explained. These works

[7] Blanqui, in his *Histoire de l'Economie Politique*, describes this as a *tendance à envahir le domaine du publiciste*, yet at the same time he acknowledges that the German method has, through the influence of German literature upon political science, become almost universal in Europe.

have derived their chief value from the discovery that historical pathology and historical therapeutics, the history of disease and of the art of healing, can only be properly presented to the world when drawn from the history of human culture as a whole. This has been done for us by the valuable works of Leupoldt, Hecker, Häser, and others.

Turning from sciences that cover the whole field of human life to glance at one department, that of *Philology*, I maintain, without any disparagement of the achievements of English or French writers, that it is chiefly the historic sense of the Germans that has given to the study of philology an extent and importance formerly unthought of, although even at the worst of times Germany could boast of a few able philologists in her universities. Yet it is only since the end of the last century—since Heyne— that philology has reached the level of a science that investigates the whole of the labours and productions of classical times and includes them in one magnificent system, of which F. A. Wolf first conceived the plan. In the great encyclopædia begun by Pauly we have a monument of German industry in the matter of philology such as no other country possesses, and such as no other science can show.

'The interest formerly taken in *Philosophy* has given place to that now taken in history.' We are compelled to acknowledge the truth of this recently expressed opinion. Systems that were the outcome of the constructive method, and were so abundant in Germany for thirty years, have fallen to pieces, and their schools have passed away. The assertion made not long ago by a very numerous and dominant philosophical party, that the coping stone had been put to philosophy by Hegel's system, now provokes a smile. The presumption that any one system could pretend to such a position would be met with derision, or at least with incredulity and distrust. This has scared away numbers of our students from the study of philosophy: it ought rather to incite them to seek out what is still wanting to complete the sequence of successive systems from the Ionic school down to that of Hegel, and thus to study the history of philosophy. Men have been slow to perceive that where there is no history of philosophy, there can be no true philosophy. The constructive philosophers, indeed, felt the necessity of accounting for history, but they did so by selecting what they wanted and disguising or suppressing, often misinterpreting and disfiguring, whatever did not suit their purpose. Meanwhile, after the appearance of many unsuccessful books, a marked improvement in the historical treatment of this wide subject has set in, and we may hope to see the history of philosophy take a fitting position in our universities, and maintain a prominent place amongst the studies essential to a liberal and scholarly education.

In the department of *Universal History* our schools are pursuing a double aim; first, that of adding to the material by drawing upon all existing sources of information and discovering new ones, and by testing and purifying these original sources by means of the strictest examination and comparison; secondly, that of mastering the facts thus ascertained, and of combining them into an harmonious whole, purified and refined by much thought and study.

Geography, in the new form which von Humboldt and Ritter gave to it by pointing out the relations between the earth and its inhabitants, and by drawing attention to the influence of geographical situation upon the life and destiny of nations, has become a welcome handmaid to historical research.

Comparative Philology, which treats languages as the most ancient records of mankind, has reached important conclusions as to the genealogical relationship of races, and promises us still greater results. And as knowledge, not only of events and facts themselves, but also of their conditions, is important, nay indispensable, to the right understanding of history, a wide field in the latter direction has been opened up by German research into the history of civilization. Owing, however, to the great difficulty of sifting and classifying the enormous mass of material collected, we are as yet only at the very beginnings of the work.

One branch of the history of culture, the history of literature, has been raised by German industry into being no longer a mere history of books, but a history of the ideas that produce books, and of the forms in which these ideas take shape.

Such being the foundation, we shall doubtless in the future possess a genuine philosophy of history, and Germans, beginning with Frederick Schlegel, Steffens, and Görres, have already made some progress towards the attainment of this end. It will be one of the noblest fruits of the growth of learning in our schools. The mistaken method adopted by Fichte and continued by Hegel is now exploded and set aside; its object was to compress the whole wide contents of history into a narrow inflexible scheme, and, by means of a purely mechanical and logical construction, to put rigid necessity in the place of the personal freedom that pervades all true history, and thus to reduce the living purport of history to mere modifications of thought. The time will come when the philosophy of history—the hardest won, but possibly the most precious, result of academic scholarship—will have to face the great task of proving that the forces that govern and fashion universal history are spiritual forces, viz. ideas; it will have to trace the forms and workings of these ideas through all times and changes, and so bring more fully to light the all-pervading plan of Divine Government which alone can make history comprehensible.

We must not here omit to mention a new feature of the work peculiar to the present day, and formerly unheard of. Since the beginning of this century a new power, growing rapidly to giant strength and proportions, has sprung up—the power, namely, of the newspaper press, which combines two modes of operation, the one immediate and instantaneous, the other slow, like the action of water dropping on stone. The daily papers have become a necessity so imperative that it can only be compared to our physical wants. Every passion, every momentary delusion, every national or controversial prejudice, is re-echoed by these organs a thousand times a day. The half-educated opinions inculcated by them flow in such a powerful stream that genuine learning has urgent need of strong defences and bulwarks to resist the impetuous current. In other countries, as in England, France, and Italy, this power has become, I may well say, boundless and irresistible. In Germany it is moderated, as regards questions of scholarship, by respect for the universities and by their influence. Public opinion still upholds them as the highest tribunal of the nation in matters of intellect. As the guardians of learned traditions, as the seat of thoughtful and methodical research, they possess and exercise the function of curbing and correcting public opinion, and of directing it, though slowly, into the right path. Thanks to the universities, there now exists a second new force among us, side by side with that of the daily press, in the shape of numerous scientific and critical reviews, chiefly written by university men. Their influence works less speedily, but is certainly more lasting; the weighty utterances of the scholar eventually turn the scale against the light coin of evanescent newspaper opinion.

Our universities continue to enjoy the confidence of the nation. Open and emphatic testimony was afforded to this feeling of confidence in the year 1848, when no fewer than 118 professors found a place in the great assembly chosen to guide the destinies of Germany, and elected for the first time in our country's history by the suffrages of the whole nation. It is true that this confidence was not justified. The exhaustive way in which rights and principles were discussed was a sacrifice of the precious interval of time during which the fate of Germany might have been peaceably settled, and the last war of 1870 avoided. Neither learned bodies nor their members are called upon or are well fitted to throw themselves into the tumults and intrigues of party politics, and whenever this happens, or where even against their will they are drawn into politics, they are sure to fail.

But since the world is moved and the history of mankind ultimately decided by great ideas rather than by material interests and by the passions of men, our schools will continue as before to fulfil their task, and to justify our confidence in their ability to do so. Now, as ever, whilst the German people continues in a state of vigorous development, they will mediate between the past and present life of the people; they will aid them now to choose the right path ; they will point out the best means of reconciling the conflicting elements that arise; in all times they will help the nation to prepare for the future.

And now, I ask the students to whom I speak, Is there any other lesson to be drawn from the story of the growth of our universities than this: that to whatever faculty you belong, the welfare and blessing of your university life chiefly depends on the acquisition and cultivation of the historic sense? Of this I have already mentioned the most splendid examples. We professors not only give, but receive. We receive from you that invigorating force that impels us forward and renews our energies to grapple with our yearly course of lectures, rousing us to pour fresh animation into our subjects, and to endeavour to improve their form, while we neglect no opportunity of enriching them by the addition of new matter. We come before you, indeed, with the teacher's authority, but we heartily desire and endeavour to enable you, in the prosecution of your studies, to dispense more and more with our authority, to stand on your own feet, so that our teaching, received at first on trust and by faith, may become your own by the testimony of personal investigation and proof.

Not everything that is set before you in our lectures will prove the pure gold of absolute truth ; far from this, it is inevitable that errors and half-truths will sometimes creep into our teaching. We professors, who have devoted our lives to the pursuit of learning, readily admit that all life is a struggle, not only against the errors of others, but against our own, which have often become dear to us. It is impossible, indeed, to discover new truth (new at least to ourselves) without having had first to overcome the error that stood in its place. No true progress, no real scholarship, can be imagined which does not involve continual rectification of faulty conceptions, and expulsion of false ones. If ever we renounce the daily intellectual effort of examining and correcting our opinions, or rest on our hardly won laurels, fresh delusions are sure to creep into our minds, engendered by selfish motives hidden even from ourselves, or by indolence, and the too hasty adoption of other people's theories. Do not then, my friends, rely too implicitly upon your master's words, even while committing yourselves to his guidance, and rest assured that the chief gain of your university education consists not so much in assimilating a certain number of facts and truths as in awakening and cultivating those mental powers which fit you to overcome the errors that may spring up from without or from within, and to discover truth by the independent exercise of your own understanding. If in your academical career you have won this costly prize, then even the errors you may have imbibed will turn to your advantage, because the effort to discover, combat, and subdue these errors will strengthen your mind and powers of perception, and will be to you a most wholesome mental training, so that you will come forth from the struggle strengthened and enriched by experience.

On this solemn occasion I feel bound to make use of an opportunity, never to return in my life, of addressing a few words to the theological students. The science you have chosen for your study claims not only to be that up to which all others lead, but to be at once the indispensable foundation and the keystone of them all. Yet theology herself can prove her right to such sovereignty only by knowing how to avail herself of the services of her sister sciences, and by being wide and unprejudiced and self-reliant enough to assimilate and make her own all the genuine refined metal that issues from our different faculties, to cull the best fruits from all branches of the great tree of knowledge, and to turn her gains to the best advantage. Woe to theology and woe to her disciples if, like a nervous woman, she shun the keen air of criticism, and if she—or rather, not she, but her theologians—reject every unpalatable fact in history as though it were a food too coarse for her delicate constitution! To theology it is of vital importance that her students should maintain, in the greatest purity, that historic sense which is preserved by the frank recognition in others of all good gifts and qualities wherever they may be found, and by turning to profit all the truths brought to light by other departments of science. Γίνεσθε τραπεζίται δόκιμοι, 'be good bankers,' said Christ to His disciples, according to an old tradition. Let us, then, practise the art of distinguishing true from false coin in the realm of intellect, whole truths from half truths, whole errors from half errors; of discovering and sifting out of each one-sided or false statement the grain of truth that is in it. Far better this than the sweeping or superficial condemnation of whole branches of knowledge, as though they were inspired by the powers of evil.

I apprehend no danger from such an enlargement of your circle of vision. Any theory that would dethrone the living and personal God of conscience and of religion, to set in His place the abstractions of pantheism, you will set aside if merely on account of its internal contradictions. In the same way, any system which openly denies free will to man, or necessarily leads up to such a denial, will have no effect on your minds, first because this freedom is too deeply rooted in your inner consciousness, and secondly because, even if ingenious reasonings should momentarily succeed n obscuring the inborn certainty of our freedom of choice, the consciousness of strife between our understanding and our will must soon restore it triumphantly in our minds. Least of all will you be tempted to let materialism attract you, and persuade you that man is but a finely organized monkey, and thought but a secretion of the brain.

Let me recommend to you as a motto : *Theologus sum, nihil divini a me alienum puto.* Nothing divine, therefore nothing that is true (for all truth springs originally from God), ought to be strange to us. All that is requisite is to be in possession of the right magnet, which invariably attracts truth from the covering that surrounds it, and draws it towards itself. It was thus that of old the great men of the Alexandrian school understood their task in the face of Greek philosophy and of natural science. Our task is, indeed, far more laborious than theirs was, owing to the daily increasing mass of material before us. The whole history of mankind in all its branches—philology, archæology, anthropology, the comparative history of religious beliefs, legal science, and philosophy with its history—all come before you with the demand for intellectual mastery. You are, as it were, in a Mohammed's paradise, where the first tree calls to the believer on his entrance, 'Pluck my fruit, for it is sweet.' But at once another calls, 'Come hither, for mine is better.' The isolated student, even with the greatest thirst for knowledge, must sink under the weight of the giant task. But what to him would be impossible will be accomplished—at least, to a great degree—by the united efforts and labours of many others like himself.

About two centuries ago a famous Italian closed his life with this wish on behalf of his own republic : 'Esto perpetua.' I will close my lecture by uttering the same wish for the republic of letters, to which I have belonged for forty years : 'Esto perpetua.'

II

FOUNDERS OF RELIGIONS[1]

WE are assembled here to-day to greet our beloved and gracious king and master with every good wish upon his entrance upon another year of his life, and to thank him heartily and joyfully for all the benefits that we enjoy through him and under his rule. We rejoice in the consciousness that the eye of the king rests on us with favour, and that he sees in this institution a society which, by furthering to the utmost its appointed work—the advancement of learning and research—strives to minister to the general welfare. For what else ought we to desire to be than the appointed guardians and servants of that high and holy fellowship which the Christian daily proclaims and yearns for when he prays 'Thy kingdom come'—the kingdom of the truth that maketh free?

I have thought it right on this day, dedicated to the king, to choose a royal subject for my theme. I venture to call it so not merely because it is a subject on which the rulers of the earth, more than other mortals, have occasion to reflect much and often, but also because founders of religions, like kings, or even in a greater degree, stand on a higher level than the rest of mankind. Dominion over the souls of their adherents has not seldom given them power over their bodies also, and just as the office of prophet has not infrequently led to that of king, so kings have sometimes

[1] [Lecture delivered in the Royal Academy of Munich, July 25, 1883, in honour of the king's birthday.]

felt the inclination and calling to become religious teachers and to found a new or purified church.

No people has ever created a religion, or received a religion, as a complete system, either at a given moment, or by gradual evolution. Families, growing into tribes, whilst still living peacefully together, and before a multiplicity of nations had arisen, already possessed religious beliefs. In short, religion is as old as humanity. The first beginning of religious development is and must remain, like the whole of the primitive history of mankind, a secret.

The question of the existence of atheistic peoples has very recently been warmly and thoroughly discussed, and the assertion of Sir John Lubbock [2] that numbers of tribes exist, amongst whom travellers and missionaries have been unable to detect a trace of religion, has been triumphantly disproved by Tylor, Quatrefages, Peschel, J. Huber, Gerland, Roskoff, and others. It has been proved that ignorance of the language, unsuitable questions, or the aversion of the savage to express himself in the presence of strangers, have been the cause of this error. But a second assertion of Lubbock's has proved equally untenable, although in this case he has such men as Tylor and Waitz upon his side. He assumes that amongst the rudest peoples religion is totally independent of morality, their religious conceptions and usages having no influence upon their ethical ideas. This is not the case; on the contrary, some connexion between the one and the other, though latent, is never wanting; although in numberless cases it may be only evil in its effects, making that appear as a religious duty which man otherwise recognises as a crime.

On the comparative antiquity of different religions nothing can be said with historical certainty. We can only hope that the youthful science of comparative philology has some future disclosures in store for us.

That religion has in all cases begun with the coarsest

[2] Lubbock, *Die vorgeschichtliche Zeit*, German by Passow, 1874, i. 237 ff.

and most degraded forms of fetichism, and has gradually, through manifold forms of polytheism, worked itself upwards to a purified monotheism, is contrary to all the evidence of history. For in the first place the most refined forms of religion are so radically different from each other, and stand frequently in such striking opposition, that it is impossible for us to assume for them any common principle of development, guiding and shaping their growth by its influence, either formerly or now. Secondly, two opposing currents show themselves in the history of religions: one which advances from lower to higher and nobler types, and becomes more and more spiritualised and purified; the other and more common example which becomes more and more corrupt, and sinks from faith into superstition as religious conceptions are gradually obscured and degraded.

Further, we submit that no founder of a religion has ever encountered a people or society who in naïve simplicity would allow themselves to be moved by his preaching if it contained an entirely new and strange revelation. Nobody, indeed, has ever undertaken simply to set aside or eradicate the received religion, and to substitute a totally new one in its place. The old religion has always been taken as a foundation in every attempt to win new disciples. A religion professing to be altogether original, and having no connexion with former beliefs, would be unintelligible and barren of results. And should any one allege to the contrary, that relations have been formed between Christian missionaries and the most degraded heathen tribes without any spiritual connexion of the sort, we reply that in such instances conversions have been won at first by force of superior intellect and education, and that the intelligent reception of what has been taught can only follow in course of time, when the forms and ceremonies of the new religion have become part of daily life.

But the term 'founders of religions' calls, to begin with, for closer definition and limitation. Is every founder of a sect to be regarded as the founder of a religion? How is a religion (by which I now mean a religious society or church maintaining its own peculiar characteristics independently of all others) related to a sect? The use of the terms is undefined and arbitrary. With many the difference is merely quantitative: a church is a larger and therefore more esteemed association; a sect is smaller, and consequently despised. Or else a church is a community recognised and privileged by the state—that is to say, an established church; whilst a sect is merely tolerated, or at any rate legally inferior. But this political definition of the difference is nowadays altogether accidental and out of date, for, as it has been said, in the United States the distinction between church and sect no longer exists. Let us, therefore, say once for all that a particular religion or church exists wherever a denomination distinguished from others by essential features and having corresponding forms of worship is to be found; whereas a sect is formed when a select minority withdraws from the larger association, in order to realise that ideal of religious fellowship which is not attainable within it; or, again, when mere discontent with subordinate points of doctrine or discipline leads to a separation from the larger communion. Still, there is always the possibility that what at first was only a sect may, in course of time, under new influences and by the introduction of important peculiarities of doctrine, develop into a new religion.

Looking back over the three thousand years which comprehend the province of religious history, we come across many abortive attempts, and many organizations extinguished after short duration, or suppressed by force; religions, too, which stood the test of many centuries, and yet have disappeared with the nations that adhered to them. We shall meet with three dominant religions of very unequal age, still outwardly holding undiminished possession of the countries and peoples which acknowledged their sway. Of these three religions, the oldest still shelters in her bosom a third of mankind; the two others have themselves been subdivided into a number of other communities, which claim the rank and importance of independent religions. We feel as though we were wandering over a vast plain covered with ruins and gravestones, and discover among them a few palaces, besides a considerable number of less important dwellings.

A glance at the past enables us to recognise certain periods when the desire for new forms of religion, the power to create them, and the disposition to receive them, were remarkably strong. One such time was from the end of the first to the close of the second century of the Christian era, when the decay of heathenism caused that fermentation in men's minds which helped to produce numerous forms of gnosticism and eclectic religions. A similar movement took strong hold of men's minds at the beginning of the sixteenth century, in the form of an impetuous struggle for freedom, for release from the fetters imposed by the powers previously dominant in every department of life, and in particular in that of faith and worship; and this movement, like a swollen stream, broke irresistibly over every obstacle and barrier that opposed its progress.

In Asia also, at the end of the same century, in the time of the Emperor Akbar, there arose an impulse to found new religions and win proselytes to them. As in the times of the Roman empire, out of the contact of the old paganism with new idolatries imported from the East, together with philosophical systems, and with Christianity and Judaism, a fermentation, fruitful in sects and religions, had been set up, so now from the friction between Islamism, Parseeism, Buddhism, Christianity, and Brahmanism with its schools and offshoots, a like movement was produced, which led equally to the formation of eclectic religions and a similar intellectual agitation. Yet all those religions, or experimental religious systems, have entirely disappeared; only one, that of the Sikhs, has maintained itself, chiefly through its hatred of Mohammedanism.

All religion rests upon authority, and this authority must be positive, historical, and derived from a source lying beyond the range of the individual consciousness. It is only at a very low stage of civilisation—possibly that of fetichism—that men content themselves with the simple conclusion, 'As our fathers believed and acted, so also do we.' Every one in a civilised community must go back to the first link in the chain of racial descent, and ask—How did our religion arise? Who first prescribed its forms of worship and sacrifice, of prayer and penance?

No people has traced the origin of its religion back to a purely human founder; it was the gods themselves who first revealed themselves to men, through their sons, the ancestors of the nations; the first generation of men lived in familiar intercourse with the gods; their first kings were gods, or heroes sprung from the gods; their first laws and social organisations, together with their first forms of worship, were divine ordinances. Amongst the Indians, Manu, the creator of the universe, is also the author of their book of laws. The Germans sang in their poems the praises of their god Thuisko, who was brought forth by the earth, and of his son Mannus, as the ancestors of their nation. In Egypt it was the first king, Menes—like other most ancient kings, also a god—who instituted sacrifices, taught veneration for the gods, and gave the first laws.

So it happened that when real human founders of religions arose, they invariably found some kind of worship of the gods existing. They were not inventors of a religion, but reformers. Such were Zoroaster, Buddha, Confucius.

Confucius, with whose history we are best acquainted, has been refused by Plath the dignity and importance of a religious founder. He certainly founded nothing new; his aim was only to raise the moral condition of the Chinese from degradation to fresh prosperity; and he was also the principal collector and preserver of the old traditions. In truth, he concerned himself less about religion than about other matters, and his utterances regarding it were made with reserve; but he nevertheless believed himself to have received a divine mission, and insisted upon the conscientious veneration of souls and spirits. For 2,400 years his precepts have maintained an unlimited sway over a nation whose idol he is; innumerable temples have been erected to him: and the emperor himself, in the character of high-priest, offers libations to him.

Zoroaster, on the contrary, was a genuine prophet, and the preacher of a remarkably pure system of religion, opposed to polytheism; but the accounts of his life are legendary, and it is only with some degree of probability that he may be said to have lived in Bactria 1,500 years before Christ.

It may still more properly be said of Buddha that in a true sense he was the founder of a new religion, in which his own personality, his mission, and exalted endowments form the central point of doctrine. But the story of his life is obscured and disfigured by a mass of the most extravagant legends that human fancy has ever invented; and investigators of this subject, such as Emil Senart, James Darmesteter, Heinrich Kern, are at present engaged either in labouring to exclude him from history as a mere sun-myth, or, with more reason and success, in sifting the genuine facts of his life from the mass of fables and exaggerations that surrounds them. In spite of all, the story of his life—partly real, partly fictitious—has been beyond all others extensive in its effect upon mankind, since two-thirds of the human race reverence in him the sublimest pattern of all virtue and wisdom.

Many elements must combine to ensure the success of a newly founded religion. The founder must possess a firm belief in his own mission, and also the gift of awakening in his hearers a disposition of mind in sympathy with his own, and of kindling in others the same enthusiasm that animates himself. Yet more, as a genuine son of his time and people, he must pledge himself to satisfy one at least of many pressing needs. He must appear at the right moment, amongst men who, perplexed by the past, wearied with the prevailing corruption or ignorance, and tormented with a sense of spiritual void, or tortured by doubts, are looking earnestly for the advent of some herald of better things, some spiritual guide to lead them. But besides all this, there is a power in religion that triumphantly breaks down every obstacle and subdues the souls of men, so that like Goethe's Iphigenia they feel most free when rendering obedience, and are raised to a higher life through the faith that is in them.

Peschel, and Schaeffle[3] following him, have started a theory in connexion with the origin of Mohammedanism— viz. that there is for the founders of religions a special zone, which, owing to its geographical characteristics, has been peculiarly favourable to the rise and development of the different historical religions. This zone of the monotheistic religions comprises the desert between 26° and 33° N. lat. There a pure air and wide horizon, with a perpetually clear sky and a scant and simple supply of Nature's gifts, nurture a contemplative habit of mind, whilst the prolonged fasts of a lonely shepherd's life beget a religious enthusiasm fed by the sense of immediate nearness to God.

It is true that the region indicated, if extended somewhat further into the interior of Asia, has been remarkable as the home of many prophets—taking the word in its Moslem sense as signifying a divinely appointed founder or reformer of religion, Mohammed being pre-eminently the Prophet. The same writers would have us believe that a series or succession of prophets, who have arisen at periodical intervals, extends through the whole course of universal history. Ibn-Khaldun, in his remarkable and instructive 'Prolegomena,' gives us in a few touches a kind of natural history of the prophetic office. According to

[3] Schaeffle, *Bau und Leben des socialen Körpers* (Tübingen), 1878, iv. 147.

him, prophets are the chosen instruments of God, the mediators between God and man. They receive their revelations sometimes suddenly and without previous training, sometimes after going through a season of preparation. At the moment of the divine communication, which usually takes place through the medium of an angel, they are rapt in ecstasy, withdrawn from the outer world; only a gentle sigh or gasp is heard. They appear to be insensible, but in reality are only absorbed in the spiritual world that surrounds them. In this condition their perceptions differ totally from those of other men, though afterwards they are again subject to ordinary human conditions. They hear the muffled sound of words and understand their sense; they see the form of the divine messenger; the ecstasy passes over, but the mind of the Prophet retains the remembrance of the revelation.[1]

This brings us to a subject in which the obscurity of the phenomena is combined with the attested certainty of historical facts, to take cognisance of which is indispensable for the comprehension of religious history—I mean that of the condition of rapture or ecstasy, with the hallucinations and visions attending it. If only to save men who are amongst the heroes and pioneers of the world's history from the vulgar accusation of lying, deceit, and hypocrisy so often brought against them, I must touch upon this subject.

I will take Mohammed in the first place. He was, to use Ibn Khaldun's expression, predisposed to become a prophet. After living for a long time alone in a cave, he was visited with illuminating dreams and frightful visions, which alternately delighted and tortured him to such an extent as to make him fear that he was possessed. He was seized with a malady resembling epilepsy, and at times he fell senseless like a drunkard, with reddened face and foaming mouth, uttering incoherent cries. The hallucinations which then presented themselves to his sight and

[1] 'Prolégomènes d'Ibn-Khaldoun,' in the *Notices et Extraits des Manuscrits publ. par l'Institut de France*, tome 19, 1862, p. 184 et 235.

hearing assumed the shape of heavenly visions and revelations. His abhorrence of the idolatry of the Arabs; all that in silent solitude and fasting he had thought out respecting God, and his countrymen as sons of Abraham, and their religious calling; all that he had appropriated as true out of Judaism and Christianity, came before him as a message from heaven and confirmed his mission to proclaim it. He had long seen his people, the hereditary guardians of the true faith, sunk into a state of barbarism and disunion; the abominations of idolatry that he witnessed around him roused his indignation, as did the ceaseless feuds amongst the tribes, who ought to have been united by the brotherly bond of common descent from Abraham.

Arabia stood in need of a deliverer and reformer in religion no less than in its political and social life; and naturally the next step was to believe himself called to this work. Forthwith an excited fancy created the form of the angel and the sound of words, which he believed to be uttered by the heavenly messenger, but which, in reality, were only the expression of his own thoughts. To him they were a heavenly revelation; and this firm belief, which accompanied him to the end of his life, gave him the endurance, the confidence, and the self-possession required to transform a man of timid, undecided character into a wise statesman and a conquering general, to raise him to undisputed sway over a people who, beyond all others, had hitherto been remarkable for their intractability and for the proud assertion of their independence.

Mohammed did not always maintain the high moral standard which he had set up in the first days of his mission. He allowed himself more than once, as time went on, to stoop to falsehood and deceit, and was not ashamed to have recourse to various immoral means to secure his end. The belief by which such a man is possessed that he is divinely inspired, chosen from amongst millions to be a special instrument in God's hand, is in itself, as the history of all religions proves, a dangerous temptation; it loosens on occasions the obligations of the moral law, sanctifies objectionable means, and conceals human avarice and passion under the cloak of divine guidance, or permission, more particularly if, as is usually the case, the prophet is, or in the interests of his mission thinks he is bound to become, the ruler.

More than ten centuries later the condition, during the last years of his life, of Swedenborg, the founder of a small yet still existing community, the Church of the New Jerusalem, presents an instance of a visionary state of mind more enigmatical than that of the Arabian prophet, but one so fully attested that any suspicion of imposture is out of the question. Here is a man of powerful intellect, in full possession of his faculties, held in general esteem, of great learning, and deeply versed in natural science, who asserts that, transported into another world, he has been initiated by angels into the secrets of the universe and of the Bible, and proceeds to fill many volumes with the narrative of these revelations concerning nature, mankind, and the spiritual world, combining the whole into an organised system as the divine order of the universe. For twenty years Swedenborg lived under the conviction that he was constantly holding intercourse with angels and with the spirits of departed worthies, and that he owed to them his knowledge of the visible and the invisible world. He died at an advanced age with this assurance on his lips.

Even our sober-minded Germany has fostered in her bosom in the last, as well as in the present century, a number of so-called inspired communities, the members of which, after being first seized in their assemblies with violent convulsions and contortions of the body and limbs, received whilst in an unconscious condition of ecstasy communications or revelations, to which they afterwards gave utterance either in a typical kind of speech or in short, broken sentences.[5]

[5] M. Göbel upon 'Inspirations-Gemeinden,' in Herzog's *Real-Encyklop.* 2 ed. vi. 764 ff.

It is a remarkable and very striking fact, recurrent in almost all religions and churches, that trance or ecstasy— that is to say a condition of emancipation from the bodily senses, coupled with visions—is regarded on the one hand as the best way of becoming the subject of divine communications and influences, and on the other as the highest possible aim in life.

The philosophers of the Alexandrian or Neo-Platonic school practically founded a new religion when seeking to restore the old paganism of Greece in an entirely new form. The highest aim of this religion—its supreme excellence—was said to consist in a condition of ecstasy, as being that of thorough purification, or of fusion with the Deity, a beatific state only attainable through complete detachment from all external objects, and through the suppression of all personal thought and will and consciousness. Plotinus has described this condition, manifestly from his own experience.

The Alexandrian Jew Philo, a contemporary of the Apostles, also availed himself of counsels received whilst in a state of ecstasy for the construction of the system of philosophy by which he sought to weld the Mosaic religion into harmony with the theories of Greek philosophers, more especially with those of the Pythagorean and Stoic schools. Here was abundant material for the formation of a new religion similar to those created soon afterwards by the founders of the Gnostic sects. But Philo's allegiance to his people and their faith was too strong for him to admit the thought of such an undertaking, even if its accomplishment had not been precluded by the approaching rise of Christianity and the predominance of Pharisaic doctrine amongst the Jews which quickly followed it. Philo describes the condition in which he often found himself whilst engaged in writing, as one in which, whilst thoughts flowed into him from above, he became so enraptured that he forgot all outward matters and everything around him— nay, even himself. He seemed to himself to be a passive instrument in God's hand; he declares this to be a mystery revealed only to especially favoured men.

Meanwhile, in every age, in prehistoric times as well as in the present day, among many peoples, the systematic production of such states of ecstasy has been widely understood. The art of falling into a state of trance has been, and is still, frequently practised in the East. Thousands of years ago the Brahmins made use of the magic drink *soma*, as the Zoroastrians did of *haoma*. The effects were so enchanting that not only was this *soma* offered in sacrifice as the most costly gift, conveying strength even to the Deity, but even itself became an object of enthusiastic worship. Haschisch, opium or bhang, and similar strongly alcoholic drinks and preparations, have long been used in the East, and still continue to be used by the Moslem orders of monks and by the Sufis, as means for inducing a condition of religious ecstasy.

But in such visions, and in the voices heard at such times, the substance of the communication is usually derived from subjective ideas latent in the mind of the recipient himself. Thoughts, wishes, presentiments, and hopes which lie hidden in his mind, and of which he himself may be unconscious, suddenly assume shape and expression, and penetrate his consciousness through the sense of sight or of hearing. These ideas present themselves in the garb most suitable to the time, country, and point of view of the seer. All the heroes, angels, and spirits of the other world, with whom Swedenborg was in the habit of communing, were, after all, as Emerson aptly puts it, only Swedenborgians. It has been observed, also, that people mentally afflicted mistake their own thoughts for communications made to them by others. The seer himself has no criterion whereby to test such conditions and their relations to everyday life. The circle of his disciples is equally indiscriminating; his inspired words kindle in the sensitive minds of his devoted followers unquestioning belief in him, while their own confident longings have already prepared and disposed them to receive the magic influence that flows from him. Thus the new religion comes into existence.

In our own days the great Tae-ping rebellion in China, which shook the empire to its foundations and threatened to overthrow the dynasty by eleven years of civil war, first broke out in consequence of a series of visions which its leader, a village schoolmaster named Hung-siu-Tsuen, had seen for forty days during an illness brought on by overstudy. In these visions he imagined himself to have received a commission from God to uproot idolatry (the worship of demons) in China, and to introduce a new religion—a mixture of Christianity with the old Chinese traditions. In one vision a sword was presented to him by God, and he and his followers explained this as a command from God to exterminate his adversaries. This was the commencement of a war, certainly the bloodiest that the nineteenth century has witnessed,[6] in which the Imperial Government was finally victorious only through the aid of the English and French.

It was natural in the earlier periods of the world's history that kings should be founders of religions, but in the civilised states of the present day this would be impossible. Passing over the Greeks, whose religious systems extend back into pre-historic times, we find the belief current in Rome that after the first foundation of the state, Numa Pompilius, the second king, a disciple of Pythagoras, organised the religion of the infant state. His reign of thirty-nine or forty-three years seems to have been entirely devoted to this object. But this royal high-priest is one of the mythical heroes so abundant in early Roman history. The Romans really worshipped the same gods as the Latins and the Sabines, from whom they were descended. In an old civilised state where the religious beliefs and customs had been long established, a monarch could only become

[6] Thomas Taylor Meadows, *The Chinese and their Rebellions* (London, 1856), p. 77.

the founder of a religion by introducing the worship of a foreign divinity hitherto unknown to his people. This the Persian king Artaxerxes Mnemon did when, apparently under female influence, he set up the worship of the Asiatic goddess of Nature, Anaitis, throughout his whole realm. To the Magian priesthood the arbitrary introduction of an element so totally at variance with the spirit of the established Zoroastrian worship must have been hateful and repulsive.

Six centuries later the Emperor Heliogabalus made a similar attempt in Rome. The endeavour to make the Syrian sun-god, whose high-priest he was, supreme amongst all the gods of the earth was the only serious occupation of his reign. All the sacred relics of the Romans were conveyed into the temple of this god, and his marriage with Astarte-Luna was celebrated as a great festival throughout the empire. The worship of any other gods was forbidden, and even Jews and Christians were to be compelled to join in the worship of the sun-god. However, the new religion was but short-lived, for Alexander Severus, the successor of the youthful emperor who had been speedily put to death, proceeded without delay to purify the desecrated city, and to re-establish the old Roman worship.

Henry VIII. of England must also be counted amongst the sovereigns who have sought to be the founders of a religion, notwithstanding that his work was likewise of very short duration, collapsing at once at his death. He banished the papal power from his kingdom, and caused himself to be recognised as the head of the English Church, but in other particulars he desired to retain the old religion as it had been handed down from the Middle Ages. His youthful training had led Henry to regard himself as a theologian, and as such, in the character of a priest-king, he desired to govern the English Church. He did not perceive that he thereby cut the ground from under the old religion, and that in the path which he was following it would be impossible for him to pause. The new church which he had created could as little pretend to be the continuation of, and identical with, the old English Church, as might a statue of Socrates, whereon a head of Alcibiades had been set, do duty as the statue of the philosopher.

Had Napoleon lived in a time of religious ferment, he would probably have attempted to become the founder of a religion. The religious fibre in him was indeed very weak, but his opinion was all the stronger that a self-made ruler who was determined to exercise unlimited power must have even the faith and conscience of his people under his control. He intended to keep the head of the church in his power, and to use him as his tool. Through the enthusiasm displayed by the French for his victories, he hoped to incite them to the worship of his person. Unquestioning obedience to the emperor was to pass for the highest moral law. How well he understood the method of making religious ideas serve political ends he had already proved among the Mohammedans in Egypt. Having formed the plan of founding a French empire upon the banks of the Nile and in Western Asia, he represented himself to the Moslems as a prophet—a Mahdi—with a divine mission to release Egypt from the tyranny of the Mamelukes, and to confirm the laws of the Koran. He affected the pompous, dignified manner of speech usual in the East, but the battle of Aboukir annihilated his bold and ambitious designs.

I am much tempted to reckon amongst founders of religions—although certainly not in the ordinary sense—another of England's rulers, the Protector Cromwell, a man who surpassed many kings in power as well as in political insight and serious religious conviction. He was not the founder of any particular church or denomination, but became a member of a sect with which he felt himself particularly in sympathy—that of the Independents. Yet he was the first amongst the mighty men of the world to set up one special religious principle, and to enforce it so far as in him lay; a principle which, in opposition to the great historical churches and to Islam, contained the germs of a distinct religion—the principle of liberty of conscience, and the repudiation of religious coercion. It must be clearly understood how great the gulf is which divides the holders of this principle from those who reject it, both in faith and morals. He who is convinced that right and duty require him to coerce other people into a life of falsehood, hypocrisy, and habitual dissimulation—the inevitable consequence of a system of religious intolerance —belongs to an essentially different religion from one who recognises in the inviolability of conscience a human right guaranteed by religion itself, and has different notions of God, of man's relation to God, and of man's obligations to his fellows. It was in those days no insignificant thing that the ruler of a powerful kingdom should proclaim the new doctrine, which, nevertheless, has required the growth of a century and a half in public opinion to become strong enough to command even the acquiescence of its still numerous opponents. The Evangelical Alliance, which now embraces two continents, and has happily realised a principle of agreement between churches formerly unknown or held to be impossible, may well regard Cromwell as its prophet and preparatory founder. Yet it is only of this one doctrine that Cromwell can be called the prophet, for he adhered upon all other points to the tenets of the Independents; yet the doctrine of liberty of conscience has struck deeper into the course of events, and has had a larger share in the development of modern religious feeling, than a dozen dogmas, sprung from theological schools, that affect merely the intellect and not the soul—that is, the will—of the believer. The constitution of the United States of America has been built up upon Cromwell's doctrine; and there is every prospect that, as one of the great powers of the world, it will leave its mark upon the future of mankind.

The temptation to a monarch to become the founder of a new religion never can have been stronger than it was to the Emperor Akbar, the Great Mogul of India, who died in 1605. Possessed of an inquiring mind and of a wide store of knowledge, this monarch broke the hierarchical power of the Ulemas; the religion of Mohammed, in which he had been brought up, did not satisfy him; he had adopted the belief, widespread in Asia, of the purification of the soul through transmigration. He had collected at his court the adherents of the most different religions; he had summoned Jesuits from Goa; and frequented the society of Buddhists, of Brahmins, and of Parsees. A society or order was thus eventually formed, of which he was the moving spirit, combining the learning and customs of the Brahmins with unquestioning submission to the emperor, for whom, as God's vicegerent, its members declared themselves ready to make any sacrifice. There is hardly another instance on record of a Moslem prince severing himself so completely from Islamism as Akbar did, and attacking it so boldly. But the result of his action is only another proof that this religion, where it has once taken root, never allows itself to be supplanted; with Akbar's death the whole scheme collapsed.

Let us now turn our consideration to the great schisms which led to the rise of new churches and forms of religion in Christendom.

It has at all times been a just reproach against Christianity that it has been unable to maintain its unity and internal peace, but has split up into so many churches, denominations, and sects. We must not, however, in looking at the dark side, which both in past and present looms out luridly enough and confronts us with the gloomiest pictures, forget the bright side. Even the divisions of Christendom bear witness to the inexhaustible wealth of ideas with which Christianity more than any other religion is pregnant. Whoever dispassionately reflects upon the various Christian churches and denominations wherever they have been free to grow and flourish unchecked by a daily struggle for existence, will surely not fail to admire the fulness of the gifts ($\chi\alpha\rho\acute{\iota}\sigma\mu\alpha\tau\alpha$), to use St. Paul's expression, distributed and developed among them. Each one ought to be willing to borrow from another: even the greatest churches, such as are most penetrated with the idea of their own excellence and sufficiency, would do well, in taking account of the spiritual wants of their members, to repair the breaches and defects of their household by appropriating the advantages of other bodies. Thus, in the United States of North America, the existence side by side of so many denominations is productive in each of a wholesome rivalry, promotes continual comparisons, and gives rise to an endeavour to imitate the good points of others; the consciousness of agreement upon the chief articles of faith, in spite of differences in subordinate matters, is a bond of union conducive to the preservation of all.

Luther must doubtless be reckoned amongst founders of religions, although he would have entirely disclaimed this appellation; a reformer was all he wished to be. But it has always happened that attempts at reformation have struck out fresh systems of religion, or have developed them in course of time. The mere re-establishment of the old landmarks of earlier times is as impossible in religion as it is in politics. The community drawn together by the teaching of Wittenberg recognised this fact, and unhesitatingly spoke of the 'Lutheran religion,' both in books and in daily intercourse.

Luther is the only religious founder that the German nation has produced; nevertheless, in all his aims and actions, in his good and bad qualities, he is a genuine typical German. Next to him Count Zinzendorf might perhaps be mentioned, the founder of the Moravian Brotherhood, a dwarf in comparison with Luther if judged by results, but a man to whom a gift was imparted which was denied to the Wittenberg reformer—the gift of social organisation. It may truly be said of Luther that he was capable of founding a religion, but not a church.

The French reformer Calvin also excelled the great German prophet in this respect; Calvin stands before us like a Janus, with two faces, the one theological, the other political. He was at least as much the founder of a religion, in the full sense of the word, as Luther was. But his theological system, governed by the theory of Predestination in its most extreme form, is now almost forgotten even by those communities in Switzerland, England, and America, that otherwise hold the memory of Calvin in high esteem. Yet in the sphere of church politics, his action rather than his teaching—that is to say, the organisation of his community in Geneva—has exercised an influence far wider than he ever anticipated. In the republican theocracy which he set up in Geneva, the English and Scotch Puritans saw the pattern of a Christian state which was capable of realising the purposes of human association after God's ordinance, and in accordance with His laws, and which would therefore not merely have regard to material wealth and the protection of life and property, but would also control and foster all the higher obligations of life. They carried this ideal with them across the ocean to America. The first Anglo-Saxon colonies were founded in accordance with its principles.

Gradually the theocratic element was lost, as it came into conflict with Cromwell's doctrine of liberty of conscience; and there is much truth in the eloquent description that Bancroft, the classical historian of the United States,[7] gives of the young French fugitive, versed in theology and civil law, taking refuge in Geneva, and founding a party based upon principles of strict church discipline combined with republican simplicity, the English members of which subsequently found an asylum in New England. Here religious and civil liberty were combined in theory and practice; thence they became naturalised in France, and

[7] *History of the United States* (Boston, 1879), i. 203.

gradually spreading over all European states drew them irresistibly into the movement.

The impulse towards fresh developments in religion has in our own days also been productive of new systems, though some of these have already passed away, and others are without vitality, or maintain a precarious existence without prospect of success, or of an increase of converts in the future.

In Persia the sect of the Sikhs, which was intimately connected with Sufism, was destroyed in a general massacre; its founder, Bab, at the age of thirty-seven, preferred to die rather than to disown his teaching.

The new church which bears the name of its founder, the Scotch preacher Irving, was marked at first by the appearance of ecstatic conditions, and amongst others of the gift of tongues, like that displayed in the Apostle's time at Corinth. Soon, however, the renewal of the Apostolate and of the prophetic office, after the pattern of the primitive church, combined with expectations of the millennium, became the distinguishing mark of this religious community, which is entirely confined to England and Germany.

In France two successive attempts have been made to found new religions to supplant or supersede Christianity. The first was that of Saint-Simon, or rather of his pupils, under the leadership of Enfantin, the self-constituted high-priest of the new doctrine. Saint-Simon was to be honoured as the highest Messiah, the Moses and Christ of humanity, the mediator between material and spiritual monotheism, the living union of spirit and flesh. But when the Saint-Simonians, emboldened by the revolution of July to express themselves with less reserve, proclaimed the rehabilitation of the flesh and seriously thought of restoring the ancient worship of Aphrodite, the measure of their perversity and blasphemy was full; many deserted them for very shame, and the sect fell to pieces.

Subsequently there arose the founder of that philosophic system which has received the name of Positivism, and which is now widely diffused, and counts many adherents in France and England. The project of Auguste Comte was to organise a system or religion suited to the present standard of science. According to him, the theological period is for ever past, the idea of God overcome. Since, however, mankind cannot exist without religion and a form of worship, ecclesiastical buildings and the rites and ceremonies of the Catholic Church ought to be retained, although beneath it all lies only atheistic materialism. Any attempt to put this religion of ghosts and phantoms into practice has not, to my knowledge, been made; it exists only upon paper, and would hardly deserve to be mentioned here had not men of such importance as Littré, Lewes, John Stuart Mill, and others yet living, who shall be nameless, reckoned themselves amongst the number of the Comtists or Positivists.

The signs of the times indicate the approach of serious religious changes. The great and difficult problems which lie unsolved before us, such as the social question, the relation of church and state, and others of a like nature, contain material enough to call forth new church organisations, or at least to transform the old.

New religions are certainly likely to arise in the future wherever religious and moral feeling awake to new life, and develop strength and energy sufficient to carry the new-born faith through its first struggle for existence. North America is a region peculiarly favourable to such new developments. Such a grotesque monstrosity as Mormonism would certainly find no footing in old Europe, but it is, judging by the past, not improbable that in America and Asia similar phenomena, like festering sores upon the human body, will yet again break out. Signs are not wanting which portend wide and comprehensive changes in the great churches of the present day. On the one hand, the exclusive spirit seeks by every device to widen and deepen the gulf of separation, and levels the weapons of its newly created dogmas like spears and lances against those outside its pale. On the other, there is at work in the religious world a growing desire for peace and mutual understanding, which is moving bodies, hitherto at variance, if not to unite, at least to live side by side in brotherly love.

It is usual, both in books and pictures, to represent the church as a ship tossed upon stormy waves. Retaining the metaphor, I should say that the ship which will glide peacefully and safely over the billows of ocean is that which is not too deeply laden with the burdens of the past, nor depressed by the recollection of guilt. Amongst the reefs and rocks upon which even a three-masted vessel may make shipwreck is the rock of History.

III

THE EMPIRE OF CHARLES THE GREAT AND HIS SUCCESSORS.[1]

I. THE FALL OF THE OLD EMPIRE IN THE WEST.

AFTER the death of Theodosius (A.D. 395), who had held the empire together with a strong hand, the partition into an eastern and a western empire had become a settled thing. The main cause of this was that, in the face of accumulating dangers and assaults from without, no prince was found with sufficient confidence in his own powers to preside with success over the whole realm, and at the same time to maintain it against the rebellious attempts of powerful generals. The partition had the great advantage that treason or revolt in one division of the empire, the temptation to which was always strong, owing to the want of a fixed hereditary succession, could at once be checked by the arrival of the emperor of the other portion to assist or to avenge.

When the sons of Constantine divided the empire into three (A.D. 337), the share which fell to the eldest, Constantine II., was neither Rome nor Byzantium but the western portion, namely, Gaul and Britain. Valentinian I. (A.D. 364) again divided the empire, which Constantius, Julian, and Jovian had reunited. Retaining the West,

[1] [The two treatises upon the Empire of Charles the Great grew out of a ecture delivered by Döllinger in the historical class of the Academy at Munich, November 15, 1862.]

with Rome, for himself, he ceded the eastern part to his
younger brother, Valens. Since that time no one had
cared to rule alone, at least for any length of time, over
an empire threatened on all sides by terrible dangers.
The government and defence of such a realm seemed
to surpass the powers of any one man. Even the strong
Theodosius, after raising his elder son, Arcadius, although
still a minor (A.D. 383), to the dignity of Augustus or
co-emperor, had abandoned to him and to the statesmen
he had appointed to guide him the administration of the
East. The younger son, Honorius, became Emperor of the
West at the death of his father (A.D. 395).

The West had now become far the most difficult and
dangerous portion of the Roman world to govern. Exposed
to the attacks of the barbarous tribes pressing onwards
from the north; weakened by the depopulation of its centre,
Italy; constrained, so to speak, to cut diamond with diamond—in other words, to meet the invading Germans and
Slavs with legions composed of the same material—the
West resembled a body from which one limb after another
was being torn off.

Rome itself, where at the close of the fourth century
heathenism was still stronger than Christianity, had long
ceased to be the ordinary residence of the emperors. They
lived at Treves, Vienne, Milan, or Ravenna, as though
they shunned the vicinity of the Senate and the Roman
populace. Meanwhile the New Rome of Constantine was
rising in importance, and with it the oriental portion of the
empire, which was more united, less threatened, and less
disturbed. The Roman West became in its distress and
helplessness the dependent of the East.

Constantine had not himself succeeded in making his
favourite creation, the New Rome of the East, equal Old
Rome in importance and extent. That it would take precedence of the latter as a permanent imperial residence
he did not anticipate; all that he looked for or announced
as a principle was an equality, and this inevitably contained

the germs of a lasting separation, or possibly of two confederate kingdoms. The Senate which Constantine had established in Byzantium was a long way from attaining to the dignity, or winning the respect, which the old Roman Senate still possessed, although the latter had now become but a shadow of the ancient body. After Diocletian the continued absence of the emperors from Rome enabled the Senate to re-assert a certain amount of power. The Senators could still flatter themselves that their assembly was the refuge of the whole world,[2] whilst the Senate of the new capital, a creation of yesterday, oppressed by the weight of a despotic court, which stifled free deliberation or decision, was so lightly esteemed that it was reckoned a degradation rather than an honour to belong to it.[3]

But the New Rome possessed two great advantages over the Old. In the first place, it was an entirely Christian city, whereas in Old Rome a considerable portion of the population, especially of the senatorial families, clung with singular persistency to the old Roman gods and to heathen superstitions. Secondly, situated as it was upon the confines of two continents, commanding the splendid waterway of the Bosphorus, and possessing one of the largest and most sheltered harbours in the world, it was of all cities the most certain to attract riches and a large population. Whilst Old Rome was easily subdued by every serious assault made upon her by her enemies, and within 142 years (A.D. 410—A.D. 552) was eight times besieged and taken,[4] the eastern capital withstood for nine centuries every attack from north, east, or south, made by Germans, Slavs, and Saracens. It is, then, quite

---

[2] *Ammian. Marcell.* xvi. 10.

[3] Themistius, *Orationes*, ed. Dindorf, p. 57 : ἡ τιμὴ (τῆς γερουσίας) τιμωρίας ἐδόκει μηδ' ὁτιοῦν διαφέρειν. Comp. p. 225, the request to Theodosius that, by conferring additional honours and rights upon the Senate, he would veritably transform his city into a second Rome.

[4] In 410 by the Gothic prince, Alaric; 455 by the Vandals under Genseric; in 472 by Ricimer, who put the Emperor Anthemius to death, *cum gravi clade civitatis* (*Marcellin. Chron.*); again in the year 536, by Belisarius; 546 by Totila, 547 by Belisarius, 549 by Totila; finally, in 552, by Narses.

credible that Constantinople, as stated by Sozomen, who lived there, was only a hundred years after her foundation, both in riches and population, considerably in advance of Rome, which had lately been sacked, although in Julian's time she had still been far behind her elder sister.[5]

After the death of Honorius (A.D. 423) the supremacy of the empire in Constantinople over the West became more and more marked. The actual power in the West fell into the hands of a Germanic chieftain who had both money and troops at his disposal. Hence Ricimer, the Sueve, was able four times to bestow the dignity of emperor, and three times to withdraw it. When the house of the great Theodosius became extinct at the death of Valentinian III. (A.D. 455), there followed, in the space of twenty years, nine emperors, most of them mere shadows, who were deposed and murdered so soon as they attempted to avail themselves of their position, and so came into collision with the greed and selfish interests of the foreign mercenaries and their leaders. One only, Majorian (A.D. 457), a man who might be compared with the Antonines, by his personal merits threw a passing gleam upon the sinking *imperium* of the West, which was reduced at last (A.D. 473) to Italy, Dalmatia, and a part of Gaul.

In theory, the Roman Senate still possessed the right to elect the emperor, or to confirm him upon the throne. The Senate, since Stilicho had restored to it somewhat of its former dignity, had become the only real support of the state. It represented the Rome of the past in laws, and administration, and in continuity of political order, in contrast with the lawless domination of Germanic military leaders such as Ricimer, Gundobald, and Orestes. It was backed by the authority of the imperial throne in the East, which, though distant, was nevertheless honoured and recognised by the barbarians and their chieftains. Even in these latter times the Senate could take upon itself to

---

[5] As Julian himself says, *Orat.* i. p. 14.

condemn to death two prefects of Gaul, Arvandus and Seronatus (A.D. 468).

A peculiar state of things had arisen in relation to the succession to the throne. In the East, for a hundred and sixty years (A.D. 450–610), no son ever succeeded his father; twice a nephew succeeded his uncle, and twice a son-in-law succeeded his father-in-law. In other cases it was the army, or the intrigues of the women and eunuchs of the palace, that determined the succession. Amongst the last emperors of the West, not one was connected with his predecessor by any bond of relationship. Emperors whom the Roman Senate, and the ruler of the East, had not acknowledged, were regarded as usurpers, and could not maintain their position. When, after the fall of Maximus, Avitus of Auvergne was proclaimed emperor (A.D. 455) by the Visigoths at Toulouse, the Senate did homage to him, and an embassy [6] sent to Constantinople succeeded in persuading Marcian to recognise him as co-emperor. Upon the elevation of his successor, Majorian (A.D. 457), the world beheld once more, and for the last time, the rare spectacle of an election ratified in accordance with the Roman theory by all the competent powers. The people, the army, and the Eastern emperor, Leo, acknowledged him. Majorian himself afterwards wrote to the Senate, expressing the hope that the high assembly that had made him emperor might continue to favour him. The insignificant Severus, on the contrary, whom Ricimer put forward as a puppet, and soon afterwards set aside, was not recognised by Leo, and after his death (A.D. 465) events merely led up to the policy of Odoacer. Ricimer found that he could rule without hiding himself behind a nominal emperor, and so the imperial throne remained empty for more than a year and a half. None desired the perilous dignity, and the legions, which formerly had so often proclaimed their general *Imperator*, had ceased to exist.

[6] *Pro unanimitate imperii*, says Idacius, and *Marcianus et Avitus concordes principatu Romani utuntur imperii.*' Ed. Roncall, p. 38.

At last, yielding to the urgent entreaty of both Senate and people, Leo sent the Greek Anthemius to Rome. He was proclaimed Augustus in the neighbourhood of the city (April A.D. 467), and the two emperors, in the laws which they subsequently made, gave formal expression to the position which the one assumed towards the other. Anthemius styling Leo his 'lord and father,' Leo calling Anthemius his son.[7] For it was Leo who had conferred upon him the imperial dignity. This was a fresh confirmation of the suzerainty which circumstances and the helplessness of the West had assigned to the emperors of the East.[8]

Since Valentinian III. had ceded Illyricum to Theodosius II. (A.D. 425), the hopeless weakness of the Western empire, which now possessed no footing east of Italy, had become evident. For Dalmatia, where the Emperor Julius Nepos, after flying out of Italy to escape Orestes, vainly tried to maintain himself, was quite unimportant.

Olybrius, whom Ricimer, after the murder of Anthemius, proclaimed emperor (A.D. 472), had also been sent from Constantinople by Leo, but not in any way as already designated for the imperial throne.[9] Before Leo had time to declare his intentions, Ricimer and Olybrius died, within a few months of each other (the latter in October A.D. 472). Leo repudiated the election of Glycerius, whom Ricimer's nephew and successor, Gundobald, had put forward in Ravenna as emperor after several months' interregnum. His *protégé* Nepos, to whom he had given his

[7] Upon this, *Vales. Rer. Francic.* i. 204. Leo is styled by Anthemius *Princeps sacratissimus*, but the latter by Leo only *Princeps serenissimus*.

[8] The Westerns felt this superiority, and spoke openly of it. Thus Sidonius Apollinaris :
Facta priorum
Exsuperas, Auguste Leo, nam regna super stat
Qui regnare jubet. Melius respublica vestra
Nunc erit una magis, quæ sic est facta duorum.

Carm. 2, p. 6, ed. Savaron [*Mon. G. Auct. Ant.* viii. 174]. One sees that he emphasises the unity of the empire under the two emperors.

[9] Although Theophanes, i. 101, p. 183. ed. Bonn [ed. de Boor, 118, 9], in opposition to older statements, asserts that he was. Cf. Chron. Pasch. 321.

niece in marriage, was proclaimed in Ravenna as Cæsar by Domitian, acting under orders from Byzantium, and in Rome as Augustus. But the death of Leo, which happened shortly afterwards (February A.D. 474), left Nepos without support. Orestes, the patricius and general, dethroned him, and nominated as emperor his own son, Romulus Augustus, a mere boy. He had soon, however, to give way to one stronger than himself. The Germanic mercenaries, who felt themselves the real masters of an otherwise defenceless land, having insolently requested him to give them possession of a third part of the Italian soil, upon his refusal, revolted. Their leader, Odoacer, having taken Orestes prisoner, caused him to be executed. Romulus received a castle in the Campagna and a pension, and the Germanic chieftain, whom his troops greeted as king—i.e. as *their* king—was for ten years able to rule over a depopulated Italy, making Ravenna his headquarters. As Cassiodorus remarks, he abstained from appropriating the royal insignia because he did not wish to found an Italian kingdom, and he certainly never called himself King of Italy, although later writers so describe him and affirm that he assumed the title. The old writers knew nothing of the kind;[1] they call him King of the Turcilingi and Rugi, or else king of the Goths. To the first he belonged by birth, and they appear to have been the first to make him their chief or king;[2] the rest—the Heruli and Skiri—also, after his victory over Orestes, greeted him as theirs. Amongst his troops, composed of various tribes, there may have been Goths; and because

---

[1] *Rex gentium*, he is rightly called by Jordanis, p. 163, ed. Closs. [*M. G. Auct. Ant.* v. i. 120]. *Nomen regis assumpsit*, says Cassiodorus; others, *Rex factus est—levatus est rex—regiam arripuit potestatem*. None imply a new kingdom of Italy. They rather consider him to be *Rex Gothorum*, or *Rex Turcilingorum*. Or they say, from his time onwards kings of the Goths possessed Rome. Paulus Diaconus, at the end of the eighth century, was the first to say, *Totius Italiæ adeptus est regnum*.

[2] *Sub regis Turcilingorum et Rugorum tyrannide Hesperia plaga nunc fluctuat*, so Jordanis, p. 194 [p. 132] makes Theodoric say.

Goth was the name given in Italy to the invading Germanic tribes from the North in general, he also came to be known as King of the Goths.[3]

The Eastern Emperor, Zeno, despoiled of his throne, and expelled for twenty months from his capital by the usurper Basiliscus, had been unable to interfere with the course of events in the West. But in July 477 he was again in possession of the imperial power, whereupon the Senate, at the instigation of Augustus, who had become the willing tool of Odoacer, sent an embassy to Zeno. They needed (so ran the message) no emperor of their own; Zeno, as the sole emperor of both portions of the Roman empire, was sufficient for them. They besought him, therefore, to confer the patriciate upon their chosen leader, Odoacer, and to cede to him the government of the Italians.[4]

Odoacer himself also sent ambassadors, and from Zeno's answer it appears that he had already been nominated patricius by Nepos. Zeno praises him in that, by applying to Nepos for the patriciate, he had conducted himself in accordance with the constitution of the Roman empire. When, in the document drawn up at Odoacer's request, the emperor gave him the title of patricius, it was not to bestow the dignity upon him, because, in his opinion, Nepos had already done so.[5] Zeno, at the same time,

---

[3] The Skiri and Rugi are expressly reckoned by Procopius, *Goth.* i. 1, and iii. 2, amongst the Gothic tribes.

[4] Malchus, p.235, ed. Bonn. This somewhat differs from what Gregorovius (*Gesch. Roms*, i. 239) relates as to the message of the Senate: '*Er* (Odoaker) *zwang . . . den Senat zur Erklärung, dass das abendländische Kaiserthum erloschen . . . sei.*' The Senate also did not beseech Zeno to invest Odoacer with the 'kingdom of Italy,' but τὴν τῶν (Ἰταλῶν) τούτῳ ἐφεῖναι διοίκησιν, thus, only the jurisdiction over, or government of, the Italians. The Senate certainly never thought of a kingdom of Italy, seeing that they had just done homage to the Eastern Roman emperor as their supreme lord, and desired no more for Odoacer than his appointment as an imperial official. [In a later edition Gregorovius has somewhat altered his statement (vol. i. 3 ed. p. 233)].

[5] The statement of Malchus, p. 236, ed. Bonn, must be thus understood, for Zeno's behaviour would otherwise come into inexplicable opposition with

recommended the reinstatement of Nepos, who from Dalmatia was soliciting his help. In Rome Zeno's supremacy was acknowledged by the erection of his statue in different parts of the city.[6]

Thus, between Zeno and Odoacer a regular relation was established of imperial supremacy on the one hand, and of voluntary submission on the other. This became clearly evident when some Gauls who still dwelt within the limits of the empire (no doubt in a part of Provence) revolted against Odoacer's rule, and sent an embassy to Zeno appealing for help. In the report of Candidus, of which we have only extracts, it is not said whether they desired to come directly under Zeno's rule, or to receive a prince at his hand. Zeno decided in favour of Odoacer, who nevertheless resigned the province to the Visigoths. This circumstance doubtless contributed to the misunderstandings which subsequently arose between Zeno and Odoacer, and which induced the emperor to summon Theodoric to make war upon the latter.

The assumption that the deposition of Romulus Augustulus marked the extinction of the Roman empire and the beginning of a new era, which is common to later writers and has served to determine the division of historical periods, is shared by only one contemporary writer, the chronicler Marcellinus. From all other ancient sources, from Cassiodorus, from the 'Chronicles' of Cuspinian and Ruinart, the old 'Imperial Catalogue' which closed with Justin I., the anonymous chronicler of Valois, Marius of Avenche, Victor and Isidore, and from Bede, we learn nothing of the kind. The occurrence did not appear to them in that light. Ruinart's 'Chronicle' refers to the murder of the valiant Aetius, twenty-two years previously (A.D. 454), by

his words, which Lebeau, *Hist. du Bas-Empire*, ed. de Saint-Martin, vii. 95, has needlessly assumed.

[6] *Zeno . . . senatu Romano et populo tuitus est, ut etiam ei imagines per diversa loca in urbe Roma levarentur.*—*Anon. Vales.* 663. That, however, could only happen with the consent of Odoacer.

Valentinian III. as marking the 'fall of the Hesperian Empire,' which after that could never be restored.[7]

Nor did Procopius see any such decisive occurrence in the elevation of Odoacer. It was not until the end of the eighth century that Paulus Diaconus took up the view of Marcellinus, and he was followed in the ninth by the Greek Theophanes. It is, in point of fact, scarcely possible, after the death of the great Theodosius (January 17, A.D. 395) and the division of the hitherto united empire, to fix upon any period when an independent Western Roman Empire existed in any degree equal to that of the East. Possibly this might be said of the early part of the reign of Honorius. In the general opinion it was self-evident that there were not two Roman empires, but that only one *Imperium Romanum* could exist, even though divided between, and governed by, two emperors. When the whole of Illyricum became a part of the East, and when Britain, Spain, Africa, the greater part of Gaul, as well as the countries between the Danube and the Alps, had fallen into foreign hands, the eyes of contemporaries necessarily turned towards the East, and looked for the real Roman Empire in the countries of which New Rome was the centre. Italy was nothing more than an appendage or offshoot of the empire, which the latter now reappropriated.

As general of the imperial forces, and invested with the title of patricius, Theodoric the Ostrogoth, who had been educated in Byzantium, marched into Italy and overthrew Odoacer's rule. The Emperor Zeno, his adopted father, had already formally made over Italy to him by a pragmatic edict (i.e. one issued with the consent of the nobles), and had especially commended him to the Senate and people of Rome by bestowing upon him a decoration (a purple veil). Theodoric, even at the height of his power,

---

[7] Ed. Roncall, p. 261. Yet this chronicler had Marcellinus before him, for he borrows from him the description of Aetius as *magna occidentalis reipublicæ salus*.

never ceased to acknowledge the supremacy of the imperial dignity. In his eyes, and in those of his Goths, his kingdom formed a portion of the Roman Empire. There are two republics, he says, in his address to the Emperor Anastasius, the one governed by himself, and the East Roman; but yet there is only one Roman Empire.⁸ On his side Anastasius looked upon the king as governing by the power he had conferred upon him.⁹ Constantinople gladly saw in Theodoric, the delegate of the emperor, the guardian of the bounds of the empire, and in the Roman Senate a body of officials subject to the emperor. The Senate protested that they were greatly pleased and honoured by receiving an order from the emperor, and added that Theodoric himself, the emperor's son, had charged them to obey such commands.¹ The emperor called the Roman Senate 'His Senate,' and it responded unhesitatingly to the term.

Theodoric publicly declared his kingdom to be merely a copy of the Eastern Rome, which all rulers regarded as their model. He had learnt in Constantinople how to rule the Romans with justice, and in the manner in which he followed the emperor he was in advance of other nations. He caused coins to be struck with the impression of the imperial effigy, and allowed the Senate to do the same. Roman institutions and political offices were retained, and the entire continuity of Roman jurisdiction preserved. At

⁸ *Pati vos non credimus, inter utrasque Respublicas, quarum semper unum corpus sub antiquis principibus fuisse declaratur, aliquid discordiæ permanere.* . . . ROMANI REGNI *unum velle, una semper opinio sit.* Cassiod. *Var.* i. 1. The Roman Senate also speaks of the goodwill shown by the Emperor Anastasius *in utraque republica concordanda.—Epistolæ R. Pontif.* (Romæ, 1591), i. 448. Upon his part the emperor uses the expression, *pars reipublicæ vestra.*

⁹ *Excelsum regem, cui regendi vos potestas vel sollicitudo concessa est,* is his expression in a letter to the Roman Senate (*Epistolæ R. Pontif. l. c.* 447).

¹ *Maxime cum ad hoc et animus Domini nostri invictissimi regis Theodorici filii vestri mandatorum vestrorum obedientiam præcipientis accederet,* ib. The question was, to be sure, a purely ecclesiastical one which the Arian Theodoric willingly left to the pope to settle with the emperor.

a later period, when the Goths wished to demonstrate the injustice of the war begun against them by Justinian, they appealed to the fact that neither Theodoric nor any other of their kings had made laws,[2] but that all the offices of the state had remained in the hands of Romans to the exclusion of Goths, and that the Romans had also been allowed to receive the yearly nomination of their consuls from Byzantium.

Theodoric's kingdom was far larger in extent than that of the last nine emperors of the West; yet he would not accept the title of emperor, however great the temptation may have been, and in spite of the charm that the name possessed to the German ear. He contented himself with the title of king, although every petty chieftain of that time who ruled over a tribe or a portion of a tribe, or who could boast even of a few followers, styled himself a king.[3] His emperor was the monarch in Constantinople. Even Jordanes, the Gothic historian, rates the dignity of the regular office of consul conferred by the emperor upon Theodoric as the highest in the world, and the joy of receiving it as the greatest. But according to the standard of opinion in Byzantium, this German kingdom upon Roman soil was always a foreign institution or a usurpation; and just as Procopius had called Odoacer's rule a 'tyranny,' so he can only say of Theodoric, however highly he may rate him, that he was in very deed a true emperor, but in name only a 'Tyrannus.'[4]

---

[2] Procop. *Bell. Goth.* 2, 6, p. 170 ed. Bonn. Neither a written nor an unwritten law, they said, existed.

[3] So that Ennodius, naturally with rhetorical exaggeration, says of Theodoric: *Tot reges tecum ad bella convenerant, quot sustinere generalitas milites vix valeret.* *Paneg. Theod.* [*M. G. Auct. Ant.* vii. 207].

[4] *Bell. Goth.* i. 1: ἔργῳ δὲ βασιλεὺς ἀληθής. The title ῥήξ hich the Byzantines adopted in the Latin form to describe a barbarian or Germanic ruler (βασιλεύς was only used of an emperor, or of the Persian king), had the signification of mere military power, not of a sovereignty founded upon political order. Hence even by Asterius the combined use of ῥήξ and τύραννος: ὥσπερ ἐν τοῖς πολέμοις πλῆθος βαρβάρων ὁπλίζεται, οἱ πάντες δὲ τοῦ ἑνὸς νεύματι τοῦ ῥηγὸς, ἢ τοῦ τυράννου ἕπονται.—*Homil. in Psalm. vii.*

The ruin which befel the Ostrogothic kingdom was not by any means due to the fact that Theodoric 'dared not trample on the rotten husk of the empire in Italy'—on the contrary, had he made the attempt to do so, he would but have hastened the downfall of his rule; for the Goths were not in a position to establish another order of government and legislation in the place of the Roman; the attempt could only have brought about a state of chaos. The weakness of the kingdom lay in the circumstance that the Goths, being Arians, remained always isolated, instead of becoming, like the Franks in Gaul, amalgamated with the old population of the country. They were, and they remained, a foreign military colony, and as such they had not the mass of the people on their side. The people were in favour of Justinian and Belisarius, although the Byzantine rule brought upon them greater evils, and an intolerable oppression, and the Goths, reduced to their own insufficient resources, succumbed in spite of their bravery (A.D. 552).

The conviction that the imperial sovereignty was the only true Imperium, that the governing power flowed from and could be transmitted by it alone, was shared with the Goths by the other Germanic princes who had settled in the provinces that had once been Roman. The Germanic peoples could imagine no fabric of political organisation except in the Roman form, with Roman institutions and laws. The Visigoth King Ataulph at first nourished the design of founding a great Gothic Empire upon the ruins of the Roman—of setting up a *Gothia* in the place of the *Romania*—but he became convinced that to raise such a political edifice out of the raw material of his Goths would be an impossibility, and that without Roman institutions a state could not exist; he therefore preferred to devote himself to the preservation and restoration of the Roman Imperium.[5] Submission, even servility, is breathed in the letter that Theodoric's contemporary, the Burgundian King Sigis-

[5] Orosius, vii. 43.

mund, caused to be written by Bishop Avitus to the Emperor Anastasius!—'To you belong my people,' he says, 'to serve you rejoices me more than to rule over them. I and my forefathers have always prized the titles we received from the emperors above the royal title we inherited. Your empire is our home.' Even the dignity of a Roman general[6] appears to have been more precious in the eyes of Germanic kings than their royal descent. Even Clovis the Conqueror himself (A.D. 508) gladly received from the Emperor Anastasius the titles and dignity of patricius and consul.[7] According to Procopius, Justinian formally resigned Gaul to the sons of Clovis—in other words, confirmed the transfer of it from the Goths to the Franks. The Frankish kings in Arles consequently introduced the *ludus Trojanus*,[8] which was held in high esteem in the times of the empire, and was considered as peculiarly Roman. They availed themselves, besides, of the imperial privilege of striking gold coins with their own likeness. It must have been on account of this surrender or abdication by Justinian that when the Comes Syagrius was sent by the Burgundian King Guntram to Constantinople (A.D. 587) and was nominated patricius by Mauritius, the emperor was obliged to rescind the nomination, because it had been irregularly granted.[9]

[6] *Magister militum.* Pope Hilarius, in a letter to Leontius, Bishop of Arles, designates the Burgundian king Gunderich by this title only, and Sidonius Apollinaris (*Epist.* v., 6) gives the same title to his son Chilperic without ever calling him king.

[7] Gregor. Tur. lib. ii. 38.

[8] καὶ νῦν κάθηνται μὲν ἐν τῇ Ἀρελάτῳ τὸν ἱππικὸν ἀγῶνα θεώμενοι. Procop. *Bell. Goth.* iii. 33, p. 417, ed. Bonn. This is the *ludus Trojæ* which the sons of the Roman senators and knights carried on (Sueton. *Aug.* 43, Virg. *Æn.* v. 545).

[9] Fredegar. *Chron.* lib. iv. c. 5 ad a. 585. *Cœpta quidem est fraus, sed non processit.* That certainly may mean, the nomination remained without effect.

II. Rome and Italy in the Time of the Lombards.

The Beginning of the Frankish Supremacy.

The downfall of the Gothic kingdom was followed in Italy by a melancholy period of disorder and of historical obscurity—the period of the Lombard rule, which lasted for two centuries. The general position had completely altered since the times of the Gothic dynasty. The empire continued to maintain itself in Italy, but in the stunted form of the Byzantine exarchate in the North-east, in the coast district of the March of Ancona, and in the two dukedoms of Rome and Naples. The Lombard kingdom, which comprised by far the largest part of Italy, was divided from north to south into two almost equal, but loosely united, parts, and possessed no definite boundaries, natural or otherwise. Italy became the theatre of ceaseless strife, which the Lombards carried on with great barbarity and with their characteristic love of destruction. As they recognised no fixed succession to the throne, and as their powerful dukes were continually giving rein to their ambitious designs, or grasping at royalty, the history of the Lombards in Italy during those two centuries is but a narrative of revolts, of struggles for possession of the throne, and of the rise and fall of factions. Of five-and-twenty kings, sixteen died a violent death or were dethroned. The Lombards seemed to have gained nothing by abandoning Arianism, which they had brought with them into Italy, and which they shook off between 618 and 711, while their Arian bishops, we scarce know how, disappeared. The feeling of the 'Romans' towards the converted Lombard Catholics was one of deep hatred mixed with contempt. Scenes such as Gregory the Great had witnessed when Romans were dragged from their homes by Lombards, with cords round their necks like dogs, to be sold for slaves in Gaul, these and horrors of a worse description had been many times repeated. The Lombard kings had not, like Theodoric, learnt from the Romans to rule over Romans; their relations with the East Roman Empire were always unfriendly, even when there happened to be peace. Of recognising the empire they had no thought. They always styled themselves kings of the Lombards, never kings of Italy. Except by the assumption of the title of *Flavius*—a title borrowed from the imperial house of Constantine—they do not seem to have laid any claim to the old imperial power, or to the obedience of the Roman population. The best and wisest of their kings, Luitprand, might perhaps have succeeded, during his reign of nearly thirty-three years, in undertaking the work of reconciling and fusing together Romans and Lombards; but even he did little as a lawgiver to benefit the Romans, whilst the laws of his predecessor, Rothari, were not framed with the smallest consideration for them.

Rome, Ravenna, and Pavia had now become the centres of Italian life. Pavia was the residence of the Lombard kings, Ravenna the seat of the Greek exarch. The latter, usually a general, governed despotically with military law, but was removable at the will of the emperor. He issued his orders to the *duces* of Rome and Naples, and ill-treated the inhabitants of the scattered imperial territory by his exactions. The latter, however, continually pressed by the Lombards, and but little protected by the mercenaries of the exarch, had in the course of the seventh century recovered their warlike spirit, and had learnt how to defend themselves.

Rome, with her territory, the Duchy, hemmed in by the two great Lombard dukedoms of Spoleto and Benevento, was dependent upon Ravenna as well as upon Constantinople. The clergy and people were compelled to apply in humble terms to the exarch for the confirmation of their election of a pope, and to solicit the intercession of the Archbishop of Ravenna. Once again, after the lapse of two centuries, the Romans saw their emperor, in the year 663, when Constans II., the only Greek Imperator who ever visited Rome, came thither from Sicily. Submissively, and with religious pomp and every sign of homage, pope and clergy were compelled to receive the fratricide and persecutor of the Catholics, the man who had dragged Pope Martin from dungeon to dungeon, and had left him to die far away in exile. He came, as it appears, only for the sake of robbing the town, so often plundered and laid waste, of the few objects of value that remained.

The succession of Greeks and Syrians in the papal chair, lasting with only a single break from 685 till 752, during which a Roman (715-731), Gregory III., was pope, sufficiently shows the overwhelming influence of the exarchs, and how little freedom was left to the Romans even in their most important right, the papal election.

Nevertheless, ever since the beginning of the eighth century a spirit of independence, of self-help, and ere long of resistance, had sprung up amongst the Italians of the imperial provinces, which pointed to the approaching end of the Byzantine rule in Italy.

The conviction that the *Respublica Romana* was still extant in Italy had been always kept alive, most especially in Rome, and in the eyes of Italians the popes were the representatives and administrators of this commonwealth. The bishops under Lombard rule, whose sees lay within the provinces formerly called *suburbicarian*, and who were therefore ordained in Rome, took a vow that they would do their utmost towards the preservation of peace between the Respublica and the people of the Lombards.[1] This Roman Respublica was indeed a very vague conception; but whilst the people of Constantinople knew no more of the Romans or Italians under the Byzantine sway than that they belonged to one of the eighteen exarchates of the empire, Romans and Italians, with a self-reliance most displeasing to the Byzantines, wished to be regarded as citizens of the Republic, upon which the honour and rights of ancient

---

[1] *Lib. Diurn.* p. 72, ed. Paris [ed. Sickel, 1889, p. 81] : ' Ut semper pax . . inter rempublicam et nos, hoc est, gentem Langobardorum, conservetur.'

Rome were entailed. In the Roman 'Book of Formulæ,' which gives us an insight into the affairs of the seventh and eighth centuries, we find that the popes and the Romans in their intercourse with Constantinople and Ravenna always spoke of the Roman Imperium; and Byzantine Italy is only mentioned as 'the subject Italian province.'[2] But on all other occasions the Roman legal phraseology, especially when dealing with Italians, ignores the Imperium and substitutes the Respublica; and the pope exacted a promise from the suburbicarian bishops whom he ordained that they would at once inform him, the pope, not the exarch, of any plot that was being formed against the respublica or against the emperor.[3]

In Rome, the term 'Respublica of the Romans' seems sometimes to have meant the city, together with the neighbouring district (which had not become Lombard, and since 711 had been called the Roman Duchy) sometimes to have included also the province of the Exarchate and the Pentapolis with the Duchy. Pope Stephen complains in the year 755 that the Lombard king has not yet surrendered a hand's breadth of territory to St. Peter, the church, and the republic of the Romans; and again immediately afterwards he speaks of the towns and districts of which restitution should be made to Peter, the church, and the republic.[4] Paul I. relates how he sent plenipotentiaries to King Desiderius with orders to come to a settlement of exchange, or mutual restitution of revenues and rights for the benefit of the Romans living in the Lombard towns, and *vice versa*.[5]

[2] 'Ad dispensationem hujus servilis Italicæ provinciæ,' *Lib. Diurn.* p. 20 [ed. Sickel, p. 54].

[3] *Lib. Diurn.* p. 70 [Sickel, p. 79].

[4] Cenni, *Monum. Domin. Pontif.* i. 75. [The places here quoted and those from the Cod. Carolinus in notes 11 and 14–18 are also to be found in Jaffé, *Bibl. Rer. Germ.* iv.; here *Ep.* 6, p. 35 s.]

[5] 'Volens (Desiderius) per hoc dilationem inferre, ne pars nostra Romanorum propriam consequatur justitiam.' Troya, *Codice diplom. Longobardo*, v. 225. These must have been profitable or lucrative rights in the towns which were under the Lombard rule, appertaining not to the imperial *Fiscus* in Byzantium, but to the municipality of Rome.

The popes regarded themselves, and at that time acted, as the first citizens and leaders of the populace of Rome, as the protectors and representatives of the Roman or Latin commonwealth in face of the Lombards, and as the defenders of the idea and rights of the Roman Empire. In Rome itself the conviction was indelible that the city, which had been the cradle, was also the rightful upholder, of the Imperium; no Roman could ever forget this, or contemplate the distressed situation of Italy as otherwise than transient.[6] Two circumstances had combined to bring the popes into a political position so prominent that at the fall of the Byzantine rule the secular powers, the dukes or great landed proprietors, held relatively a subordinate place. The first was the wealth of the Roman Church, which enabled the popes to provide for the multitude of poor in Rome and its environs, and so to surround themselves with a thoroughly devoted population; the other was the religious consideration in which they were held by both Lombards and Franks. Consequently all Italians or Romans looked upon the pope as their advocate and representative in the face of the foreign rulers. Even the Byzantine officials felt and occasionally availed themselves of this influence, and in the draft of a petition to be addressed to the Exarch of Ravenna upon the occasion of the election of a new pope, a reason put forward for the speedy confirmation of the election is that the Lombards, who are not to be overcome by Greek weapons, readily submit to the exhortations of the pope.

Meanwhile the position occupied by the popes with regard to the Greek emperors down to the year 796 was one of merely nominal subjection. When the Italians,

---

[6] In the confession of faith of a newly elected pope, composed about the year 690, it is said: 'May the emperor *una cum fidelissimis et fortissimis Romanæ reipublicæ Italiæ exercitibus* overthrow the rebels and enemies of the empire.'—*Liber. Diurnus.* p. 51 [ed. Sickel, p. 110]. Thus the emperor on the one hand, and the *Romana Respublica Italiæ* with its *exercitus*—i.e. urban aristocracy—on the other, were leagued together against the common enemy (the Lombards).

incensed by the arrogance of the iconoclast Emperor Leo, desired to choose an emperor of their own, they were hindered from doing so by Pope Gregory II. who exhorted the Romans 'not to fall away from their love and fealty to the Roman Empire.' That, certainly, was not love for the corrupt Byzantine rule, but for the 'Romana Respublica,' for the tie that bound together all Italians who were not under the Lombard sway, and for the idea that out of that part of the ancient edifice which still remained a complete palace would be reconstructed—a reconstituted imperial system, in which Rome would regain her dignity, and the Romans the rights which they had never resigned.

For the present, however, the citizens of the Roman Respublica were in considerable danger of being crushed between the upper and the nether millstone of the Lombard and the Byzantine powers. The popes were well aware that in the idea of the Roman Imperium and the power of that great name lay their shelter and refuge, and their anchor of hope for better times. The attitude of the emperors in Byzantium was sometimes hostile, when as iconoclasts they were in theological opposition to the popes; at other times indifferent, when they were exhausted by the dangers which on two sides threatened the Eastern Empire. The intermediate dignity of the patriciate was for this reason created and bestowed on the royal house of the Franks. The popes and the Romans had not the slightest intention of casting off thereby their allegiance to the Imperium in Constantinople. But they had already so often been abandoned by that court and thrown upon their own resources that they were ready, as no other means were at hand, to use this expedient for warding off the yoke of the hated Lombards. Now this patriciate was a dignity of the Roman Empire, and in bestowing it upon the Frankish princes, the Romans, and the pope at their head and in their name, thus making the bearers of it prominent members of the Roman Respublica, acted under the sense that the Roman people could, in time of need, confer an office or dignity without being empowered to do so by Byzantium. It was the first step, which, logically, was followed thirty years later by another—the bestowal of the imperial dignity. Meanwhile the patriciate did not confer any governing or judicial powers over the Roman Dukes.[7] The meaning conveyed was—'Be thou the shield and sword of the Roman Respublica in the whole of Italy, and the guardian in particular of the Roman Church.'

The patriciate thus had nothing in common with the Roman or any other Duchy. There were many dukes then in Italy; we meet with the dukes or the duchies of Ancona, Osimo, Benevento, Ferrara, Fermo, Naples, Parma, Perugia. They were not in general, however, patricii, although the patriciate, as a dignity held for life, but without any definite powers, was frequently combined with an office, especially that of exarch, or sometimes even with that of Duke. Next to that of Cæsar the patriciate was the highest dignity of the empire, that the emperor was wont to confer; the patricius received the golden fillet and the insignia of his dignity either directly from the hands of the emperor, or from special officers of state (*spatharii*) sent from the capital. According to the Byzantine form of appointment, the patricius was an assistant to the emperor, but more especially the guardian of the church and the poor; thus in the dignity lay the idea of advocacy, and this explains how it was that the Romans and the pope came to elect Pipin and Charles as their patricii. Upon their part it meant no more than that they honoured the Frankish princes as their protectors, and desired their assistance against enemies and oppressors. The first 'Patricius of the Romans' spoken of in history was the

[7] As Hegel supposes (*Ital. Städteverfassung*, i. 209): 'According to this there is nothing more to be understood by the " Patriciate of the Romans " than the governorship in the Ducatus of Rome, &c. But he is quite right when he says that Stephen, in appointing the Frankish kings patricians, only hoped to gain in them powerful protectors who would be satisfied with the honour an title of lordship over Rome.

Exarch Gregory of Ravenna (from A.D. 666 to A.D. 678). But as Paulus Diaconus, who mentions him, nowhere else uses the title of patricius, it is difficult to affirm that by the designation 'Patricius of the Romans' he wished to imply a peculiar relation. In the 'Liber Pontificalis' and elsewhere the expression is only used with reference to the Frankish princes. Other patricii style themselves 'imperial patricius,' as, for example, Gregory of Benevento in A.D. 792, and the distinction and opposition between the Roman Patricius Charles, in Rome and Central Italy, and the imperial Patricius Gregory, in Benevento, must not be ignored. In the same way, at a later period (cir. 911), the Prince Landulf and his son Athenulf call themselves 'patricii of the Lombard people and of the empire.'⁸ The imperial patriciate was conferred upon them as a mere title from Constantinople; the patriciate of the Lombards—that is to say, the guardianship of the Lombard population in Southern Italy—must have been founded, like the patriciate of Charles, at the wish and by the choice of the people.

Of the Roman dukes in the seventh and eighth centuries none bore the title of Patricius of the Romans; indeed, none of them had the title of patricius except the last, Stephen, who is mentioned in the 'Liber Pontificalis' only as 'formerly patricius,'⁹ probably because at the time of the Italian insurrection against Byzantium the emperor had deprived him of the dignity. After all, Pipin, Carloman, and at the first Charles also, did not consider the Roman patriciate conferred upon them as of much importance. Whilst the popes were careful in every letter to put the title first, the Frankish princes made use of it in none of their documents. When, however, he had acquired

⁸ Gattula, *Hist. Abbat. Cassin.* p. 1. sec. v. Waimar, Prince of Salerno, calls himself, in a document printed by Gattula, *Princeps et Imperialis Patricius*. Comp. Gentili, *de Patriciorum Origine* (Romæ, 1736), p. 275.

⁹ 'A Stephano quondam Patricio et Duce omnis exercitus Romani.'—*Vita Zach.* c. 2. Under Gregory II. a *spatharius*— i.e., an officer of the Imperial bodyguard—was a Roman *dux* (*Vita Greg. II.* c. 14).

the kingdom of the Lombards, Charles adopted both titles in his documents; up to that time the patriciate of the Romans had for him little significance, nor was it in his power to fulfil the mission therewith entrusted to him of acting as the guardian of the Roman—that is, of the non-Lombard—population. He most certainly never supposed that he had become through his patriciate the servant or dependent of the emperor. Nor did the Romans think that by conferring the title they encroached upon the emperor's rights, or had broken their connexion with the empire.

Thus the new patriciate gave no power to the holder of it even over a single village; it was a guardianship, but not merely of the Roman Church or of the papal chair— for in that case Charles would have been named Patricius S. Petri, or Patricius of the Roman Church, and not uniformly Patricius of the Romans. If the new King of the Lombards was Patricius of the Romans and disposer of the Frankish power, the temptation to regard his patriciate and to maintain it in the same manner as he did his kingdom must have been very great—all the greater because by that time the exarchate had passed away, and the people of the non-Lombard provinces of Upper and Central Italy had been left to themselves, and were defenceless. The pope and the Romans would readily have entrusted Charles Martel with the patriciate, and have laid upon him the obligation of coming to make war against the Lombard kings; but Charles, who stood on a very friendly footing with those princes, and had too much on his hands in his Frankish dominions, appears to have declined the office. Pipin and his son Charles, on the occasion of their consecration, allowed Pope Stephen to connect the Roman patriciate with the royal title,[1] and to insert the title patricius in the papal letters, and they were disposed to fulfil at least

---

[1] So the *Annals of Metz* say: 'Ordinavit secundum morem majorum unctione sacra Pippinum . . . Francis in regem et Patricium Romanorum,' and in the year 773 the same of Charles.

a part of the obligations which in Rome were conceived to be attached to the patriciate; but they were resolved to make the extent of these obligations, and the use which they might make of the patriciate, coincide with Frankish interests. To Charles especially, after the year 774, the consideration of the establishment and demarcation of his Lombardo-Italian kingdom must have become a matter of chief importance.

When Adrian in one place makes mention of his own patriciate [2] side by side with that of Charles, it is clear that the pope is there making a very vague use of words, and is comprising two dissimilar things under one term. The patriciate of the pope included very definite rights of government, and the power at that time (790), notwithstanding the nominal sovereignty of the Greek emperor, lay almost entirely in his hands. Charles, on the contrary, as Patricius could only lay claim to such power as the weaker party by submission cedes to a protector in its own interests, and in proportion to the greater or less need for defence. Yet his power in Rome at that time was certainly very great, for the city could not have maintained itself even for three weeks against a combination of the Byzantine forces with those of the South Lombard duchies. The pope had really no choice; in all political and military matters he was forced to yield to the will and to submit to the regulations of the king.

With regard to the position assumed by the Lombard conquerors towards the old inhabitants, very opposite opinions have even recently been formed. Upon one side von Sybel asserts, that 'the Lombards, after they had long been settled in the country as a German and Arian colony, came Catholic and *Roman*, and in a short time were thoroughly fused with the people of the provinces.' Hegel has in detail expressed the same opinion. On the other

---

[2] Cenni, i. 521 [Jaffé, *l.c. Ep.* 98, p. 290]. The pope says, as always, *Patriciatus beati Petri;* Pepin allowed this, and Charles confirmed it. In describing the papal rights in the donated provinces no conclusion must be drawn from the parallel use of the expression.

side Cantù writes : 'Italy was to them the spoil of victory, never a home; they remained for two centuries upon our soil, like the Turks upon the soil of Greece, and like the Magyar masters over the plebeian multitude in Pannonia.'[3]

The last opinion is further from the truth than the first ; for, as a matter of fact, the Lombards gradually adopted the Roman language, and to a certain degree Roman customs and civilisation ; and even intermarried with the Romans. Nevertheless, even in the time of King Luitprand, on the occasion of a desolating march towards Rome, many noble Romans were taken, shaven and dressed in the Lombard fashion.[4] The conquered Romans were indeed incorporated with the ruling race, but possessing unequal rights, as tributary vassals, or as bondsmen, although in the towns legal equality may gradually have become general. In Rothari's edict, as Hegel remarks, the name of Roman only once occurs, coupled with an expression of deep contempt. If, as the same learned writer says, the Romans worked their way out of the state of servitude or helplessness into which they had fallen, the process was certainly not completed until towards the end of the Lombard kingdom, and even then the majority of the Roman population was still in an oppressed condition. The amount of property of which, even at this later period, they were wholly or partly deprived must have been very great. Taking into account the continual internal quarrels and the ceaseless wars, it must be admitted that the history of the Lombards is little more than a chronicle of warfare, carried on with unabated barbarity for two centuries, against Byzantines and Romans. All this gives a gloomy insight into the condition of the people under the Lombard sway. The fact that the Byzantine yoke, in spite of its fiscal exactions, appeared more tolerable to the Italians than the Lombard, shows how incorrect it is to speak of a complete fusion and reconciliation of the two peoples. The

---

[3] *Storia degli Italiani*, iii. 88.   [4] *Vita Gregorii III.* p. 55, ed. Vignoli.

church, which during the Lombard period might have played a distinguished part in bringing about such a reconciliation and transformation, never attained the importance and political influence that she possessed in Spain, in France, or amongst the Anglo-Saxons. Considering that in the time of Paulus Diaconus the Gepidae, Bulgarians, Sarmatians, Pannonians, Suevi, Norici, and other tribes who had come into Italy with the Lombards, still possessed settlements, to which they gave their own names, in a country that had so often been laid waste and covered with ruins, we can understand the savage character of the hordes to which the defenceless population was a prey. The people were compelled, besides, to find wages and landed property for the foreign soldiers and adventurers who were continually joining the Lombards. It is easy to see how impossible it was in two hundred years for a united nationality to be formed out of elements so incongruous. The facility with which Pipin, and afterwards Charles, subdued the Lombards, and conquered Upper and Middle Italy, is chiefly to be explained by the hatred in which the Lombards were held by the whole Roman populace.

The connection between the House of Arnulf and Rome and the papal chair had become closer and closer. Pope and king had need of each other; each gave to each, that he might in turn receive; the pope needed protection and help, the Frankish princes leant for support upon the religious authority of the pope. But soon the situation was changed; a conflict of interests set in; the dependence of the pope upon the king continued, or rather increased, while the king had less need of the pope. Zachary rendered an important service to the Franks at the foundation of the new dynasty; in the form of a decision upon a case of conscience submitted to him, he had declared the justice of putting an end to the glaring contradiction, which could not be permanently maintained between a nominal impotent right and actual power ; that consequently the Franks were justified in putting an end to Chilperic's helpless but not harmless royalty, and setting up a powerful government in the person of Pipin. Pipin, for his part, had granted the pope's request, when the latter came to France (A.D. 754) to beg for help, and had even confirmed his promise of assistance in a document drawn up at Kiersy, by which he pledged himself to surrender the Exarchate and the Pentapolis with the town of Narnia to the Roman see, whenever he should have wrested these from the Lombards.

This was the beginning of that series of demands, petitions and complaints on the part of the popes, extending over forty years, from Stephen III.[3] to Adrian, with which the letters of the Codex Carolinus are filled, in which the extension of the papal territories is always represented as the highest and worthiest obligation incumbent upon Pipin and Charles for the salvation of their souls. Rome had long been a city, without trade or industry, in an almost desert Campagna, dependent for existence upon supplies from a distance. The number of poor, for whom the popes were forced to provide, must have been very great. The maintenance of lamps and candles in the churches and before the tombs of the saints, and the support of the poor, were the reasons assigned by the popes for their unwearying demands. And it is easy to understand why the popes were so ready to treat as joint property what belonged to the Roman Church or to St. Peter, and what belonged to the city of Rome or to the Roman commonwealth, and to make the one a cloak for the other. The continued struggle with the covetous and constantly encroaching Lombards had forced and accustomed them to do so. The Lombards cared nothing for the rights or claims of the Roman municipality or the Roman state, but they had some degree of reverence for the Roman Church, and for the apostolic

---

[3] [The pope, whom Döllinger calls Stephen III., is usually, and that even by Gregorovius and Reumont, described as the Second, his namesake and predecessor having reigned for a few days only.]

princes, and had a certain dread of committing sacrilege.

The form and motives of Pipin's donation are wrapped in obscurity, since the document has never been forthcoming. It included the Exarchate, the Pentapolis, and the town of Narnia. From the letters of Stephen III. and Paul I. it appears that this donation in the first place was demanded by the popes as a *restitution* which was admitted by the king,[6] and that, secondly, the pope received it in the name

[6] The usual term is *restituere* or *reddere*, in the earlier papal letters before Adrian. Thus Cenni, i. 75 Jaffé, Ep. 6, p. 35 s. : 'Ecclesiae et reipublicae civitates et loca restituenda confirmastis.' In the letter of the year 757, Cenni, 105 Jaffé, Ep. 11, p. 64 , it is St. Peter to whom Desiderius has promised *restitution* of the towns ; but to Pipin it is urged that the people could not live without the possession of those territories and towns *quæ semper cum eis sub unius dominii ditione erant connexæ*, and this is twice repeated. It is not a case, therefore, of a former right of the church or of St. Peter to these provinces and towns, but of a claim of the people of Italy who were not under the Lombard dominion, and the provinces and towns were, out of consideration to the wants of the people (the Respublica), to be made over as a deposit to St. Peter. Stephen's successor, Pope Paul I., again says that the Lombards refused *justitiam b. Petri restituere*, Cenni, i. 137 Ep. 11. p. 74 ; then Desiderius promises to '*restore*' Imola, 150 [Jaffé, Ep. 16, p. 76], and p. 219 Ep. 20, p. 89 Paul's grievance against Desiderius lies in the fact that the latter wished to prevent, *ne pars nostra, Romanorum propriam consequatur justitiam*. Here, then, there is no question of possessions or rights of the Roman Church, but of those of the people, the Respublica ; but St. Peter was answerable at that period for these also, and the letter in which Desiderius resigned his rights or claims is another proof to the pope that the king had no fear of St. Peter. What the *justitiæ b. Petri*, which were continually demanded, exactly were, Paul puts more plainly than Stephen or Adrian ; they are the *patrimonia, jura, loca, fines, territoria civitatum nostrarum reipublicæ Romanorum*, 163 [Jaffé, Ep. 19, p. 87] ; these Desiderius at last *restored*. By these, as by some other passages in Stephen's letters, it is plainly shown that before Charles's victories, the popes, on principle, as guardians or heirs of the Roman Respublica, claimed everything in Italy which did not belong to the old Lombard territory, and over which Byzantium could no longer maintain any hold. Pipin would not have made any great sacrifices for the Respublica alone; but as St. Peter was always held up to him as the patron of the Respublica, and all wants and claims were put forward in this name, it may be taken as the true expression of his feeling if, as the papal biography reports, he declared to the Greek ambassadors that he had drawn the sword not to recover for the Greeks the countries they had lost, but out of love for St. Peter.

both of the Roman Church and of the Roman Respublica. Against this is the fact that in the numerous letters of Pope Adrian which refer to this donation, or put forward new claims, there is no longer any mention of restitution or of the respublica, but exclusively of St. Peter, to whom territory and towns ought to be simply given or surrendered. Pipin must, therefore, have conceived that the Exarchate, with the Pentapolis, had once belonged to the Roman Church, in which case it might be supposed that the 'Donation of Constantine,' which is first heard of about this time, must have been cited to him as a title to possession. But this is contradicted by the prominence given to the Respublica, and by the fact that even at a later date the demands made in Rome were limited to certain parts of Italy.[7] The most correct view of the matter, then, is that

[7] The testimony of the *Liber Pontificalis* is decisive as to the fact that Pipin, in making over the Exarchate and the Pentapolis, had no intention of founding a spiritual principality or ecclesiastical state, but that he desired to give these territories in trust to the pope as representative of the Respublica in opposition to the Lombards or the Greeks, and that this was also the form in which the pope and his clerical and lay followers had proffered their request to the king. The Biographer of Stephen II. [III.], in this collection, shows himself so well informed as to the journey of the pope to North Italy and France, and is so exact in giving dates and localities, that we must suppose that he accompanied the pope on his journey, or had before him the diary of some one who did so. Now, he reports that Pipin, even at the first meeting at Ponthyon, had solemnly sworn to 'restore' the Exarchate and the other districts to the *jus reipublicæ*, in compliance with the wish of the pope (ed. Vignoli, p. 105). That *respublica* does not mean especially the Roman Ducatus, as some have assumed, is clear, and has been already noted by Savigny and Waitz (*Verf. Geschichte*, iii. 82). In the letters St. Peter, the church, and the Respublica of the Romans are usually named together—to them ought *civitates et loca* to be restored. Cenni, i. 74, 75 [Ep. 6, p. 35]. The Senate and the people of Rome, in the year 757, pray the king, first for the glory of the church (naturally the Roman), but next for *dilatatio hujus provinciæ a vobis de manu gentium ereptæ*, p. 144 [Ep. 6, p. 35]. Immediately afterwards Paul I. prays for *perfectam redemtionem istius provinciæ et exaltationem ecclesiæ* [Ep. 24, p. 100]. This certainly only refers to the Roman Ducatus. Once (in A.D. 761) Paul appears to narrow the signification of the *justitiæ Petri*: Pipin, he says, is fighting for the restoration of the lamps of St. Peter, i.e. for the recovery of the Patrimony, out of the revenues of which the lamps were maintained. According to Stephen IV., p. 287 [Ep. 47, p. 163], *propria ecclesiæ et Romanæ reipublicæ* ought to be restored by the Lombards.

Pipin made over these lands to the pope as the representative of the national Italian Respublica, so that only the patrimony within these provinces fell to the church; and further, that he and the popes used the expression 'to reinstate' because the Byzantine dominion over the provinces was regarded as a usurpation, begun long ago by the conquest of Justinian, which had interrupted, but not abolished, the right of self-government belonging to the Italico-Roman Respublica.* The Lombard conquest and the subjugation in turn of that people by the Franks had reawakened the pretensions of the Respublica, and had stirred it into new life, and from this point of view Pipin's act was in truth a restitution. But the pope at that period was the only power that, as the natural guardian or patricius of the non-Lombard Italians, could take charge of the restored territories. However, as soon as the Frankish king had become king of the Lombards, and, like his Lombard predecessors, was necessarily forced to extend his authority over Upper and Central Italy, the terms 'Respublica' and 'restitution' disappeared from the papal letters; for now Charles, and not the Pope, was the natural heir and protector of the Respublica. From this time forward the definitions contained in the letters of the popes, especially Adrian's, become confused; the *Justitia B. Petri* is used as a mantle to cover terms of a wide and undefined extent, and it is not clear whether the pope regarded himself as the lord of the Roman Duchy or merely as its guardian, whether he speaks in the name of the sovereign city of Rome or in his own.

It appears from the document of Kiersy (754) and the treaty with Astolf in 755 that Pipin made over to the papal chair only the Exarchate and the Pentapolis; and in the new donation of 756 these districts only were appropriated

---

* [Gregorovius, in his 2nd ed. (ii. 278 f.), adopts Döllinger's interpretation of the expression 'restitution,' but does not admit that the Byzantine rule was regarded as a usurpation.]

to the pope. Charles, on the contrary, on his first visit to Rome in 774, drew up a deed of donation, or rather of promise, as Adrian's biographer says, by virtue of which the pope was to be put in possession of a great deal more—of more, indeed, than the half of all Italy, comprising territory that Charles had not as yet conquered. What motive could have induced the king to make a promise politically so inexplicable deserves especial investigation. As a matter of fact, Charles left unfulfilled the greater part of the promise he then made. The first district which he at once—*i.e.*, in 774—made over to the pope was a part of the Lombard dukedom of Tuscany and Spoleto.

In the year 781 the Sabine district was made over to the pope; Benevento was also given then or in 787. Istria and Venetia were never surrendered; neither did Corsica ever come into the possession of the popes. From Adrian's utterances it is evident that documents from the Roman emperors, or from the Lombard kings, were laid before the king in proof of a legal claim over the districts coveted by Rome. It is important to remember that imperial documents, if genuine, could only contain donations of patrimony, not of sovereign right over towns and districts. In the duchies of Spoleto and Benevento the Roman Church had, even of old, possessed considerable patrimonies; but the claim was now made to the whole duchies, and neither Charles nor the plenipotentiaries whom he sent to Italy were in the least disposed to satisfy the demands of the pope to the full extent. How little authority was conceded to the pope in the district of Spoleto, which had been given to him in 774, is proved by his petition that the king would allow a particular kind of wood to be sent from thence to Rome for the repair of St. Peter's Church, as in his own territories it could not be grown.[9] And after Charles had given over the town of Capua to the pope, Adrian made the Capuans swear fealty not only to

[9] Cenni, i. 379 [Ep. 67, p. 211].

St. Peter and to himself, the pope, but to the king besides.[1]

So long as the Frankish power had not secured a footing in Italy, all that was not subject to either the Greeks or the Lombards claimed to be Roman, and to belong to the Respublica, desiring to be placed under the guardianship of the pope, the only national and morally strong power in Italy. But when the Lombard crown, with all its historical titles and the pretensions dictated by the claims of self-preservation, had been transferred to Charles, his Roman Patriciate then for the first time acquired significance and importance; then for the first time he coupled the despised title with that of King of the Lombards, concluded treaties with the pope as to the rights of his patriciate, and requested Adrian, not without reproach, to be more careful to respect them. Charles never called himself King of Italy, but King of the Lombards; yet practically he reigned over Italy, and even in the towns and provinces which had been made over to the Roman Church he made his supremacy felt,[2] although Adrian still nominally recognised the Byzantine emperor as his sovereign.[3]

[1] Cenni, i. 184, 187 Ep. 85 and 86, pp. 258 and 260.

[2] His imperial supremacy even in the Exarchate, is clearly shown in the affair of Archbishop Martin of Ravenna. When Pope Leo III. wished to compel the Archbishop to appear in Rome, in order to impose upon him certain restrictions, he first sent a Legate to the emperor to obtain his approbation. The latter, however, sent Bishop John of Arles with instructions to conduct the Archbishop to Rome and to assist him when there, when the Archbishop excused himself on pretext of indisposition. This induced the pope to release him from obeying the summons. (Agnellus, in Muratori, ii. 182.) Prior to this (c. 783) the people of Ravenna had appealed to the king against the pope, and Adrian had declared himself satisfied that any of his subjects should appeal to the king as umpire. (Cenni, i. 521 Ep. 98, p. 201.) Adrian's letters contain other frequent proofs of his submission to Charles's authority; Adrian exculpates himself when complaints are made against him, hastens to submit to Charles's demands, and renders account as to matters of justice and fealty. Here then is the xplanation, where some have chosen to see a contradiction, of the fact that Charles, according to the pope's assertion, made a donation of the Dukedom of Spoleto to St. Peter (Cenni, i. 341 [Ep. 47, p. 191]), but at the same time continued to exercise over it the full rights of sovereignty.

[3] Adrian also wrote to the Empress Irene and her son quite in the

The situation of things in Italy urgently called for some solution to relieve the uncertainty and the strain caused by these relations. Charles was already regarded by his contemporaries as the master of Rome. Paulus Diaconus plainly says that Charles had incorporated Rome with his realm, and this was long before the imperial coronation. That Charles was already in possession of Rome was at a later period (800) one of the chief reasons for choosing him emperor.[1] The new pope sent to the king in 796, with the gift of the keys of St. Peter's tomb, also the banner of the city of Rome; and the request accompanying these tokens —that Charles would send one of his nobles to Rome to administer to the Roman people the oath of fealty and independence leaves no doubt as to their significance. The manner in which Charles, in his letter to the new pope, defines their respective duties is characteristic. He appears to see in the pope only the high priest and intercessor. 'My part,' he says, 'is to defend the church by force of arms from external attack, and to secure her internally through the establishment of the Catholic faith; your part is to render us the assistance of prayer.' Charles declares, at the same time, that he has been well pleased to receive from the pope the humble assurance of his obedience and fidelity.[5]

The attack upon the pope Leo III. by Adrian's nephews brought Charles for the fourth time to Rome, and the result of this visit was the 'renovation of the Roman Empire,' as a coin struck at the time to commemorate the event describes it. On Christmas Day, in the year 800, the pope, suddenly after mass, placed the crown upon Charles's head, and the acclamations of the people announced to him that he was Emperor of the Romans. This, for the next ten centuries, was the most important day in the history of the world.

style of a subject, saying of the imperial letter: διὰ τῆς ὑμετέρας κελεύσεως, ἐν τῇ εὐσεβεῖ ὑμῶν κελεύσει.

[1] *Annales Lauresham.* Pertz M.G., S.S., i. 38.

[5] 'Gavisi sumus . . . in humilitatis vestræ obedientia et in promissionis ad nos fidelitate.' Mansi, xiii. 980 [Jaffé, *Bibl. Rer. Germ.* iv. 354].

IV. The Coronation of Charles as Emperor.

There are several questions to be answered and several points to be investigated in order to elucidate the event of Christmas Day, A.D. 800, in its motives, aims, and consequences.

In the first place, with regard to the personal action of the pope, it has been customary to combine the Frankish reports with the Romish account given in the Liber Pontificalis, in such a way that the one supplements the other. But there are strong objections against this mode of proceeding. For the matter, unanimously reported in one fashion by the Frankish chroniclers, is differently represented in the papal annals. According to the Frankish accounts, the course of events was as follows: Paschalis, Campulus, and their numerous followers amongst the Roman nobility, had first condemned the pope as guilty of a pretended crime, had then proclaimed his deposition, and afterwards had committed the outrage. The Frankish delegates, who by Charles's command escorted the pope back to Rome, proceed forthwith to an investigation of the matter, and send the authors of the outrage as prisoners to France. Seven days after his arrival in Rome, Charles convenes an assembly and informs it of his reason for coming, and occupies himself daily (for several days, therefore) with the matters that have brought him. Amongst these, the most difficult and important is that already begun (by Charles's delegates), the investigation of the crimes of which the pope had been accused. Charles had brought the pope's enemies, Paschalis and Campulus, back with him from France. It now appeared, upon judicial inquiry, that they were not in a position to give any formal proof of Leo's guilt; Charles perceived, therefore, that hatred was the motive which had induced them to make the accusation. Thereupon he and the bishops announced to the pope that the accusation having fallen through, it now depended upon the pope whether he would choose of his own free will, not as the consequence of a legal verdict, to take the oath of purgation. Leo took the oath. Such is the unanimous account of the annals of Fulda, Lorsch, and of Eginhard, as well as of the chronicle of Moissac.

Very different is the statement made in the Liber Pontificalis, and it is impossible to avoid the inference that the story has been throughout intentionally tampered with ; it passes over some points in silence and misrepresents others.[a] The statement, to begin with, that Leo's election had been unanimous amongst all classes, is, judging from later events, more than doubtful. Next, it is related that Leo was twice mutilated by his enemies ; the first time, in the street, when his tongue was cut out, and as it was believed he was blinded by his eyes being torn out ; the second time, immediately afterwards, when Paschalis and Campulus dragged him into the church of a monastery, and completed the tearing out of both eyes and tongue. But afterwards, during his confinement in the monastery of St. Erasmus, his eyes and speech, through God's grace and the intercession of St. Peter, were in a wonderful way restored. The biographer evidently intends that the reader should believe an actual miracle to have taken place, although he does not venture to mention the word, but he forthwith proceeds to represent a very natural occurrence as a 'great miracle,' viz., that one of the Pope's partisans let him down by a cord from the wall of the monastery, whence he escaped to St. Peter's, and thence to the Duke of Spoleto. The double mutilation, which would certainly have needed an unparalleled miracle to repair, is a fiction ; the Frankish annalists say nothing about it. Afterwards when Leo returns under Frankish protection, the whole

[a] [Simpson, *Charles the Great*, 169², 229¹, and Exc. i., agrees with Döllinger in considering the Frankish annals throughout as the most worthy of credit. Gregorovius, in his 2nd ed. (ii. 483), has also adopted Döllinger's opinion that *das Buch der Päpste den Process (gegen Leo) verschleiere.* Ranke, *Weltgesch.* i. 182 and 187, follows the *Liber Pontificalis.*]

population streams out to meet him, overjoyed to have him back again, so that one cannot understand why in the first instance in Rome not a single hand had been lifted in his defence, and why no one but the Duke of Spoleto should have afforded him shelter. The clerical and lay envoys sent by Charles, having escorted the pope back to Rome, institute an enquiry, which lasts more than a week, and interrogate Adrian's nephews as to their accusation against the pope; but they, being unable to say anything, are sent to France. When Charles himself arrives, he calls a great clerical and lay assembly, which he commissions to decide the question of the crime laid against the pope. But the bishops and abbot unanimously declare: 'We cannot venture to judge the Apostolic chair, whose office it is, rather, to judge us; according to ancient tradition, it cannot be judged; to the pope's declaration, whatever it may be, we will yield canonical obedience.' Thereupon the pope offers to take the oath of purgation. It is evident that things have here been given quite a different colouring. According to the Frankish reports, Charles institutes a formal enquiry into the pope's conduct, which lasts several days. When nothing can be proved against Leo, he is given free choice whether he will still take the oath of innocence. Charles, in conjunction with the bishops, undoubtedly sat in judgment upon the pope and delivered a verdict. But, according to the Romish chronicler, the bishops, both Frankish and Italian, will not allow the proceeding to go so far, but cut the whole matter short by declaring that a pope cannot be subjected to a legal sentence; in fact, Charles, by implication, receives a rebuke for having set on foot an illegal undertaking—the trial of a pope. The later occurrence of a fresh conspiracy of the Romans against Leo, the execution of several of the conspirators at the command of the pope, and the interference of the Emperor Ludwig, are passed over in silence by the Liber Pontificalis.

The next point which comes under consideration is the

relative position which Charles occupied on the one side to the pope, on the other to the Greek Empire and imperial throne.

Charles did not doubt, for he had been brought up in that belief, that the pope was the successor of St. Peter, the bearer of the highest ecclesiastical authority, the first in rank of all the bishops of the world. Yet this authority was in his eyes confined within narrow limits, and the king often set himself above the pope not only in civil, but even in ecclesiastical matters. He made the pope feel that he was dependent upon him, and must even occasionally obey his commands. Besides this, he had learnt by experience that Rome and the popes were for ever approaching him with fresh claims, and desiring only to avail themselves of his strong arm for their own purposes. He was well aware that the papal chair was unable to stand without support, and that without him it would become a prey to the factions of the Roman nobility, as it had before to the Lombards. The heads of these factions had already appropriated to themselves the most important clerical dignities in Rome. Even as a youth Charles had seen the pope imploring help, prostrate before himself and his father, Pipin.[7] Later on, his bishops, returning from the Roman Synod (769), had reported to him how Pope Constantine II., after a reign of thirteen months, had been blinded, deposed, and personally assaulted at the synod by bishops and priests. Charles had then learnt that the very same men who, for more than a year, had served the pope at the altar, and had celebrated mass with him, now declared all the acts of his pontificate to be invalid, and constrained the bishops and priests whom he had ordained to submit to a fresh ordination. He had also heard how the new pope, Stephen IV., with the rest of the Roman prelates, had thrown themselves on their knees in presence of the whole synod, and had there confessed themselves guilty of having received the communion at the hands of

[7] *Chron. Moissac.* Pertz [Mon. G. SS.], i. 293.

Constantine, and had submitted to the penance imposed upon them.[a] Adrian, whose letters to Charles were chiefly filled with petitions and claims for grants of land and towns, had incurred Charles's displeasure by his participation in the Synod at Nicæa (787), and his confirmation of the resolutions there passed on the worship of images. Without any reference to the pope or his legates, the Nicene decrees were rejected at the great synod summoned at Frankfort by Charles, and a deep wound was thereby inflicted upon the papal authority.

Charles's personal ascendency, even in ecclesiastical matters, obscured and repressed the papacy at that time. Rome was suffering from the miseries consequent upon centuries of devastation in Italy. The citizens had become brutalised. Very few amongst them had any intellectual cultivation. The bishops of that time saw in Charles not only the powerful guardian, but the reformer and director of the church. During the winter of 801, while Charles was in Rome, Paulinus of Aquileia recommended not the pope, but the new emperor, to urge the bishops to the investigation of Holy Scripture; the clergy to better discipline; and the monks to piety, and thus build up and restore the church." The synods were assembled at his bidding, not at that of the pope,[1] and what is more, the pope obeyed a royal command when he held a synod in Rome to consider the Adoptionist controversy.[2] The king,

[a] 'Projiciens se in terram sanctissimus Stephanus Papa cum universis sacerdotibus et populo Romano, c'amantesque, Kyrie eleison, cum ingenti fletu peccasse se omnes professi sunt . . . sicque ex hoc omnibus indicta est pœnitentia.' Even the Acts of the Council, which Constantine had confirmed, were now burnt. *Concilium Lateranense*, ed. Cenni, Rom. 1735, p. 10.

[b] Paulini Aquil. *Opera*, ed. Madrisins, p. 189.

[1] So the Frankfort Synod records that it was assembled 'præcipiente et præsidente . . . Carolo rege, ad renovandum cum consilio pacificæ unanimitatis . . . ecclesiæ statum.' Sirmondi.*Conc.Gall.* ii. 175 [comp. Simpson, ii. 63⁵].

[2] Two synods were held by Charles's order upon the Adoptionist matter, the one by Adrian, the other by Leo. With respect to the first, Leo said before the Council of 799 : 'Et olim quidem a prædecessore nostro Hadriano Papa, et ex auctoritate sedis apostolicæ, ejusdem regis magni jussione synodali tramite sub anathematis vinculo putabatur esse exstincta.' Sirmondi,

not the papal legates, who were present, presided at the great Council of Frankfort. The Synod of Altino (799), or rather Paulinus in the name of the synod, declared itself ready to alter its decrees according to Charles's pleasure, or to abandon them altogether.³ Even the new pope had to put up with the exhortation sent him by Charles through his ambassador, Angilbert, to lead a moral life, to observe the canons, and do away with simony. The popes, on their side, might have had frequent occasion of addressing like exhortations to the king, who, even in old age, continued to indulge in sensuality; but it is not found that they did so. It is also remarkable that even at a later time Pope John VIII. not only acknowledged the mission of Charles as a powerful reformer of the church, but warmly praised him as having understood his mission, and having purified the church of that time from errors.¹

Charles himself readily styled the pope his spiritual father, but in the guidance of the church he assigned to him a task very subordinate to that which he appropriated to himself. For himself he arrogated the responsibility of edifying the church internally by causing the recognition of the Catholic faith; the pope's mission was to pray for Christendom and for him.⁵ He often, nevertheless, sought the pope's advice upon ecclesiastical matters, and on one occasion even obtained a dispensation to withdraw a bishop from his diocese and to retain him as chancellor; yet every-

Conc. Gall. ii. 224. Of the other, Felix of Urgel affirms that it was 'præcipiente Carolo, præsente Leone Apostolico,' with fifty-seven bishops in Rome (799). Sirmondi, i. c. 226 [comp. Simson, ii. 35³ and 157²].

³ Paulini *Opera*, pp. 191 and 235.

⁴ Discourse of the pope at the coronation of Charles the Bald, Bouquet, vii. 695 : ' Qui cum omnes ecclesias sublimasset, semper hoc erat ei in voto, semper in desiderio—ut S. Romanam ecclesiam in antiquum statum et ordinem reformaret.' Evidently the numerous donations made by Charles to the Roman Chair are principally referred to. But further on it is said: 'Religionis quippe statum . . . sacris literis erudivit . . . erroribus expurgavit, ratis dogmaticis saginavit,' &c. This zeal of Charles for the internal purification of the church had been praised by Alcuin also, *Epist.* 84, p. 124 [ed. Jaffé, Ep. 111].

⁵ Bouquet, v. 626 [Ep. Carol. Jaffé, *Bibl.* iv. 356

thing, after all, was decided and carried out at his will and pleasure. Theodulf, Bishop of Orleans, accordingly affirms that St. Peter has entrusted the keys of his church to the king, 'for it is Charles who administers the affairs of the church, and who governs not only the people, but the clergy.'[6]

The position of Charles in relation to the East Roman Empire and the Byzantine court was decided by his conquests in Italy, and his aspiring to the imperial dignity; after that it could only be hostile, especially on the side of the Greeks. The struggle for the possession of Istria, Liburnia, Venetia, and Dalmatia went on. Charles had gained possession of Istria (789); but the Greeks still held the command of the Adriatic, which was of the utmost importance to the Byzantine Empire, and, in order to maintain it, were obliged to hold on to the protectorate over Venetia, and the possession of Liburnia and Dalmatia. At the same time their hold of the provinces of Lower Italy seemed to depend upon Charles's good pleasure. Charles did not disguise from himself that, so long as he was not emperor, the right of the Eastern Roman emperor over the Italian territories was held in public opinion to be better founded, as being more ancient and respected than his own. Byzantium, besides, had not formally resigned anything. Even in Rome the nominal supremacy of the eastern emperor was still recognised; by a single lucky campaign, even by the landing of an army at an unfortunate moment for the Franks, this supremacy might have again been transformed into a reality. The constant alliance of the Venetians with Byzantium was a continual menace to the neighbouring districts subject to the Frankish king. For in Venice the party favourable to the Greeks was in the majority. The pope had been consequently forced at Charles's bidding to expel all the

---

[6] Bouquet, v. 421 [also M. G. P. *Car. I.*, 524].
  Tu regis ecclesiæ (claves), nam regit ille (Petrus) poli.
  Tu regis ejus opes, clerum populumque gubernas.

Venetian merchants from the Exarchate and the Pentapolis; upon their part the Greeks had blinded the Bishop Mauritius in Istria as being a partisan of the Franks,[7] and probably for the same reason had caused the Patriarch John of Grado, the son of the Doge of Venice, to be thrown from the tower of his castle.[8]

Thus, the entangled state of affairs in Italy pressed the king to grasp the imperial crown. Thereby everything would be simplified, and every possession and every claim would acquire a well-founded right in the opinion of the people. His patriciate laid obligations upon him, without giving him corresponding rights or fixed powers. It must have appeared to him as a stepping-stone, upon which he ought not to remain standing, but from which he must advance to the higher and clearer position and dignity of the imperium.

It is in itself highly probable that Charles, long before the year 800, had already formed the idea of becoming emperor, and had begun to foster the wish to restore the empire to Rome and to combine it with the Frankish kingdom. He regarded the empire certainly, in its high religious importance, in the same light as did his spiritual teachers, contemporaries, and friends. These having been brought up in familiarity with the writings of the fathers, could not conceive of the Christian Church without the Roman Empire; the imperium was still in their eyes ordained of God to be the basis and support of the church; it must exist so long as the church exists; its fall would be a sign of the approaching end of all earthly things. The decline and visibly increasing weakness of the Eastern Roman Empire was to them a disaster, a disgrace to Christianity; and it must have appeared an unnatural state of things, as well as a misfortune for the Christian Church, that the might and dignity of the Roman Empire should rest in the feeble and incompetent hands of the Byzantine monarchs. Had

---

[7] Bouquet, v. 588, 559.
[8] Lebret, *History of Venice*, i. 121 [Simson, ii. 293].

not the ancient Christians especially prayed for the preservation of Rome because she was the keystone of the imperium, and because she was the city which upheld and maintained all?[9] Providence itself seemed to have ordained that the strong, flourishing Frankish Empire should take over the inheritance of the Roman Empire without any violent breach of continuity, and that the Roman Imperium should again find its legitimate centre in Rome.

But Constantinople, with its young Emperor Constantine, stood in the way. The thought of a partition of the empire into east and west, similar to that which had taken place for a time in the fourth and fifth centuries, was foreign to the ideas of the age. That partition had long passed away; for centuries only one emperor had been known, the one in Byzantium. Peaceful overtures had been made: the Empress-mother Irene (781-2) had sued for the hand of Rotrude, the daughter of Charles, for her son, the youthful emperor. But the negotiations after some years had been broken off; Irene, to whom, because she was determined to govern alone, the daughter of the powerful Frankish king was unwelcome as a daughter-in-law, gave Maria of Amnia to her son for his wife at the end of 788.[1]

Charles believed that he had found a pretext which would enable him to declare the imperial throne vacant and after that to claim it for himself, and to this end he

---

[9] *Illa est civitas, quæ adhuc sustentat omnia.* Lactantius, *Opp.* i. 584. Lactantius was convinced that the Roman Imperium could never be severed from Rome. Hilary, who was the author of the commentaries upon the apostolic epistles, although throughout the Middle Ages they were attributed to Ambrose, had a remarkable influence over the conceptions of a later date. He, Augustine, and Jerome caused the opinion to become prevalent that the *defectio* foretold (2 Thess. ii. 6, 7), after which Anti-Christ and the end of the world were to follow, would be an *abolitio imperii Romani*, the falling away of all nations from the Roman Empire. Two authors, much read in those days, Bede and Pseudo-Prosper, the author of the book *De Promissionibus et Prædictionibus Dei*, confirm this view.

[1] [For the different opinions of the historians upon the betrothal of the young Emperor Constantine with Charles's daughter Rotrude, see Richter-Kohl, *Annals*, ii. pp. 78 and 97 f.]

seized the opportunity which the Synod, held at Nicea (787) to decide upon the question of image worship, afforded him.

Charles took the liveliest interest in religious controversies, and threw himself with zeal into the discussions; but upon this occasion his mode of proceeding was altogether different from that which he had adopted in the Adoptionist controversy. He had allowed the latter to be dealt with after the regular ecclesiastical manner; in the question of images he threw the whole weight of his name and personality into the scale. It was his intention to use them as a weapon. Three years after that synod — and this is remarkable — he made Alcuin compose a treatise upon the deliberations and resolutions of the synod in which he himself led the discussion.[2] The whole composition is a solemn manifesto, a severe indictment directed in the first place against the emperor and his mother; secondly, against the Greek bishops. The arrogance of the Byzantines, coupled with their ignorance, their neglect of the western churches, their independent attitude in ecclesiastical things — all this is denounced in the strongest terms. Charles well knew that at the time of the synod Constantine was only sixteen years old, and was not therefore capable of forming a judgment in ecclesiastical affairs; but this did not prevent him casting the blame upon the youth for everything that had then happened. He purposely only speaks of him as 'king,' whilst, instead of calling himself, as he had been wont to do, King of the Lombards, he styles himself 'by the grace of God, King of Italy.' The charges made in the very first chapter, with reference to some traditional expressions used in Byzantine documents,[3] show that to attack the emperor and his mother was the primary object of the Frankish king. Irene is reproached with having offended against

[2] [Simson, 78 f., distinguishes between a treatise composed by Alcuin in his own name and the *libri Carolini* written in Charles's name.]

[3] *Libri Carolini*, ed. Heumann, 3, 14, p. 317.

the laws of God and man in having behaved at the synod as a 'directress and teacher:' both she and her son have become mad with pride.[1] Some years later, at the synod of Frankfort, the synod of Nicea with its decrees upon the worship of images was absolutely condemned, and the papal legates, if they did not give their assent, had at any rate to remain passive.

Had Charles been occupied chiefly with the religious question, he would have endeavoured above all things to bring about an agreement between the view taken by the Frankish Church and that of the pope and the Romish Church. For the difference of opinion was wide. In the Frankish kingdom the mere exhibition of religious images, without any outward sign of worship, was all that was tolerated. In Rome, on the contrary, there was entire accordance with the conclusions of the synod of Nicea, which approved the worship of images. Of this Charles was well aware, but none the less entirely ignored it in his book. He pretends that the pope is in perfect agreement with him and the Frankish bishops, and that he, the king, only raised this protest, and made these charges, to protect the rightful claims of the Roman Church against the selfish and arbitrary conduct of the Greeks. He has only the Greek Emperor and his bishops in view.

Acting upon this manifesto, or rather upon the epitome of it which was forwarded to Rome, Charles, through his confidant Angilbert, summoned the pope to declare the emperor a heretic—a suggestion which threw the pope into no small embarrassment, since he had himself approved the resolutions of the synod, and had through his legates taken part in them all. Adrian sought to evade the difficulty; he wrote a submissive letter to Charles,

[1] It is charged as a grave offence against the emperor and his mother that they use the word *divalia* in their edicts, that they say *Deum sibi conregnare*, that they assert that they seek the honour of God, and the like. Yet the popes, in their letters to the emperors, had unhesitatingly used the same expressions; for instance, Agathos, in his letter to Constantine Pogonatus: *divales apices*. Harduin, *Conc.* iii. 1075.

in which he said that he would, if the king would allow him, summon the imperial court to surrender to the Roman chair the patrimony which had been wrested from it, and the jurisdiction over the Illyrian diocese. If this were refused, then he was ready to condemn the emperor as a heretic.[5]

Had not the pope felt himself entirely dependent upon the Frankish king, it is impossible to conceive that he could have voluntarily incurred an obligation so contrary to all ecclesiastical ideas of justice or truth, which, if realised, must have had the immediate effect of causing a separation between East and West.

The subsequent course of the matter is not known; at all events, the blinding and death of Constantine (796) relieved the pope from taking any further steps. But what would have happened if that extreme measure had been taken? Is it possible that Charles remembered how the Romans in the year 712, when the Emperor Philippicus desired to revive the Monothelistic heresy, had renounced their allegiance, and had declared that they no longer would acknowledge him as emperor? And again how, under Leo the Isaurian, they had thought of proceeding to the choice of a new emperor, whom they proposed to conduct by force of arms to Constantinople? The presumption is justifiable that Charles desired to bring about his own election as emperor in the place of Constantine, who, as a heretic, had, according to the views of that period, forfeited his right to the imperial throne.[6]

Now, for the first time, the highest dignity in Christendom was borne by a woman. To the contemporary world this must have seemed unnatural, contrary to law, and intolerable. Even according to Roman law a woman was

---

[5] For the letter of Adrian see Mansi, xiii. 759. [Alcuin, *Ep.* 33 in Jaffé, *Bibl. Rer. Germ.* vi. 248. Jaffé ascribes it to the year 794—of course, after the Synod of Frankfort. [Simson, p. 78, puts Angilbert's mission and the answer of the pope before the Frankfort Synod.]

[6] [Against this opinion Otto-Harnack, *Die Beziehungen des frankisch-italischen zu dem byzantinischen Reiche* (Gött. Diss.), 1880, p. 40 f.]

incapable of reigning.⁷ We see that in 798 negotiations took place between Charles and Irene; that a Greek embassy, bearing proposals of peace, agreed with Charles that Sisinnius, the brother of the Patriarch Tarasius, who had been imprisoned, should be set free to return with the ambassadors to Constantinople—certainly not without being charged with some commission. The object doubtless was to find some combination by which the imperial dignity might be made to devolve upon Charles as the successor of Constantine VI. In those days negotiations of that kind required a long time. Wittbold and John, whom Charles had sent to Irene (785), took eighteen months on the return journey after leaving Constantinople.⁸

But the events which occurred in Rome, and the impatience of the Frankish nobles, of the pope, and of the Roman people, cut the knot which Charles had for years been vainly endeavouring to untie.

Eginhard, as is well known, records that Charles, after his coronation, was in the habit of asserting that had he been previously aware of the pope's intention he would not have gone to church on that day, in spite of it being the greatest of Christian festivals. Modern historians almost unanimously suppose such an assertion to have been impossible; the plan must have originated with Charles himself, and must have been the outcome of deliberations carried on for some time past between himself, his Franks, and the pope, so that the assertion that the affair took place by surprise and without his co-operation was simply untrue. Even the reproach of having in this greatest and most important occurrence of his life acted with unworthy hypocrisy has not been spared. Thus Gregorovius recently expressed himself strongly: 'The king gave himself, as Augustus once did, the appearance of being unwilling to accept the

---

⁷ For the passage upon this, see Grotius, *De Jure Belli ac Pacis*, ed. Cocceji, ii. 532.

⁸ *Gesta Abb. Fontanell.* 787. [*M. G. SS.*, ii. 291; comp. Abel, *Karl d. Gr.* i. 472.]

highest dignity until he could declare himself ready. The world was dazzled by a *coup de théâtre*.'⁹ The Italian La Farina,¹ and the German authors Kurz, Rettberg, and others, have vied with Gregorovius in like expressions. It has even been asserted that Charles had systematically set himself in his own person to play the part of a Roman emperor, particularly by interfering in the Adoptionist and Iconoclast controversies. Gfrörer has supposed besides that Charles had already (possibly between 785 and 795) treated with Pope Adrian upon the subject of the imperial crown. This may well have been possible, and in 794 Angilbert, besides the message entrusted to him with regard to the Greek emperor, may have been commissioned to negotiate with the pope in favour of Charles assuming the imperial crown. Yet it is generally supposed that the plan was first mooted and secretly discussed between Leo III. and Charles after the former had taken refuge in Charles's camp at Paderborn (April, 799).² Heinrich Leo³ thinks that in the consultations which Charles held with Alcuin at Tours in the summer of the year 800 the revival of the imperial dignity was further discussed, and that it appears to have been made the condition of Charles's presence and of his protection, notwithstanding that, as a matter of form,

⁹ [In the later editions (2 ed., ii. 491) Gregorovius, convinced chiefly by Döllinger's arguments, has abandoned the opinion expressed in the first. (Vol. ii. 547.)]

¹ 'Questo era congiunger all' ambizione falsità ed ipocrisia,' *Storia d'Italia*, ii. 47. In the same way Kurz, *Kirchengeschichte*, ii. 213: 'Wie weit er in dieser Heuchelei ging, ergibt sich aus Eginhard.' Comp. Luden's *D. G.* iv. 413. The French authors Des Michels, Monnier, and Henri Martin express themselves in a similar manner. The Benedictines Martene and Durand, so far as I can see, are the first who (*Vet. Monum. ampl. Coll.*, iv., praef. §1), quoting from John Diaconus, accuse Charles of dissimulation. But Sigonius, Daniel, and Gaillard also refuse to believe Eginhard's statement, or that Charles spoke the truth. [Ranke gives Döllinger especial credit for having proved the indefensibility of the opinion that the whole affair of the coronation was preconcerted. Ranke, *Weltgesch.* v. p. 2, 184¹.]

² [According to Simson, 179³, Pope Leo first came to Paderborn in July 799.]

³ *Vorlesungen über deutsche Geschichte*, i. 510 ff. He has here, like many others, followed Frid. Lorenz in his life of Alcuin.

it might be said 'to have taken place by a sudden inspiration, by a kind of prophetic act, on the part of the pope.'

Amongst modern writers Waitz[1] is almost alone in rendering to the king the justice due from an historian. 'People,' he says, 'have hardly a right to cast a doubt upon Eginhard's statement. As far as we can judge, it can only be intended to mean that the king was surprised on the day, and perhaps had not yet given his consent to the matter which was occupying the thoughts of those around him.' I share this opinion, but I should like to set aside the 'perhaps,' and to say decidedly: 'Charles was unaware of what was intended, and had not as yet given his consent.'

It seems to me quite conceivable that Charles's thoughts and plans had for years past been directed towards the attainment of the imperial dignity, and that he was nevertheless taken by surprise upon that Christmas Day, A.D. 800, and saw in the step taken by the pope and in the tumultuous manifestations of the will of the populace a precipitate act, which might make him honestly say that he would not have come to church on that day if he had known beforehand what would happen. At the moment, as I think I have shown to be probable, he was carrying on negotiations with Irene, and it was of the greatest consequence to him to make sure in the first place of the recognition of his imperial title in Constantinople, and to be reckoned as the legitimate successor of Constantine VI. The event of Christmas Day broke in abruptly upon the negotiations. The supposition in Constantinople would be that Charles had cunningly designed to put the imperial court in the position of having to give its consent to an accomplished fact.

But what evidence have we that obliges us to consider the event as having been preconcerted? It is, says Leo, incontestable from one of Alcuin's letters, that Alcuin himself knew *beforehand* of this revival of the imperial

---

[1] *Deutsche Verfassungsgeschichte* [1 ed.], iii. 175.

dignity. This, since Lorenzo made the discovery, has been the received opinion, and the conclusion is drawn that Charles had also known about it, and that his ignorance and his surprise were feigned. For Alcuin presented Charles with a splendid Bible, *ad splendorem imperialis potentiæ*, as he says in his accompanying letter, and had arranged that this Bible should be delivered at Christmas; so that he must have known in Tours that the coronation in Rome was to take place on that day. Even Waitz bows to this proof.[5] Nevertheless it fails at once, from the fact that Alcuin expressly says—'his friend Fridegis (he called him Nathanael), who was to deliver the Christmas gift, is now at Aix.'[6] Charles, therefore, was to receive the Bible at Aix, and not in Rome, nor on Christmas Day of A.D. 800; but in some earlier or later year, only before 804. The letter to Charles bears the inscription: 'To the King,' whilst Alcuin's letters, after Charles had become emperor, are always addressed: 'To Charles the Emperor.' We must therefore assume that *imperialis potentia* refers in this instance not to the power of the emperor, but to that of the empire.[7] In reality it is much more surprising that Alcuin's letters should contain no reference to the plan of assuming the imperial title, especially the letter in which he replied to Charles's communication about what had happened in Rome. Alcuin confines himself to advising Charles above all to secure to himself the possession of Rome.[8]

No weight is to be attached, even in the opinion of

[5] *D. Verf. Gesch.* iii. 175, note 2.
[6] *Alcuini Opp.*, ed. Froben, tt. 154, 248. [*Alc. Ep.* 205, 206; Jaffé, *Bibl.* vi. 697.]
[7] Thus the Italian bishops, as early as 794, speak of the proclamation of Charles to the Frankfort Synod: 'Imperii ejus decretum.' Baluze *ad De Marca, de Concord.*, iii. 177, ed. Bamberg. Even Pipin was already called imperator. [From the words 'imperialis potentia' Dümmler infers in Jaffé: 'Carolus igitur jam imperator creatus erat. Vana sunt quæ de hoc munere sibi effinxit Lorenz.' *Alcuin's Leben*, p. 236.]
[8] Charles from Saxony communicated to Alcuin what had occurred in Rome. Alcuin, still in 799, replies that the safety of the church rests now in Charles's hands alone: 'Nullatenus capitis cura omittenda est. Levius est pedes dolere quam caput. Componatur pax cum populo nefando, si

Gregorovius, to the statement in the 'Liber Pontificalis' that after the coronation Charles presented splendid consecration gifts to the Roman churches, as if they had been prepared in expectation of the occurrence. These presents of sacred vessels and other objects Charles would certainly have made, even had the coronation not taken place; besides which, it must not be forgotten that the biographer of Leo, who, as already mentioned, wrote at a considerably later time, ascribes to this occasion all the gifts that Charles ever made on his different visits to Rome, or that he sent from a distance; for elsewhere, in spite of

fieri potest. Relinquantur aliquantulum minae, ne obdurati fugiant, sed in spe retineantur, donec salubri consilio ad pacem revocentur. Tenendum est quod habetur, ne propter acquisitionem minoris, quod majus est amittatur. Servetur ovile proprium, ne lupus rapax devastet illud. Ita in alienis sudetur, ut in propriis damnum non patiatur.' How many different interpretations have been put upon this passage in the last 200 years! First by Pagi, who by the *majus* and *ovile proprium* understood the Lombard kingdom, and drew the conclusion that Rome could not as yet have formed part of Charles's territory. Froben has refuted this statement, *Alcuini Opp.* i. 118. Gregorovius (ii. 533) has recently again mistaken the passage by understanding the *aliena* to be the 'particular relations betwixt the pope and the Romans which Charles, as judge, was with prudence to set in order.' The *populus nefandus*, with whom Charles is to make peace, is also, according to Gregorovius, the Roman populace, and so on. This is all incorrect. The matter stands thus: Charles had written to Alcuin from Saxony, where he was with his army, to inform him of the assault upon the pope, and, as appears from Alcuin's answer, had declared that he was altogether taken up by Saxon affairs, and therefore, for the present, could not attend personally to Roman ones. He was at the moment occupied with the great transplantation of Saxon families into other provinces of which the Annalists inform us. Alcuin represents in answer to this that he ought not to abandon the head (Rome and the Roman chair); a malady in the foot (Saxony) must be easier to bear than one in the head. He ought, therefore, if possible, to conclude peace with the Saxons, and to hold fast what he already possessed (Rome), in order not, in acquiring the lesser (Saxon territory), to lose the greater (Rome); he ought to protect his own flock from the wolf, and so to operate in the foreign land (Saxony had not yet become a Frankish province) that he should not suffer in his own (Rome and Italy). That this rightly interprets Alcuin is clear from the next letter (ed. Froben, p. 120), where the Saxons are expressly called the *populus nefandus*, and Alcuin wishes that the Saxons would leave the king at liberty for the journey. [Gregorovius, in his 2nd ed., ii. p. 476, has given up his own view and adopted that of Döllinger. Comp. Simson, 175², and *Alc. Ep.* 114 and 118, in Jaffé, *Bibl.* vi. 465 and 483.]

the minute enumeration and description, the consecration gifts presented by the monarch are not mentioned either in Adrian's biography or in Leo's. Yet it must certainly be admitted that Charles, even before that time, had made important gifts to the Roman churches, and it is recorded that he sent by Angilbert (A.D. 796) a considerable part of the treasure taken from the royal residence of the Avars as a present to Rome; of this not a word is said in the biography of the pope.

The statement of Johannes Diaconus, that Pope Leo, when he fled from his enemies, promised the imperial crown to Charles, as the price of the protection afforded him, is unworthy of credit. This of course would have happened in Paderborn. That this author, who lived a century later in Naples—he was born about the year 870—possessed but scanty information as to the events of Charles's lifetime is shown by his further statement that Charles at once [9] marched into Italy with a large army, took possession of Rome and reinstated the pope. It is difficult to understand how it is that the evidence of a witness who thus distorts the best ascertained facts is preferred to that of contemporary historians. Yet some modern writers have placed implicit confidence in him.

The event of Christmas Day A.D. 800 was doubtless not altogether an act of sudden inspiration, nor were those present, especially the Frankish nobles, taken by surprise. The question of the empire had in all probability long since been thoroughly weighed and discussed by the pope and these nobles. This is apparent even from the chronological sequence of events.

On November 29, 799, Pope Leo, returning from Germany, and escorted by the royal envoys, seven bishops and three counts, was received at the Milvian Bridge by the Romans. The ten envoys, who were reckoned amongst the foremost and most influential of Charles's subjects,

[9] 'E vestigio,' in Muratori, *SS. Ital.* i. pt. ii. p. 312. Comp. with him Tiraboschi, *Storia della Lett. Ital.* vi. 45, ed. 1834.

remained more than a year in Rome. It is a striking fact,
indeed, that such a number of men, whose services at home
and at Charles's court could certainly not easily be dis-
pensed with, should have stayed such a long time in Rome.
No mention is made of any special business with which
they had been charged; had there been any such, one only
of the ten might have been entrusted with it. The investigation of the accusations raised against the pope and of
the outrage committed upon him was not undertaken until
after the king's arrival. The envoys were the Archbishops
Hildebald of Cologne and Arno of Salzburg, Bishops
Bernard of Worms, Jesse of Amiens, Kunipert, Otto and
the Bishop-elect Flaicus, and Counts Helingaud, Rothacar
and Germar, of whom the first and the last were entrusted
at other times with important embassies. Hildebald was
Charles's confidential adviser, his minister for ecclesiastical
affairs. Charles had caused Adrian to issue a special dispensation allowing the king to retain him constantly by
his side.[1] That Arno, Alcuin's friend, did not fail to make
use of his influence with the pope is shown by a papal
letter of this year (April 11, 800), in which the bishops,
clergy, and people of the Bajuvarian province are recommended to obey their Archbishop Arno.

A whole year later (Nov. 24, 800) Charles arrives, and
is received by the pope on the steps of St. Peter's. With
him, amongst others, is one of the most important men of
the realm, Angilbert, his son-in-law, privy councillor, and
president of the royal court of justice, and at the same time
Duke of the Frankish maritime provinces. If any one
possessed the king's confidence, it was he. Twice before
(A.D. 794 and A.D. 796) Charles had sent him to Rome to
conduct important negotiations with Adrian and Leo. The
flower of the Frankish prelates and statesmen was therefore
now together in Rome. Seven days elapsed before Charles
on December 1 announced, in presence of an assembly
called together by himself in St. Peter's, the reason of his

[1] *Synod Francof.*, 794, § 53. [Comp. Simson, 542?.]

coming, viz. to decide the matter of the accusation against the pope. Twenty-two days more elapsed before December 23, when finally Leo took the oath of purgation before the synod.[2] The coronation took place upon the next day but one.

The people and kingdom of the Franks were thus represented in Rome by a gathering of their chief men, and undoubtedly during the long interval of nearly thirteen months frequent and earnest consultations must have taken place between them, the pope, and the Roman aristocracy, clerical and lay, consultations of which the purport and design cannot have been unknown to the king. That the resolution to proclaim Charles Roman emperor was formed at a public conference between Franks and Romans, and that the meeting did not merely consist of the bishops and nobles, but that some at least of the people were present, is recorded in the Chronicles of Lorsch and Moissac.[3] It is passed over in silence in the Annals of Eginhard and in the biography of Leo, with the design, I suspect, of allowing the event to appear more entirely as a direct act of divine inspiration. Yet it is evident that with the exception of Charles, and perhaps of one or two of his confidential friends, every one was agreed and prepared beforehand, so that they must previously have arrived at an understanding. By the mere gesture of the pope placing the crown suddenly on the king's head, the people could not have recognised anything to do with the imperial dignity, which for four centuries had not been given or received in Rome, and for conferring which in former days there had been no ceremony of coronation. The people would therefore have seen in the transaction nothing more than a simple solemnity without further importance; for in those days it was customary occasionally to repeat the coronation, and the

---

[2] [Simson, 231⁵, agrees with Döllinger and Jaffé, against Gregorovius and Reumont, that Pope Leo took the oath on the 23rd, and not on the earlier day, Dec. 2.]

[3] Pertz [*M. G. SS.*], i. 38, 306.

crown itself was an ordinary king's crown, since a particular form for the imperial crown was not known.

It cannot therefore be denied that a conference had already taken place in which an understanding was arrived at between the chief Frankish and Roman ecclesiastics, as well as the secular grandees of both nationalities. The pope as well as the Romans expected to acquire advantages and increased consideration through the revival of the empire.

To the pope, who was unable by himself to cope with the factions of the nobles, and who could not even reckon upon personal safety without the aid of Charles's strong arm, an emperor with despotic power must have been more welcome than a patricius with doubtful and undefined authority. Leo, besides, had already recognised Charles as his supreme lord four years before; the position of a subject to the new emperor into which he entered, and to which he gave expression by performing the act of adoration, could not therefore appear to him humiliating, and the counterbalancing gain became the more certain through his conviction that the new emperor, and his successors, would not fix their residence in Rome. The most doubtful point to the pope must have been the prospect of the displeasure of the Greeks and its possible effect upon ecclesiastical affairs; but how little account was then taken of such matters in Rome is shown by the offer which Adrian had made to the king (see p. 117). For the present there was only a woman to be dealt with, and the expedient of a marriage between Charles and Irene had in all probability already presented itself to Leo's mind. The imperial dignity must have appeared to the pope to offer another advantage; it placed Charles under a new and higher obligation, that of devoting himself to the guardianship of the church, and naturally, above all, to the protection of the papal chair. It was this point which Leo singled out to put forward. 'We have,' he says, in a document drawn up on the day of the coronation, 'consecrated him to-day to the office of Augustus for the defence and exaltation of the universal church.'[4] Charles himself understood his duty as emperor in the same way. Besides this, the pope had reason to expect that the new emperor, who, as king of the Lombards, had hitherto shown himself so little compliant towards the demands of ecclesiastical policy, now that the whole papal territory, to whatever extent it increased, must remain subject to the imperial supremacy, would prove more compliant.

The acclamations with which the mass of the Roman people greeted the emperor were without doubt genuine. One hundred and forty years ago an emperor had been seen for the last time in Rome: but the transient appearance of that emperor, as well as the memory of his successors, was connected only with gloomy reminiscences. Old Rome had long been humiliated, ill-used, and degraded by her arrogant and selfish daughter on the Bosporus to the ignoble rôle of a distant provincial town. Formerly, so long as all hope of security rested upon the army, and brilliant victories were still achieved by the army, Rome had remained satisfied with the soldier emperors. But now victory had deserted the Byzantine standard, and a woman sat upon the throne of Constantine. The thought that the right moment had come to recall to life Rome's ancient right, which had been interrupted but never abolished, must have impressed itself upon all. And now Providence had sent the man who possessed in the highest degree all that befitted an emperor. Charles stood before them as the living embodiment of the imperial idea, the second Cæsar who, everywhere present and ready for battle, came, saw and conquered. By electing him their city would again become the metropolis of a great empire, they would bind the object of their choice to them by ties of gratitude, and by the exercise once more of their prerogative they would show to the world that the precious right still survived and might again be exercised in the future. The aristocratic faction,

---

[4] Jaffé, *Regesta*, 1913, p. 218. [2 ed. 2504, p. 310. Where, however, the records are declared to be 'spurious, and therefore historically worthless.'],

to whom it was of the utmost importance that a strong empire should not be established and that the power should remain in the weak hands of a priest, was at the moment broken and intimidated. Finally, Charles had for years past been considered as the supreme lord of Rome. Rome belongs by right of possession to the king, she is the head to the body of his realm,—so Alcuin in the year 799 clearly pronounced.

The Frankish nobles had also another point to consider, and did what in their situation any one else would have done. Both the Franks and Romans of that period felt that as Christians they were dishonoured and degraded in the face of their Moslem foes. The Mohammedan world, they said, has its Kaliph, its Defender of the Faithful, but we, the Christians, have no longer any secular head, no protector of the church. The Eastern Empire of Christendom has begun to sink, has suffered nothing but losses during the last century and a half, and has to pay a shameful tribute to the foes of Christendom. In the West, on the contrary, through the valour of the Franks, and through the sword and the wisdom of Charles, the cause of Christianity is strong, triumphant and advancing. And now Rome also, the mother of the empire, the old, genuine seat of the emperors, is under the dominion of the Franks. Besides, this new kingdom of the Franks includes the greater number of the countries which formerly belonged to the Roman Empire in the West. It is high time that the imperial dignity should be transferred to the Franks, for they alone amongst Christian nations show themselves worthy of that high office ; and none but Charles, who has subdued and converted heathen peoples and extended the pale of the church, is called to sustain the imperial dignity, and is worthy, in addition to the power of emperor which he already possesses, to receive the name and symbols of the office.

Such, according to the report of the Lorsch Chronicle, was the situation of affairs, and such were the considerations which were discussed in Rome at that time. The incapacity of the Christian Empire in the East was but a few years later strikingly exhibited, when the Kaliph Harun Alraschid overran the whole of Asia Minor in one campaign, and penetrated as far as Heraclea in Bithynia without meeting with any serious resistance, and compelled the Emperor Nicephorus to pay a yearly tribute.³ Had it not been that soon after his death the Kaliphate was divided by the revolt of the governors, Constantinople might, even in the ninth century, have become Mohammedan.

The power which the tradition of the religious idea of the Roman Empire had in former days over the thoughts and actions of men, especially the clergy, has not hitherto been sufficiently taken into account. What in those days could have appeared more urgent or more meritorious than the endeavour to raise from degradation this empire, with which the destiny of mankind was bound up—to rescue it from desecration, and from the destruction which threatened it? 'The Roman Empire is the vessel destined by God to contain and preserve the church; God has conferred such greatness and might upon it, in order that the nations who are to be called into the unity of the church may be embraced also within one wide secular bond, and that all Christians may rest beneath the shade of this wide-spreading tree. This empire will endure to the end of time, for it is the fourth and last of the great monarchies that Daniel foretold to Nebuchadnezzar.' These sentiments embody the traditional view shared by Charles's contemporaries. What was more natural than that a young, strong, and victorious people like the Franks, filled with the consciousness of their high destiny, should aspire to become the upholders of this imperial dignity, indispensable as it was to the whole of Christendom, in place of the antiquated and debilitated Byzantines? The Romans, the Franks, and the pope were united in the feeling that the strength and energy of Christianity now lay no longer in the East, but in the West, and that a powerful sovereign

³ Elmacin, *Hist. Saracen.* pp. 118–123.

and champion, practised in the art of war, was urgently needed to stand in opposition to the Heathen as well as to the Moslem world. Such a one was Charles, whose rule was now acknowledged from Barcelona to the banks of the Raab, and from the Eider to Benevento.

The Romans and the Franks did not imagine, that in Charles's elevation, the previous unity of the empire was broken, or that the intention was to set up two empires in the place of one. It was no new Western Empire that was to be erected by the side of the Eastern; Charles was not to be the successor of Romulus Augustus, but of Constantine VI., whose throne had been vacant since his death, for a woman could not be Cæsar. In Greek this view might be expressed by saying that Irene's rule was only a *tyrannis*, and not a *basileia*. In those days people certainly still held fast to the idea of the unity of the Roman Empire. If two Roman empires stood side by side with equal qualifications, then neither the one nor the other could be the real ancient Roman Empire, nor either of the two emperors the genuine successor of the great Constantine. The people of Rome might be represented as thinking thus:—' Hitherto the imperial dignity has been disposed of at one time by troops of mercenaries, and at another by women, eunuchs, and courtiers, who placed rulers over the Greeks and over us; but now it behoves us to take our ancient and indefeasible right once more into our own hands.' As early as 741 the heads of the Roman nobility had sent a formal resolution to Charles Martel to the effect that the Roman people desired to foreswear their allegiance to the (Iconoclast) emperor, and to entrust themselves to his rule.[6] Had Charles Martel acted upon this proposition and established himself in Italy, he would certainly very shortly have been proclaimed emperor. At that time the non-Lombard Italians would have liked nothing better than first to elect an emperor, and then to march with him under arms to Constantinople! Even now many would

[6] *Annales Metens.* ad a. 741. Pertz [*M. G. SS.*], i. 326.

have been quite ready, after their emperor had been proclaimed in Old Rome, to follow him to New Rome, and to help to seat him upon the throne of Constantine; but Charles well knew that he could neither march an army through Pannonia and Bulgaria, nor enter the Bosporus with his fleet, which was too weak for such an attempt.

No one, therefore, thought at first of a separate Western Empire. The fact that such had existed four centuries before, or that there had, at any time, been two emperors, had long vanished from the remembrance of later generations; the generally received idea at that period was that Constantine had removed the seat of the one indivisible empire from Old Rome to New Rome, and that, since that time, the emperors had uninterruptedly had their seat in Byzantium. The antagonism between the numerous kingdoms that had arisen within the former limits of the empire was precisely what had led to the clear conception of the necessity for a united empire. The idea prevailed not only amongst Christian nations, but was felt even to some extent by barbarians and Mohammedans, and on all sides more or less definitely, that the emperor was the secular supreme head of all Christendom, who, as the holder of the highest power, stood above all kings and dukes. The increase of authority and moral consideration which Charles gained in becoming emperor was therefore unbounded. True, his friends and enthusiastic admirers thought that, even before his coronation, Charles had attained to the highest point of worldly honour, for if there were three highest dignities in the world, the papal, the imperial, and the kingly, yet Charles excelled both pope and emperor in might, wisdom, and royal dignity.[7] This, however, was merely a tribute paid to the good fortune and brilliant personal qualities of Charles himself; the imperial dignity could alone invest him in the eyes of the nations with the nimbus of supreme authority and sovereignty,

---

[7] Alcuin, in Bouquet, v. 612, as early as the year 799 [Alc. Ep. 114 in Jaffé, *Biblioth.* vi. 464].

and bestow upon him personally the assurance that he had been called and charged with a mission to act as the guardian of the whole Christian world.

If now we ask what consideration would, according to Charles's own declaration, have withheld him from entering the church if he had known beforehand of the Pope's intention, Eginhard gives us the answer, for he immediately adds that Charles had borne with great patience the displeasure of the Roman (Byzantine) emperors, who had been much incensed at his assuming the imperial title, and that he had overcome their obstinacy by his magnanimity, sending frequent embassies to them, and addressing them in his letters as 'brothers.' Charles had foreseen the indignation of the Eastern Roman Imperial Court, and it had seemed to him not without justification. He had himself been brought up in the conviction which Alcuin, as already mentioned, expressed, viz., that the office of a Frankish king ranked as the third dignity in the world, and that the imperial dignity, which took precedence of it, had for centuries been the rightful heritage of the second Rome.* None of the German conquerors had, as yet, dared to stretch out his hand to grasp the imperial crown. Himself a monarch he felt, more keenly than did his bishops or counts, the doubtfulness and presumption of the step, and may have, therefore, responded with hesitation and in a temporising manner to the earlier overtures, solicitations, and offers of his own followers or of the pope; or he may have referred them to the negotiations with Byzantium, the issue of which was still pending. But the impatience of the Franks and the Romans, when once they had arrived at a mutual understanding, hastened the decision of the matter, and we are entitled to suppose that Charles honestly believed that he ought to accept the accomplished fact as a manifestation of the Divine will. He and the pope now sought to devise some means of conducting the matter to a peaceful issue, and of obtaining what he felt to be all-important, the

---

* *Imperialis dignitas et secundæ Romæ sæcularis potentia*, says Alcuin.

recognition of Byzantium. Charles had recently become a widower, and a marriage with Irene seemed the simplest solution of the difficulty. Envoys from the pope and from Charles went together to Constantinople to sue for the hand of Irene, in order, as Theophanes says, that the West might be united with the East.[9] Charles only wished to obtain thereby that legitimation of his imperial title which, he felt, was lacking. He could not have had the intention of either fixing his residence in Constantinople and of governing the united East and West from that centre, or have imagined that he was in a position to rule the Eastern Empire from the West. But he would have gone to Constantinople, concluded the marriage, had himself crowned by the Patriarch, and, above all, would have attempted to put fresh energy into the struggle with the Moslem, the common foe, for at that time Byzantium was paying a shameful tribute to the Kaliphs. With the aid of Byzantium he would have been enabled to fit out a fleet, of the want of which in the Mediterranean he must have long been painfully aware.

Irene would have consented had not Aetius, who was anxious to secure the throne for his brother, prevented her. Shortly afterwards, whilst the envoys of Charles and of the pope were still in the capital, she was deposed, through a conspiracy of seven eunuchs of great influence, in order to make room for the treasurer Nicephorus.

The new emperor of the East was not inclined to recognise Charles as emperor, whilst the latter showed his anxiety to obtain this recognition, and assumed for the purpose an attitude and language almost humble.

[9] It is only the Byzantine writer Theophanes who reports this [*Chronogr.*, ed. de Boor, 14 and 27], whilst the Frankish annalists are silent about it. But Theophanes was a contemporary, and well informed, and as the fact is in itself very probable, there is no reason for saying with Ideler (*Leben Karl's des Grossen*, i. 200) that the statement bears the stamp of an idle tale, or at best points to a scheme of the ambitious Irene. [Simson, 282² (against his former view and in opposition to Harnack, S. 42), doubted the truth of the statement of Theophanes.]

So thirteen years elapsed, marked alternately by wars and embassies, and Charles did not live to see the desired result. Nicephorus and his successors supposed, as Eginhard says, that the Frankish prince wished to wrest the imperial office from them and to become himself sole emperor. Charles, however, only asked to be placed on an equality with the Greek emperor. He clothed this thought in the proposal to accord him the title of brother, naturally on condition of receiving the same in return. His idea seems to have been that there should be a single Roman Empire with two emperors, just as there were already two imperial cities, Old Rome and New Rome. Two Roman Empires could not be thought of; history, as well as the religious importance which had long been attributed to the Imperium, forbade this. But it was felt in Constantinople that the recognition of the new emperor implied a kind of self-deposition, that the star of the Eastern Roman Imperium must fade before the brilliancy of the newly risen imperial sun in the West. Whilst the Eastern Empire included only a few of the provinces of the old Roman Empire; had suffered fearful losses in the course of the last two hundred years; had not made a single conquest, and was still continually losing territory, Charles possessed the greater part of the Roman Western Empire, with Spain as far as the Ebro, the old imperial towns of Trèves, Arles, Milan, Ravenna, Rome, and beyond the old Roman frontier immense tracts of territory. The sentiment of the Greeks has been expressed by Constantine Manasses, although he belonged to a later period. He says: 'Thus the old tie which united both cities was rent asunder; the mother parted from the daughter; the youthful and beautiful New Rome from the wrinkled and decrepit Old Rome.'[1]

Thus there arose a complication of conflicting interests. The Byzantine court desired to remain on friendly terms with its powerful western neighbour, or, if possible, to have him for an ally, and was anxious also to retain what-

[1] See Bouquet, v. 398.

ever might yet be saved of the Italian and Dalmatian possessions; they desired to avoid having to carry on a war at the same time against the Kaliph, the Bulgarians, and the Franks; but the price set by Charles upon his friendship, namely, the recognition of his title as emperor, seemed too high and too perilous. So several years passed, during which diplomatic negotiations alternated with open hostilities carried on along the Dalmatian and Venetian coasts. 'Charles,' says Eginhard, 'bore the displeasure of the Greek emperor with great patience, and overcame his stubbornness by magnanimity.' Yet his stubbornness was, at any rate, long in being overcome, and was even at last not entirely subdued. In the year 803 the Greek ambassadors were the bearers of a treaty of peace; they proceeded from the court of the emperor to Rome, and then returned to Constantinople, but a substantial peace was not concluded; Nicephorus made no rejoinder, and in the year 806 sent his fleet to attack Dalmatia. In 809 a struggle again took place in those waters; the Greeks vainly attacked Commacchio; the Venetians did their best to fan the flame of war, because the conclusion of a peace would inevitably have subjected them to the dominion either of Charles or of the Greeks.[2]

It appears that the Greeks, anxious to avoid recognising the imperial title, preferred to treat with Pipin, Charles's son, rather than with Charles himself. Nicephorus sent an ambassador direct to Pipin, whereupon Charles, being very desirous, as he himself says, to see a Greek envoy at his own court, could not forbear causing the ambassador to be brought to him. In a letter couched in strikingly humble terms, written in 810, the emperor declares that ever since 803 he has anxiously awaited an embassy from Nicephorus, that he might once for all be relieved from uncertainty; he would have given himself up to despair if he had not been upheld by confidence in

---

[2] *Eginh. Annal.* ad a. 809. Pertz [*M. G. SS.*], i. 196.

God.³ Charles again sent ambassadors to Constantinople, and even formally ceded Venice to the Greeks. At length, in the year 812, he experienced the long-desired satisfaction; the ambassadors of the Emperor Michael addressed him in the church at Aix with the title of emperor (Basileus). They received from his hands in return a document containing a treaty of alliance, which they afterwards caused to be again delivered to them by the pope in the church of St. Peter in Rome as the sign of its confirmation. The cession of Venice, the prospect of help against the Bulgarians, who had become too powerful in the north of the empire, and the fear of losing the South Italian provinces appear to have been the reason for these slight courtesies, which after all did not pledge the Greeks to any permanent concessions. Charles was still without any document signed by the emperor, to obtain which he despatched a fresh embassy to Constantinople. The letter from Charles, which the ambassadors, Amalarius and the Abbot Petrus, took with them, contained for the first time the phrase 'to the Eastern and to the Western Imperium,'⁴ and the assurance that Charles earnestly desired peace between the two empires. Here, then, were two empires at one moment at peace and the next at war with each other. Which of the two was the genuine, legitimate Roman Empire? This was certainly the question asked in Constantinople, and what answer could the Frankish ambassadors give? Charles did not live to see their return.⁵

The statement of Theophanes, that Charles, immediately after his coronation, had intended to make an expedition for the conquest of Sicily, is confirmed by the occurrences which immediately followed. The increasing weakness and decrepitude of the Greek Empire, and the growing power of the Saracens in the Mediterranean, must have made it

---

³ See Bouquet, v. 632 [Ep. Carol. 29 in Jaffé, *Bibl.* iv. 395].
⁴ Alcuini *Opp.*, ed. Froben, ii. 561.
⁵ [Upon Charles's relations with the Byzantine Court after his coronation, see Simson, p. 281 f., 288 ff., 394, 441 ff., 459 ff., 480 ff., 498 ff.]

clear to the Sicilians that if they did not wish their beautiful and fertile island to become a prey to the Moslems—which actually came to pass in the year 828—they must throw themselves into the arms of the Frankish power, which was alone capable of protecting them. The Balearic Isles had already given themselves up to the Frankish king in 799, in order to obtain his protection against the repeated attacks and ravages of the Saracens from Africa.[6] Thus we find that (795 and 797) envoys from the Greek governors of Sicily—Michael and his successor, Niketas—appeared at Charles' court. They were the bearers of no mission from the Byzantine emperor, for the latter almost at the same time had sent an embassy of his own, and it is remarked that Charles dismissed the Sicilian envoy Daniel at Aix (799) with special honours. Soon afterwards (801) another Sicilian, the Spatharius Leo, took refuge at Charles's court, and remained ten years in Frankish territory, returning to Sicily in 811. He must have remained so many years near to Charles, in the hope that the emperor's Sicilian expedition would take place.[7] But Charles relinquished the design, being determined to purchase peace with Byzantium, and the recognition of his title, even at the cost of some sacrifices.[8]

Rome was now the metropolis of Charles's imperium, the actual seat of the empire. Since he was already in possession of Rome (say the Frankish annals), it was both right and needful that he should be invested with the dignity of emperor.[9] Even the Franks admitted that in the revival of the imperial dignity, the decision belonged to the inhabitants of Rome, however great had been the share taken in it by the Frankish bishops and counts. In the annals of Salzburg, Weissenburg, Cologne, and other

[6] *Annal. Lauriss.* Pertz [*M. G. SS.*], i. 186.
[7] *Annal. Eginh.* Pertz [*M. G. SS.*], i. 198.
[8] [Harnack, p. 40¹, and Simson, 188 f., draw attention to ' some inaccuracies ' in Döllinger's representation of Charles's relations with the Sicilians.]
[9] *Annal. Lauresh.* Pertz [*M. G. SS.*], i. 38.

shorter chronicles of the time, the event is consequently described as the act of the Romans alone, 'the elective act of the Roman people,' as Anskar puts it.[1] 'It was the dignity to which Charles was raised by the Roman Senate which was announced' (on Christmas Day), is the expression of Flodoard (950).[2] Even the Liber Pontificalis calls attention to the fact that he was appointed emperor of the Romans by the act of the whole people.[3]

The part that the pope took in the matter was the religious act of consecration in crowning and anointing Charles with the same rites with which at the same time he consecrated Charles's son Pipin king.[4] Any particular form or ritual for the consecration of the newly created imperial dignity had naturally not been thought of; there was no precedent to follow, for the coronation of an emperor had never before taken place in Rome. Upon the election, in which the pope, as the first Roman citizen, naturally took an essential part, there followed the consecration, the religious seal, which in those days could not be omitted in connexion with so weighty and decisive an act. It was the Roman Respublica, of which the inhabitants of Rome were the representatives, and of which the most distinguished member was the pope, that after the lapse of centuries gave itself once more an imperial head. Besides this, the *scholæ*, or corporations of foreigners settled in Rome—Franks, Frisians, Saxons, Lombards, who with their banners and tokens had already received the emperor at the Milvian Bridge [5]—took part as the representatives of these nations in the act of election.

Did this involve a transference of the Roman Empire

[1] *Vita S. Willehadi*, c. 5. Pertz [*M. G. SS.*], ii. 381.

[2] Bouquet, v. 468. Conclamatur honos Romanis patribus auctus, that is, from the royal to the imperial dignity.

[3] 'Ab omnibus constitutus est Imperator Romanorum.' [*Vita Leonis III.*], Vignoli, p. 254.

[4] [Not Pipin, but the Emperor's eldest son, Charles. Comp. Richter-Kohl, *Annals*, ii. 147, against Simson, 238[1], who assumes that only the younger Charles was *anointed* by the pope.]

[5] *Vita Leonis III.*, Vignoli, p. 250.

from the Greeks to the Franks? This is the theory subsequently set up, but which no contemporary can well have entertained.

Romans and Franks did not connect the same ideas with the act which they performed in common. The Frankish nobles certainly thought that with Charles's elevation the 'noble people of the Franks' had become the upholders of the empire, that between the Franks and the Imperium an indissoluble bond had been established; they (the Franks), as they supposed, had become in a certain sense Romans—that is to say, the upholders of the Roman power and rights.[6] But it did not occur to them that the Imperium was thereby formally withdrawn from the Greeks, or that they were henceforth excluded from it. Advantage had been taken of the interregnum, caused by the fact, incompatible with the idea of the imperium, that a woman was at the head of the government. The empire was bound up with Rome, but Rome was in the power of the Franks. It was left to the emperor to reconcile the claims on both sides. Had the marriage of Charles with Irene taken place, the difficulties would for the moment have been solved, and the conflict of claims suspended. What might have happened after the deaths of Charles and Irene it is hardly necessary to inquire. If the Greeks again chose an emperor for themselves, he would certainly neither in the eyes of the Franks nor yet in those of the Romans have been a mere usurper or unlawful pretender. For in that case the Roman Imperium, which, though one and indivisible, could be held in two portions, would have been maintained in a kind of partnership by two emperors, who would have regarded each other in brotherly fashion as equal in dignity. At a later period, indeed, it seemed no longer possible to imagine any just title which could warrant the Greek emperor styling himself Imperator of the Romans. Two Roman emperors

[6] *Francis Romuleum nomen habere dedi*, says Charles in Ermold. ii. 68 [M. G. SS., ii. 480].

seemed as unnatural as two suns in one firmament. 'The
Greek emperors of the Romans have ceased to exist,' said
the Emperor Ludwig II.

The Romans on their side did not consider that they
had transferred the empire to the Frankish nation, but
only to the Frankish dynasty; they did not reckon themselves by this single act to have relinquished for ever their
own right of election, but reserved to themselves the power
of asserting and exercising it at any critical moment in the
future, such as, for instance, upon the extinction of a
dynasty. For by its origin, language, and nationality the
empire, it was affirmed in the West, belongs to the Latin
race and to the king in whose realm the Latin speech is
the language of commerce and of the church, the monarch
who rules over Italy, Rome, and the Latin race.

I therefore consider Waitz's view [7] to be incorrect:
'Neither the coronation by the pope,' says this learned
writer, 'nor the salutations of the people in the church
could, properly speaking, have conferred a formal right
upon the new emperor. Nobody in those days would have
inquired if such a right existed. Charles's right lay in the
power of the facts that had led to his elevation.' I think,
on the contrary, that in those days the formal right was
long and earnestly discussed. It is true that contemporaries did not attribute to the coronation by the pope
the significance which it had in later ages, since the idea
that the pope possessed authority to dispose of empires
and kingdoms had not yet arisen. But the mere salutation of the people in the church would have been by no
means deemed sufficient, had not the act, which the multitude then confirmed by their acclamations, been previously
well considered and deliberately consummated. The
Chronicle of Moissac designedly enumerates all partakers
in the event as follows: the pope, the whole assembly of
the bishops, clergy, and abbots, the Senate of the Franks,

[7] *Deutsche Verfassungsgeschichte*, iii. 177.

the seniores of the Romans, and the rest of the Christian people. Amongst the Romans it was said that since the Greeks had first degraded the imperial dignity by allowing it to become the spoil of soldiers, and then to fall into the blood-stained hands of a woman, the people of Rome have resumed the ancient right of choosing their own emperor. By the election by the Roman people in a great assembly of bishops and other servants of God, the imperial dignity was transferred to the commander of the Franks, because he was the master of the city which was the capital of the empire and many other countries besides, and was worthy of the title of emperor. Thus Anskar writes. But it is very natural that Theophanes, the only Byzantine contemporary writer who mentions the occurrence, should report the coronation and anointing by the pope, and omit altogether the election and consent of the people. We can detect, moreover, the desire of this historian, in adopting a tale circulated amongst the Greeks, to place the event in a contemptible or ridiculous light, asserting that the pope had anointed the king from head to foot with oil, which would have necessitated an unseemly disrobing before all the people in the church. It was customary with the Greeks for the emperor to be crowned by the patriarch of the capital, but the practice of anointing was unknown to them. At a later period they introduced the custom, evidently in imitation of the pope's use of oil at an imperial consecration, the popes themselves having borrowed the rite from the Spanish Visigoths.[8] It was not, however, supposed that in this anointing there lay any particular connection with the imperial dignity, for Charles's son, Pipin, whom Adrian had already anointed king in 781, was anointed by Leo now for the second time, of course only as king.[9]

[8] The Frankish kings before Pipin were neither crowned nor anointed; they were merely raised on a shield. In Spain, on the contrary, Erwig, the follower of Wamba, is said in the first canon of the thirteenth synod of Toledo (681), *regnandi per sacro-sanctam unctionem suscepisse potestatem.*

[9] [Not Pipin, but Charles (see above p. 138); Pipin and Ludwig had already been anointed kings by Pope Adrian in 781. Abel, 313 f.]

The Frankish annalists report, but Leo's biographer is silent on the point, that, after the coronation, the pope, prostrating himself before the emperor, did homage to him. 'Charles, according to the custom of the ancient emperors, was adored by the pope,' says the annalist. Great trouble has been taken to make this adoration into a simple salutation or embrace,[1] and Gregorovius asserts, 'it consisted not of bowing the knees, but after ancient custom, of a kiss on the mouth.'[2] But as the pope wished on this occasion to render to the new emperor that form of homage which used to be offered to the early Roman emperors, we cannot doubt that he prostrated himself before him. The best emperors of the first imperial period had indeed not permitted this, but of Caligula, Domitian, and the son of the elder Maximin it is recorded that they claimed adoration, and of Diocletian, that it was he who made this oriental practice into a permanent custom in the Roman Empire.[3] Bishops used to kneel before the Empress Eusebia, the wife of Constantine,[4] and both Justinian and Theodora required all who visited them to kiss both their feet.[5] Since then it had been usual, kneeling before the emperors, to kiss their knees or both the knee and the foot[6]—an act of homage which the Emperor Manuel at first went so far as to demand from the Emperor

[1] The old controversy on this subject was renewed in Rome in 1815. A French painter exhibited a picture of Charles's coronation in which he represented the pope kneeling before the emperor. A Roman ecclesiastic, Santelli, took occasion to write a book on the subject, *Oltraggio fatto a Leone III e a Carlo Magno*. The book is intended to prove that *adorato* simply means *salutato*.
[2] *Geschichte Roms*, ii. 548. [In the 2nd ed., ii. 493, Gregorovius has given up his opinion also, in deference to Döllinger's counter-evidence. Compare Simson, 237⁴, ⁵.]
[3] Plinius, *Panegyr.* 24; Martial, x. 72; Jul. Capitol., *in Maximo*, c. 2; Eutrop. ix. 26; Amm. Marcell. xv. 5; Aurel. Victor, 39. Of Constantine the Great it is said in his biography by Eusebius, iv. 57: γονυκλινεῖς ἠσπάσαντο. Godefroy, in the *Theodos. Codex*, 6, 8 (ed. Ritter, ii. 83), has collected several passages.
[4] Suidas s. v. *Leontius*.   [5] Procop. *Arcan.* c. 15.
[6] Constantin. Porphyrog., *De cerem. aulæ Byzant.* i. 87, describes this more exactly.

Conrad III. when he came upon the crusade, at which Conrad was naturally much incensed.[7] The popes had submitted to the custom; Agapetus, in accordance with it, did homage to Justinian;[8] and in their letters to the emperors the popes made unsparing repetition of the assurance that they approached the emperor upon their knees, or bowing the knee.[9] In the year 787 Adrian made use of this and even of stronger expressions in addressing Constantine and Irene.[1] Even to Pipin, Paul I. writes: 'I pray you on my knees,' and Stephen literally did so, and remained prostrate on the ground until Pipin and his sons stretched out their hands to raise him up. Probably the expression, that 'with the utmost humility' Pope Leo received Charles upon his arrival in Rome, points to a similar prostration.[2] Apart from this, in the controversy of that time about the worship of images, the meaning of the word 'adoration' was very carefully discussed and restricted to bodily prostration, and hence it would be inconceivable that the Frankish historian would here have taken the word in any other sense.[3]

[7] Arnold, *Lubec. Chron. Slav.* 3, 10 [*M. G. SS.* xxi., 122 *lib.*, 1, 10]. Mascov, *Comm. de rebus Imperii sub Conr.* iii. p. 204, considers Arnold's statement incorrect, but without sufficient reason, so far as I can see. The silence of Cinnamus, who studiously casts all the blame upon Conrad, proves nothing, and Odo of Deuil, *De Prov. Ludov.* vii. 3, 31, tends to confirm Arnold's report by the words 'Neuter pro altero mores suos aut fastus consuetudinem temperavit.'

[8] 'Ο ἀξιωθεὶς τῶν εὐσεβῶν ὑμῶν ἴχνων, it is said of Agapetus, in the letter of the bishops and monks to Justinian, *in Alemanni not. ad Procop.* p. 173, ed. Bonn, p. 467.

[9] Agatho, in letter to Constantine: 'Flexo mentis poplite suppliciter vestram clementiam deprecamur.' Harduin, *Conc.* iii. 1078. And still earlier, P. Hormisdas to the Emperor Anastatius: 'Vestigiis vestris advolvor.' *Epistolæ Pontif. Rom.*, 1591, i. 446.

[1] *Tanquam præsentialiter humo prostratus et vestris Deo dilectis vestigiis provolutus quæro.* What would Charles have said if he had read this expression of the popes, addressed to a youth of sixteen and to a woman?

[2] 'Occurrit ei pridie Leo Papa, et summâ eum humilitate summoque honore suscepit.' *Annal. Fr. Bouquet*, v. 52 [*Ann. Lauriss.*, M. G. i. 188].

[3] Thus, for example, in the *Libri Carolini*, 4, 13, p. 537, a special protest is made against the identification of *osculari* and *adorare*.

After the establishment of the empire the custom, otherwise so foreign to the German peoples, became prevalent in the Frankish kingdom. The nobles of the empire used not only to kneel before the emperor, but even to display their respect by observing the oriental fashion of kissing the foot.[1]

Through this act of homage, the pope most unquestionably declared that, with the reception of the imperial title, Charles had become the sovereign of the pope as well as of Rome, and that the pope was the subject of the emperor. For it was then, and not until then, that, in the eyes of the Romans, Charles stepped into the place of the Greek emperor. Whenever a man should again occupy the throne of Byzantium, Charles must either be recognised by the new Eastern emperor as his associate in the imperial dignity and co-regent, or the Romans and the pope must declare the Eastern emperor to be a usurper, who, since Charles had come into Irene's place as sole and rightful emperor, could have no right to the imperial dignity. For it was not possible to relinquish the idea of the unity and indivisibility of the Roman Imperium. This empire, as the centre and safeguard of Christianity, might be governed by two emperors, reigning together as colleagues, but it ought not to be allowed to fall into two independent empires, each claiming to be the genuine Roman empire.[5] Charles was thoroughly aware

---

[1] It is said of the Duke of Toulouse when he proposed in the assembly of the year 801 to make war against the Saracens (Ermold Nigell. i. 138), [*M. G. SS.* ii. 469]:
    'Poplite flexato lambitat ore pedes.'
And of Eginhard at the assembly of 813 [Erm. Nig., 2, 33, l. c. 479]:
    'Hic cadit ante pedes, vestigia basiat alma.'
'Flexis omnes precamur poplitibus majestatem vestram,' say the Frankish nobles. Baluze, *Capitul.* 1, 405.

[5] I cannot, therefore, agree with Herr v. Lancizolle, when he asserts in his pamphlet, 'Die Bedeutung der römisch-deutschen Kaiserwürde' (1856), p. 11: 'The object was a real reorganization, a continuation or appropriation (through a fresh severance from East Rome) of a separate West Roman Empire.' On the contrary, I think that this thought, in the beginning at least, was far from those who took part in the act.

of this, and in Rome it was also understood; hence the papal embassy to Irene. Now, seeing that the Byzantine emperors persistently held themselves aloof from the new co-emperor who had been obtruded upon them, the consistent course would have been, after having revived the elective right of Old Rome, to proceed incontinently to the declaration that New Rome had forfeited her right to the imperial office. Against this, however, there were strong and numerous objections, and the first consequence would have been a perpetual warfare between East and West. In the present ambiguous situation, a step having been taken which could not be recalled—an institution created which could not easily be allowed to drop, it was necessary for Rome at once and in earnest to submit herself to the new emperor, for the whole reality and legality of the new empire rested upon its relationship to Rome, and if Charles were not truly emperor in Rome, i.e. really master there, then his imperium was, so to speak, a nonentity, in spite of the wide territory which he possessed.

Charles himself had not the slightest intention of resting satisfied with the mere title and the moral consideration which the highest secular dignity in Christendom brought with it. It was not without design that he styled himself from henceforth in his documents not merely 'emperor,' but 'ruler of the Roman Imperium.'[6] Where was this imperium? What were its constituent parts? Not the states which he had long before either inherited or conquered; he styled himself, and remained as before, King of the Franks, and King of the Lombards, whilst he dropped the title of patricius. When, in the year 806, he divided his empire amongst his sons, neither Rome and the Roman duchy, nor yet the empire were mentioned. Charles would not as yet decide these points, because at

---

[6] *E.g.* documents of the year 801. Brunetti, *Codice dipl. Tosc.* ii. 332 [M. G. LL., *Cap. Tom.*, i. 211]: 'Carolus serenissimus augustus a Deo coronatus magnus et pacificus imperator, Romanum gubernans imperium, qui et per misericordiam Dei rex Francorum et Langobardorum.'

that time he still regarded the imperial dignity as conferred
only upon himself personally, and so would do nothing
without the assent of the Romans ; in which case his views
upon this point must seven years later have undergone a
considerable change. Or it may have been that he feared
to excite jealousy and discord amongst his sons. In his will
Rome stands as the first amongst the capital towns of his
empire. Even Pope John VIII. declared Rome, and the
surrounding territory, to be the central point of the empire, and admonished Charles's grandson that, if he did
not protect the Roman territory, the nations would say,
Where then is our emperor ?[7]

It may have been very generally expected at that time
that Charles would select Rome as his permanent residence,
build himself a palace, and govern his great empire from
there. Charles did not do this ; he preferred to live not
near to the southern frontier of his dominions, but in the
north, near to the Saxon country, where the greatest
danger lay, and where the most unremitting exertions were
called for. Yet Rome was still as ever the sacred city for
the whole of Western Christendom, the city of the apostles
and martyrs, of the sacred tombs and relics, the seat of
the primate amongst bishops, the successor of Peter.
However subordinate the position might be which the
pope occupied towards the new emperor, and although Leo
looked up to Charles as his protector, his judge and
sovereign, it would be scarcely possible for both to continue
to rule in the same place. The pope would have sunk
more and more into the position of a mere subject, and
would have forfeited more of his authority in the public
opinion than even Charles would have wished or allowed.

Charles was not an arbitrary despot grasping at unlimited power. He possessed the imperial instinct and
loftiness of political view, and he understood his times far
too well to desire to see the pope degraded into a submissive

---

[7] *Et hanc terram, quæ sui imperii caput est, ad libertatem reducat, ne-
quando dicant gentes: ubi est imperator illius?* Epist. 31 (Mansi, xvii. 29).

court bishop. He appreciated the papal dignity too highly for that, and felt it to be indispensable, although he was well aware of the failings which beset the bearers of the office, and their ceaseless demands and petitions were offensive and wearisome to him.

Yet he felt that Rome must be the capital, the metropolis of his empire, the city on which the greatest honours, gifts, and adornments must be lavished. A permanent *missus* or legate must reside there, and administer justice in the emperor's name, superintend the papal elections, and protect the pope against the nobles of the city and its environs.

Charles spent a whole winter (801) in establishing his power in Rome and in the regulation of affairs, both ecclesiastical and secular. In conformity with Byzantine usage, and in accordance with the acclamation of the people on Christmas Day, he now styled himself 'Emperor, crowned by God,' but, not without design, he also made use of the expression 'Emperor by divine appointment.'[8] The idea of church and state had by this time completely penetrated the Frankish kingdom, and the authority which Charles already exercised in ecclesiastical matters as king was now strengthened and confirmed by his imperial dignity. All his subjects who had passed their twelfth year were called upon to take a new oath of allegiance to him as emperor, and his famous capitulary of the year 802 exhibits him as both ecclesiastical and secular legislator and judge. The pope addresses him in writing as his 'most gracious master,' and is attentive to his slightest hints, as well as to his bidding.[9] Sent by the emperor on a mission to Mantua to enquire into the genuineness of some pretended relics, he comes thence at his summons to the imperial court at Kiersy, and

---

[8] *Divino nutu coronatus*, in the *præfatio* to the *Capitulary* of 801. Bouquet, v. 658 [M. G. LL., *Cap. Tom.*, i. 204].

[9] *Dominus piissimus et serenissimus;* also *vestra clementissima præcelsa regalis potentia.* Adrian had only written *Domino excellentissimo.*

after a time, being *dismissed* by the emperor, is suffered to return to Rome.[1] Paulinus of Aquileia having complained to the emperor and to the pope of the devastation of his diocese, the emperor, upon the advice of the pope and the bishops, bestowed upon him six neighbouring bishoprics, transferring to him his (the emperor's) own right over them, and empowering him alone to appoint bishops to them, with what rights he should think fit.[2] Had Charles's successor been a man similarly gifted and equally capable of governing, the church would certainly soon have experienced the pressure of political fetters, and have bewailed her servitude despite the imperial favour.

'To govern the church' was the chief task which Charles impressed upon his son Ludwig when, in 813, he associated him with himself in the empire.[3] Upon the advice and at the request of the nobles of the empire, with whom he took counsel, Charles summoned Ludwig to him to Aix, and resolved to raise him to the dignity of emperor. He acted in doing so entirely upon his own imperial authority; neither the pope nor the Romans were consulted, nor called upon to take any part in the matter. The Franks must have intended to show that the empire now belonged to them.

With the crown upon his head, Ludwig entered the church, upon the altar of which his father had caused another crown to be placed. After promising obedience to his father, Ludwig was commanded by him to take the crown from the altar and to place it upon his own head. This plainly signified: Whereas we—the nation and I— have chosen thee as an associate in the empire, there is no need for any papal intervention. God has given thee the crown; accept it from His hands. Accordingly, after his

---

[1] *Unde absolutus Romam repedavit.* Annal. Fuld. in Bouquet, v. 332 [*M. G. SS.* 1, 353. Simson, 315⁹, protests against this interpretation of Döllinger's].

[2] *Append. Actor. ad Paulini Opera*, ed. Madrisi, p. 259.

[3] Thegan, c. 6. Bouquet, vi. 75 [*M. G. SS.* ii. 591].

father's death (January 28, 814), Ludwig's title was recognised throughout the whole empire, and in the following year in Rome he found occasion to make good his claim to imperial authority, even over the pope. It happened that Leo had caused certain distinguished Romans to be executed because they had entered into a conspiracy against him. Ludwig was scandalized at this act, and sent his nephew, King Bernhard, to Rome to investigate the matter; but in the meanwhile three envoys from Leo appeared at the emperor's court, bringing the pope's excuses for the crime of which he was accused.[4] For the Romans had already accused him to the emperor. Leo's death, which happened shortly afterwards, solved the difficulty. The new pope, Stephen V., at once administered to all the Romans an oath of fealty to the emperor, sent his envoys with an apology for having allowed himself to be consecrated at once, without awaiting the emperor's consent, and afterwards travelled in person to Rheims, where (October, 816) he placed a crown, which he had brought with him, upon the head of the emperor, who was already in the second year of his reign, anointing him at the same time.[5]

The imperial authority now far exceeded that of any other earthly power, and feared neither foe nor rival. But Ludwig in no way resembled his illustrious parent; he was unable to maintain the dignity of the Imperium, or to enforce the respect due to it, even from his own sons. The events of his reign seriously undermined the strength of the empire, and so long as the sceptre remained with the Carolingian house it never recovered.

[4] *Astronomi vita Ludov.* Bouquet, vi. 98 [*M. G. SS.* ii. 619 f.]. The great disturbance which broke out in the Campagna on the news of the pope's illness was brought about and diligently fomented by the papal authorities. This is evident from the statement in Eginhard's *Annals*: *quae sibi erepta querebantur violenter, auferre (statuunt).*

[5] [Thegan, c. 17 l. c., p. 514.]

SECOND TREATISE.

THE CORONATION OF CHARLES AS EMPEROR, AS REPRE-
SENTED BY THE CHRONICLERS AND PUBLICISTS OF THE
MIDDLE AGES.

It is well known that there is an agreement on one side
between the Frankish annals and Eginhard, and between
accounts from Roman sources on the other, in the representation of Charles's coronation as emperor. The 'Liber
Pontificalis' is silent upon the one point, the act of adoration, by which the pope did homage to the newly crowned
emperor. All the other annals and chronicles we possess
of the ninth and tenth centuries have drawn their information chiefly from the annals of the empire, and have
noted, in the briefest form, the fact of Charles's accession
to the imperial dignity as being mainly the work of the
Romans, omitting any particular mention of the pope. *A
Romanis Augustus est appellatus*, say the Annals of *Würz-
burg*, of *Weissenburg*, *Fulda*, and *Cologne*, without any
notice of the pope's share in the transaction, because he
was simply regarded as the instrument for carrying into
effect the decree of the Roman people.⁶

Amongst the annals of the ninth century, only those of
Xante vary in this particular. Prior to the year 831 they
are not original, only giving extracts from Eginhard and
the Frankish annals, and on this point with an unmistakable bias. The healing of the pope is recorded as a divine
miracle, and the coronation of the emperor is ascribed to
him alone, with this comment : ' as the custom is.'⁷

Eighty years after the death of Charles, the *Monk of
St. Gall* first furnishes us with the mythical version of the
occurrence, as it had taken shape in the popular mind.⁸
The pope has applied for assistance against his Roman

⁶ Pertz [*M. G. SS.*], i. 97, ii. 240 ; [*M. G. SS.* iii.], 40, 117*. Regino,
who died in 915, has here merely transcribed from the *Annals of Lorsch*.
⁷ Pertz [*M. G. SS.*], ii. 223. ⁸ Pertz [*M. G. SS.*], ii. 743.

enemies in the first instance to the emperor in Constantinople. The narrator calls him Michael, who did not come to the throne until 811. Michael sends the pope a message to the effect that, since he (the pope) has an empire of his own which is better than that of the Greeks, he may as well help himself. Upon this the pope, obeying a divine suggestion, summons Charles to Rome and appoints him emperor and guardian of the Roman Church. Charles unwillingly accepts the dignity, for he is afraid that the Greeks, in fear of being subjugated by him, may do some mischief to his territories.

In this account the unconscious endeavour to bring facts into harmony with current conceptions and to methodize history is apparent. The imaginary colouring results from the desire to account for the emperor in Constantinople having forfeited his empire, which, without possession of Rome and of Italy, could no longer be the genuine Roman Empire, and to explain with what right Charles stepped into his place. Hence arises the discovery that the pope had first applied to the Greek ruler for help in order that neglect of duty by the Greeks might appear as the reason for the transference of the empire to Charles.

In the West-Frankish kingdom Bishop *Ado* of Vienne (d. 874) exactly follows in his 'Universal Chronicle' the narrative of the annals of Eginhard; does not omit to mention the adoration by the pope, nor the subsequent coronation of Ludwig without the pope; and, like most of the lengthier chroniclers, calls attention to the fact that Irene sent an embassy to Charles with proposals of peace after his elevation,[9] which seems to be understood to indicate a formal acknowledgment of his title by the Eastern Roman Empire. *Honorius of Autun* (c. 1123) puts this clearly when he says: Charles was proclaimed emperor by the Romans and crowned by the pope, and the Greeks forthwith made peace with him. He assigns as the cause

---

[9] Bouquet, v. 321 [*M. G. SS.* ii. 315].

of the event a divine revelation received by the pope.[1] In another learned composition the same author[2] says the pope, because the imperial throne had become vacant through the blinding of Constantine, by the advice of the princes, and with the consent of the clergy and people, transferred the imperial sceptre to Charles.

The first trace of an intentional and not legendary falsification of the facts shows itself very early, in the annals of *Enhard*, a monk of Fulda (cir. 839), who combined material borrowed from Eginhard's chronicle with selections from the Chronicles of Lorsch and the Life of Charles.[3] By not naming the pope, he makes the adoration after the coronation appear as a general act of homage performed by all present; whereas the source from which he draws represents the pope alone as performing the act of adoration. The otherwise unknown librarian *Petrus* has copied his narrative.[4] The monk who compiled the Annals of Metz in the tenth century, and whose account of the time of Charles is merely a transcript from Eginhard's annals, with a few additions from Regino and the Chronicles of Moissac, nevertheless suppressed the fact that it was the pope who prostrated himself before Charles;[5] and the priest *Magnus*, who wrote the Chronicles of Reichersperg (cir. 1195) in a very hostile spirit to the Hohenstaufen emperors, did the same. He copies the account of Charles's coronation, word for word, from the Frankish annals, but in describing the act of adoration he leaves out the pope.[6]

The Hohenstaufen view of the matter is reproduced in an (unprinted) *Biography* of Charles written at the com-

---

[1] *Imago mundi.* Pertz [*Mon. G. SS.*, xii. 129.
[2] *Summa gloria de Apostolico et Augusto* (Pez, *Thesaurus*, ii. 196).
[3] Pertz [*Mon. G. SS.*, i. 352. [Enhard is no longer considered as the author of the first part of the *Annals of Fulda.*]
[4] Pertz [*M. G. SS.*], i. 417.
[5] Bouquet, v. 350.
[6] Ed. Gewold Monachii, 1611, p. 113. [Simson, 237¹, leaves it undecided whether the adoration was intentionally omitted in the above-mentioned annals.]

mand of Frederick I., and from this source it is copied into the *Annals of Marbach*. It is to the following effect:

Valentinian III. was the last emperor resident in Rome; after him the Hesperian Empire fell, and for 348 years no one again became Augustus in Rome until Charles. On this man, who had already filled the whole world with his fame, the Romans conferred the mighty Roman imperial dignity, and besides this the right of nominating the pope. But Charles, beset by the prayers of the pope and of the princes and nobles of his realm, allowed himself at length, in compliance with the will of God and of men, to be consecrated and crowned by the pope and greeted as emperor by the people.[7]

In sharp contrast with this account stands the opinion of writers on the side of the papacy at the time of the quarrel about Investitures. They purposely omit the fact of the imperial coronation. The most striking instance of such an omission is in *Bonizo*, Bishop of Sutri, who in both his writings[8] describes only the first visit of Charles to Rome, and omits the last, and to suit his object abbreviates or enlarges the account given in the Liber Pontificalis, which he evidently has before him. Thus he makes Charles first swear fealty and due reverence to the 'representative of St. Peter' before he is raised to the rank of patricius. The appearance of Charles in Rome as judge and imperial ruler Bonizo attempts to set aside, by asserting that Charles's son Ludwig, who, it is known, never came to Rome, was the first of all the Frankish kings who was elevated to the dignity of emperor.

As Bonizo had open to him the older sources, especially the Liber Pontificalis, and must therefore have had before him the account of the occurrence in Rome of the year 800, he must have been guilty of deliberate falsehood, and

---

[7] *Annales Marbac.* Pertz [*Mon. G. SS.*], xvii. 147.
[8] In the *Liber ad Amicum*, Watterich [Jaffé, *Monum. Gregor.* p. 614], and the *Libri Decretorum*, from which Mai, in the 7th vol. of his *Nova Patrum Bibliotheca*, has given extracts. On Charles, P. iii., p. 44.

it is only astonishing that he should have thought it possible to mislead public opinion as to one of the best known and most important of all recent events. He even believed that the rightful Roman Empire, which, according to the Pauline prediction, still delayed the coming of Antichrist, was the Greek; for, in the West, the Roman Empire had been ruined by the arrogance of kings and the pride and avarice of their subjects, and Old Rome was under servitude to barbarians (the Germans) and did not live under her own laws. Bonizo truly had formed for himself a peculiar theory about the empire, utterly at variance with the facts of the time. According to him, the right to appoint the emperor belonged not to the pope, but to the seven principal Roman ecclesiastics, whom he calls Judices Palatini. These govern concurrently with the emperor, so that without them he can regulate nothing of importance. So confused had the conceptions of the time become, in consequence of the quarrel over the right of investiture. Bonizo's theory, starting from an ex-parte assumption, and devised to meet a definite object, might be called the Latin-clerical theory. It was set up in Italy at a time when the succession of a series of German popes was still fresh in people's memories. Yet it is evident that Bonizo was not a thorough Gregorian. An aristocracy of Roman ecclesiastics, restraining and tutoring the emperor and even the pope, such as Bonizo imagined, was not the object which Gregory strove to attain.

If it be asked how Bonizo could have formed so extraordinary an opinion as that the Roman Empire, which was still at that time so strong and extensive, had perished in the West, and that the rightful Roman Empire only existed in Constantinople, the reason for it may be easily found in the contemporary situation of affairs, and in the tendencies of his party. It was still the prevailing opinion that the highest power in Rome belonged by right to the Roman emperor, and that such an emperor, having nothing to do with Rome itself, and divested of all authority in his metropolis, must be an absurdity. The Roman Empire in the West had sunk to ruin, in order that in Rome there should remain no other authority but that of the ecclesiastical aristocracy. For any one who could not satisfy himself, like Bonizo, with the theory that the Roman Empire continued to exist in the East, this opinion must theologically lead to the assertion that Antichrist and the end of all things were at hand, that Antichrist was indeed already born—and such accordingly was the assertion of Bishop Ranieri of Florence (A.D. 1071–1080). His statement was refuted by the great opponent of Bonizo and Hildebrand, the archbishop and subsequent anti-pope, Wibert of Ravenna. The refutation lay in demonstrating that the Roman Empire, upheld by the Germans and acknowledged by the greater part of Italy, still existed in full force, that the emperor (Henry IV.) was obeyed by all, and that Rome in particular, notwithstanding the turbulent behaviour of the factions in the city, remained subject to the one emperor ; and that consequently the falling away from the Roman Empire, which the Apostle had prophesied would precede the coming of Antichrist, had by no means taken place.[9]

Bonizo's contemporary, the imperialist *Bishop Waltram of Naumburg*, naturally considers that the Romans proclaimed Charles emperor, and crowned him by the hands of Pope Leo. They had, said Waltram, according to general opinion, already fallen away from the Greek emperor, because he had not given them timely and effectual help against the tyrants (these must be the Lombard kings), and they now took advantage of the opportunity which the government of a woman afforded them.

Old Rome, as the mother, said the bishop, said farewell to her daughter, New Rome, when the emperors of the

---

[9] Lami had Wibert's letter printed in Florence from a MS. in that place, and inserted amongst his *Novelle letterarie*, 1768, p. 771, 803. Wibert says, moreover : ' *Nec ideo diminutum imperium æstimes, vel defecisse putes, quod Pseudo sit Papa*' (Gregory VII.). ' *Papam non Romanorum generalitas, sed paucorum Romanorum cupiditas ordinavit.*'

latter city became heretical, and even persecutors of the Catholic Church, and chose for herself better sons amongst the Gallic and Germanic peoples.[1] Thus everything is attributed to the city; the pope, in prevailing upon the reluctant Charles to accept the imperial title, acted merely according to the will of the city.

Waltram's contemporary, *Sigebert* of Gembloux, who was of the same way of thinking, and whose much-used chronicle, long considered as of great authority, was written about the year 1106, likewise represents the occurrence as entirely the act of the Romans, as whose instrument the pope acted. He, like Waltram, mentions[2] the previous change of opinion and the utilising of the justifiable pretext that the government was in the hands of a woman. He is followed, in the thirteenth century, by *Helinand*[3] and *Alberich*[4] in their compilations from the chronicles. The former observes that the Roman Empire was at that time separated from Constantinople.

The facts are differently represented by Abbot *Hugo of Flavigny*, who was almost contemporary with Sigebert and Waltram. He had already separated himself from the Gregorian party, and joined the opposition. According to him, Charles himself takes the initiative and assumes the imperial title, and he mentions neither pope nor Romans.[5]

The Irish monk *Marianus*, who lived in Germany, and his contemporary *Lambert* of Hersfeld, who both wrote impartially, simply say that Charles was proclaimed emperor by the Romans. The Abbot *Ekkehard* of Aurach in his chronicle (c. 1106) also follows the Annals of Lorsch and Eginhard in describing the homage done by the pope. Is it by chance or design that he not only represents Charles as crowned by the pope, but also as formally proclaimed by him as emperor (*imperatorem pronunciavit*)? One opinion is

---

[1] Schard, *Syntagma de jurisd. imper.*, Basil., p. 2.
[2] Pertz [*Mon. G. SS.*, viii. 336.
[3] Tiffer, *Bibl. Cisterc.* vii. 102.
[4] Leibnitz, *Access. Hist.* 131. [*Mon. G. SS.* xxiii. 720.]
[5] Bouquet, v. 374.

peculiar to him, and he is evidently only led into it by the events of his time, namely, that the cause of the Roman revolt against Pope Leo was that the Romans had wanted to appropriate the rights of the imperial dignity, and that Leo had resisted them.[6] In this the narrative of *Otto* of Freising, who has made great use of Ekkehard, follows his narrative, only it is shorter. Whereas Ekkehard says that the Roman Imperium, from the time of Constantine the Great, remained with the Emperors of the Greeks, until it was transferred through Charles to the Frankish Emperors, Otto writes, 'it was in Constantinople, and has now been transferred to the Franks (meaning to the nation).'[7] A contemporary of his, *the monk of Weingarten* (about 1188), is one of the first to use the word 'transference,' without, however, ascribing the transference to the pope, and he goes further than Ekkehard and Otto, for 'in Constantinople,' he says, 'there remains only a "Regnum,"—a government with the mere name of the Imperium.'[8] In the Annals of Strasburg also, certainly in the later compilation of Urstisius,[9] the Romans 'transfer the most mighty Roman Empire, together with the right of nominating the pope,' to the already illustrious Charles.

The idea that it was the pope who, acting in his own power, restored the imperial dignity in Rome, and invested Charles therewith, found expression only once or twice prior to the Decretal of Innocent III. The first instance was when Bishop *Wido* of Ferrara (c. 1080), as the agent of Gregory VII., appealed for the justification of the step taken by this pope against Henry IV. to two fables ; the one setting forth that Pope Sixtus had previously excommunicated and deposed the Emperors Valentinian and Honorius ; the other, that Pope Stephen had escorted Charles to

[6] Pertz, viii. [*Mon. G. SS.* xi.], 168.
[7] *Hist.* 5, 30, 31. Tissier, *Biblioth. Cisterc.* viii. 68. [*Mon. G. SS.* xx. 226.]
[8] Leibnitz, *SS. Brunsvic.* i. 797.
[9] *Rer. German.* ii. 77, ed. 1670. Böhmer puts it in the 14th or 15th century.

Rome and deposed King Desiderius, and had then made Charles Emperor.¹ Wido, indeed, did not believe these things himself, but had heard them, it appears, from the Gregorians, and introduced them with the desire of impartially representing the *pros* and *cons* in the great dispute from his own point of view.

With a more serious intent Bishop *Arnulf* of Lisieux stated, before the Synod of Tours, that the emperor was under a special obligation to recognise the supremacy of the church, since, according to the testimony of 'ancient histories,' his predecessors had received the empire solely through the favour of the Roman Church, and could therefore claim no greater right to it than was conferred upon them by the favour of the bestower.² Arnulf had studied canon law in Italy, and had adopted the lately discovered theory with which two years previously Cardinal Roland had astonished the Germans—the same Roland who now, as Alexander III., was presiding over the synod. It was a time of great bitterness of feeling, when French and English alike were exasperated by the arrogant and selfish conduct of the German Emperor toward the papal chair, and people in the West eagerly seized any weapon that offered against the pretensions of Frederick. Yet a considerable time elapsed before this theory, invented by the jurists of Rome and Bologna, made its way into history.

One sees that even if the quarrel about investiture had not affected the representation of history, this would have happened in a still greater degree after the middle of the twelfth century, when the movements and pretensions that had arisen in Rome, and the opposition upon the imperial and German side, began to be felt. Arnold of Brescia had successfully preached to the Romans not only their freedom from the secular power of the pope, but also their hereditary indefeasible right to the empire and to the choice of the emperor. The Arnoldist Wetzel had written to the German king that the empire and the emperor belong to

---

¹ Pertz, xiv. [*Mon. G. SS.* xii.] 158.   ² Harduin, vi. ii. 1594.

the Romans, and not the Romans to the emperor.³ Upon the other side a Cardinal Legate had let fall the expression before the emperor and the German princes: 'From whom else, but from the pope, does the emperor hold "the imperium"?' The names of Charles and of Leo, so far as I can see, are not mentioned in the public documents of the time, but the chroniclers were not uninfluenced by the controversy.

Archbishop *Romuald* of Salerno (c. 1180) contents himself with following exactly and impartially the account in the Frankish annals.⁴ But his contemporary *Sicard*, Bishop of Cremona,⁵ and the German priest *Gottfried*,⁶ who lived in Viterbo, the former probably misled by the latter, have adorned the account of the occurrence with fables of a marked tendency. It is easy to perceive how the claims at that period again strongly put forward by the Byzantine emperor, and the attempt made through the pope by the Emperor Manuel to unite once more the Western with the Greek Empire, influence these writers. Charles, it is here stated, decides to assume the imperial crown, and to have himself anointed by the pope. The Roman people submit to him. But he thinks he is not yet rightly emperor so long as the emperor in New Rome does not abdicate in his favour, and he prepares to seize upon the Greek Empire. The reigning emperor is terrified into concluding a permanent peace with Charles and a league for mutual defence, with the name of brother granted on either side, the Greek Emperor continuing in possession of the East and of Constantinople, whilst Rome and the West are secured to Charles and his successors. Thereupon Charles marches by Constantinople to Jerusalem, and from thence by Calabria and Apulia back to Rome.⁷ Here, then, is the complete acknowledgment of

³ Martene, *Ampl. Coll.* ii. 556.
⁴ Muratori, vii. 153.   ⁵ The same, vii. 579.
⁶ The same, vii. 417. [*Mon. G. SS.*, xxii. 219.]
⁷ The same, vii. 579.

the Western Empire by the Eastern dressed up as history.

Entirely different is the account given by the three Englishmen, *Simeon*, a monk of *Durham* (c. 1130), *Orderic Vitalis*, a Norman monk, and *Gervase* of Tilbury, at the court of the Emperor Otto of Germany (c. 1210). All three are agreed that Charles was chosen emperor by a Roman plebiscite. According to Simeon it is the whole Roman people which confers upon him the dignity of emperor of the world, but the pope invests him with the purple and places the sceptre in his hand.[a] Orderic and Gervase make pope and people combine in the election. Orderic states that pope, senate, and people, after long deliberation upon the position of the Respublica, resolved to throw off the yoke of the Byzantine Emperor, because these emperors were sometimes heretical, sometimes not legitimately chosen by the people, having usurped the throne through the murder of their predecessors or kinsmen, and, besides, they had proved incapable of protecting even half the empire against the barbarians.[9] Gervase, like the contemporaries of Charles, appeals to the fact that government by a female had rendered the throne vacant; besides which, he thinks that the Roman Empire, owing to two rulers bearing the same title, has been thrown into terrible confusion, and its power weakened by division. Since, as an official under the Emperor Otto, who had been raised by Innocent III. to the throne, he was entirely under the influence of the received Roman theories, he points out at the same time how much better the position of the Greek Emperor is, who holds his dignity and undivided authority solely from God, whereas the Western Emperor must submit to regard his office as a gift from the pope, and not even to receive the imperial insignia at his coronation, the pope reserving them for himself. For

---

[a] *Monumenta Hist. Brit.*, Lond. 1848, i. 663. [Comp. Simson, 235⁵.] Matthew of Westminster has copied him.

[9] *Historiæ Normannor. Scriptores*, p. 367.

this evil, Gervase adds, the Donation of Constantine is to blame.[1]

Of the recognition by the Greek Emperor, Gervase says nothing, whereas Orderic, like most of the chroniclers, makes Nicephorus conclude peace at once with Charles; but Simeon, to make the matter still clearer, states that an embassy from Constantinople arrived in Rome at the moment of the coronation, with a formal petition to Charles to accept the empire.

Two other English chroniclers, *Roger de Horeden*[2] and *Radulf de Diceto*,[3] write of the elevation of Charles as the act of the Roman senate or people, at whose desire the pope performed the ceremony. Also in the chronicle of *Richard of Poitiers*, a monk at Cluny (1160), Charles is nominated emperor by the pope and the whole people.[4] The Eastern Empire, says Richard, had almost entirely collapsed, nothing but the name was still retained in Byzantium, when Charles set up the Western Empire. The *Chronicle of Tours*, composed in the beginning of the thirteenth century by a canon of that place, adopting the narrative of the Frankish annals, gives the coronation, the adoration of the pope, and so on, merely adding the observation that from that time onwards the emperors in Constantinople had only been styled emperors of the Greeks.[5]

Quite apart from other writers stands the author of the *third chronicler* of the Belgian abbey of *S. Tron*, which was certainly not written before the latter half of the fourteenth century. He generally copies Sigebert, but as to the event of the year 800 he has his own views. For Charles, he asserts, deposed Irene from the imperial throne, after which she was banished by the Romans, who, depriv-

---
[1] Leibnitz, *SS. Brunsvic.*, i. 941. [*M. G. SS.* xxvii. 378.]
[2] *Rerum Angl. Scriptores*, Lond., 1596 f., 233. [*Mon. G. SS.* xxvii. 138.]
[3] Twysden, *Rerum. Angl. Scriptores*, p. 347. Radulf has only transcribed from Sigebert. [Comp. *Mon. G. SS.* xxvii. 264.]
[4] Muratori, *Antiq. Ital.* iv. 1081.   [5] Martene, *Ampl. Coll.* v. 557.

ing Constantinople of the Roman Imperium, gave themselves an emperor in the person of Charles.⁶

In Italy, after the thirteenth century, the Guelphs as well as the Ghibellines based their theories upon the act of election, which the Roman people had accomplished by the elevation of Charles to the imperial dignity. Dante, and the Ghibellines with him, merely asserted that the empire of the world, having passed out of the possession of the legitimate authority, who had held it by Divine right, was at that time conferred by the Roman people, freely and directly, upon Charles and his imperial successors; but the Guelphs believed that the Roman people, through the mediation of the pope as their delegate, had made over the right of election to the German princes. If the authority of the pope or people to do this be denied, says *Matteo Villani*, then the imperial power is a mere matter of fact, and of the right of the stronger, without any legitimate foundation.

The Florentine *Giovanni Villani* manages to give a formal, preconcerted air to the course of events by asserting that the pope held a council with his cardinals at which, in accordance with the will of the Romans, the Roman Imperium was taken from the Greeks, and Charles, on account of his virtues, elected emperor, so that even the Greeks were henceforth subject to his ' *Signoria*.'

Meanwhile, by about the middle of the thirteenth century, that decay of the historic sense already frequently alluded to had set in, and displayed itself in the treatment of the history of Charles and the beginnings of the empire. All that happened in Rome was more and more frequently either passed over as unimportant, or not understood, or it was fancifully adorned or distorted to suit a particular bias.

It is astonishing that the most comprehensive historical compilation of that time, the 'Mirror of History' by *Vincent de Beauvais*, does not so much as mention the setting up of the empire. It is only briefly stated, in the

⁶ Pertz xii. [*Mon. G. SS.* x.] 327.

words of Sigebert, that Charles was the first Frankish
emperor; yet the legends of Carolingian invention are related with all the more detail as history. *Martinus Polonus*
proceeds apparently with equal thoughtlessness, but in
reality not without design. Both in his account of
Charles and in that of Leo the course of events in Rome
is passed over in silence. This silence proceeds from the
same motive as that of Bonizo. Yet Martinus's work
became the favourite book, the standard historical com-
pendium of the clergy of the fourteenth and fifteenth
centuries.

Ricobald of Ferrara (c. 1312) has also his own theory.[7]
The Roman Empire succeeded to the Assyrian, the Græco-
Macedonian, and the Carthaginian, as the fourth world-
empire. For better defence against the attacks of the eastern barbarians, the emperors transferred their seat to the
Thracian city, Constantinople. But since they rendered
no assistance to the Romans when pressed by the Lombards, the former, with the consent of the Emperor Constantine (this is twice repeated), and with the connivance
of the pope, divided the empire and set up an emperor for
themselves over the empire of the Romans, which is called
the Empire of the West. This Western Empire is now the
more important of the two, for the Roman people and the
senate established it; and it rests, therefore, on the authority of the Roman people, of the senate, and of the pope.

Similar, only with a more papal colouring, is the
view taken by the Brescian doctor, *Malvezzi*, who wrote
his chronicle a century later (c. 1412). The vitality of the
Roman Empire under Nicephorus was exhausted. But
when Charles had restored the rights of the pope and had
renovated the city of Rome, the Romans divided the empire and created a western emperor in order that the pope,
by the sword of the latter, might be in a position to withstand the frequent assaults of his enemies.[8]

[7] *Hist. Imperatorum*, Muratori, ix. 112.
[8] Muratori, xiv. 853.

The famous Decretal of Pope Innocent III. had a decisive influence upon the majority of later chronicles, from the thirteenth into the sixteenth century. By the removal of that document from amongst the pope's instructions to his legates in the year 1201, and its later enrolment in the collection of decretals, a lasting triumph was secured to those papistical views of theology to which it for the first time gave definite expression.

The pope therein bases the whole of his assumed right of disposal over the empire, and over the German royal and imperial elections, upon the supposed fact that the papal chair had transferred the imperium from the Greeks to the Germans in the person of Charles. In the year 1200 he had already, in his instruction to the Archbishop Conrad of Mainz,[9] declared it to be well known that the imperial dignity stood at the disposition of the papacy, in consequence and by virtue of the act decisive of coronation, namely, the papal imposition of hands;[1] for thus through the pope, and on account of the pope, that is to say for his defence, it was transferred from the land of the Greeks to the West.

So long as this memorandum of the pope was not included among the decretals, it exercised, so far as I can see, no influence upon historical narratives. It was only after the middle of the thirteenth century, and particularly after a commentary had been written on it in the *Glossa ordinaria* of Bernhard of Parma (c. 1260), that it was made use of as an authority and criterion by the chroniclers and others in discussing the relations between empire and papacy, and in favour of the latter.

Under the powerful influence of the Glossa it became necessary to alter history, and to place at a date much

[9] Raynald, ad a. 1200, §27.
[1] *Principaliter et finaliter.* The coronation is described as an imposition of hands, in order to liken it to the episcopal ordination of priests, and to be able to draw therefrom the conclusion that the acceptance or rejection of an emperor belonged to the pope in the same way that to the bishop belonged the power of admitting or excluding a candidate for ordination.

earlier than the year 800 the transference of the imperial dignity. For the author of the Glossa says: 'We read in the chronicles that the Roman Church, oppressed by Aistulf, begged assistance from the Emperors Constantine and Leo in Constantinople, but as they would render none, Pope Stephen II. transferred the empire to Charles, the son of Pipin, in the year 766 (this is surely meant for 756), and fifteen years later (*i.e.* in 781) he was crowned by Leo III.'

If this Glossa is the work of Bernhard of Parma, it must have been written about the year 1260–65, but I can mention no Chronicle from which this extraordinary perversion of history could have been derived. It was certainly not invented by a simple unprejudiced chronicler, but by a jurist who desired thereby to come to the help of the new theory of the transference. All the historians who have been persuaded to attribute the transference to Pope Stephen, and to throw the occurrence back to the year 765, or rather 756, do so, as it appears to me, on the authority only of the Glossa, coupled with that of the Decretal.

In order to satisfy the ideas of that period, it was needful to discover some sufficient ground to justify the pope in the exercise of such an unparalleled act of supremacy as the transference of the imperial dignity would imply. Innocent believed, as can be seen by his writings, in the Donation of Constantine, and one of his predecessors, Leo IX., had already declared in his dogmatic brief sent to the Patriarch Michael of Constantinople (A.D. 1054)[2] that Constantine the Great had long ago made over to Silvester and all succeeding popes that which he had himself received from God, namely, the imperial power and dignity together with the insignia, so that the Roman Chair was as surely in possession of the earthly as of the heavenly imperium. Whether Leo really supposed that Constantine had abdicated, and had appointed the pope universal emperor of

[2] Harduin, vi. 933.

the East and West in his stead, is not clear. He certainly derived from the Donation of Constantine the right to dispose of and to transfer the imperium, which in that case could only be a papal fief. Whether Innocent believed this is less certain. He did not, at all events, when the Latin Empire was erected at Constantinople, lay claim on behalf of the papal chair to any special right, but only expressed his joy that the Imperium of Constantinople should have passed from schismatics to Catholics, and from the Greeks to the Latins.[3] But Innocent did not regard the Roman Empire as a re-erection of a Western Empire, though justification for this might easily be found in the Donation of Constantine. He believed in a transference of the indivisible Roman Empire from the Greeks to the Germans. Such a spoliation of the Greeks, such an ejection of a great people and realm from the legitimate possession of many centuries, could only receive apparent justification through some weighty and imperative motive. Moreover, the inference had been drawn that if former popes had renounced the Donation of Constantine in favour of the new empire, they would also have relinquished the government of Rome to the emperors, a position which it would have been very hazardous for the Curia to maintain. Consequently, some other legal principle had to be found. Innocent was the first to set up the sweeping and far-reaching principle that wherever the point in question was a sin, or one side in a dispute could be accused of sin, the papal chair had the right of disposal. This principle might at all events have been applied in the case of Irene, who was accused of having blinded her son, the emperor; but it was felt that this pretext was not adequate to justify the permanent spoliation of the Greeks and the transference of the empire. Only the most grievous crime, apostasy from the faith, or heresy, could warrant such a measure. The transference was accordingly dated back to the time of the iconoclast Emperor Constantine Copronymus

[3] Epistolæ, ed. Bréquigny. p. 576.

(A.D. 741–A.D. 775). Antedating the event by thirty or thirty-four years made the imperial right to the supreme power in Rome appear at least doubtful, for the empire would then have existed several decades without such a right having arisen.

The papal penitentiary and chaplain *Martinus Polonus*, towards the close of the 13th century, was therefore, as it seems, the first to attribute to Pope Stephen II. in the last year of his pontificate the intention of transferring the imperial dignity to the person of King Charles. That would have been in 755 or 756. Martinus, as already remarked, says nothing of the coronation in the year 800. He refers to the Decretal of Innocent,[1] as later writers habitually do. In the same way as Godfrey of Viterbo had intimated that every historical work ought first to be submitted for examination to the papal chair, so from the beginning of the 14th century it appears to have been taken for granted that when once an important historical fact had been given a definite form in a papal document, the historians were forced to adopt it. At any rate it so happened in the case before us. The authors of subsequent papal histories, *Bernard Guidonis* and *Leo of Orvieto*, appeal to the Decretal and represent the transference as the act of Stephen. In *Tolomeo of Lucca* (cir. 1312) the conflict of better knowledge with the opinions exclusively received in his own circle is very noticeable. He takes the story of the coronation from the earlier accounts, but omits the homage by the pope, which in his day had come to be no longer considered possible. The journey to Mantua undertaken by the pope at the demand of Charles, and from thence to Charles's court, is so represented that the dependent position of the pope does not appear; Leo uses the occasion only to secure the emperor's support against his Roman enemies, and Tolomeo has discovered in 'other books of History' that the emperor not merely sent an escort, as the Frankish annals say, with the pope

[1] Ed. Klimes, 1859, p. 94.

on his return through Bavaria as far as Ravenna, but that he accompanied him in person from Rheims as far as Rome, so that the author here calls the attention of his readers to the devotion of the emperor. However, immediately afterwards, in relating how Charles invested his son Ludwig with the imperial title, the author's conscience reproaches him, and he adds: 'Charles may have been authorised by the pope to do this, but it is not recorded.'[5]

On the subject of the transference, this fundamental fact of the new order of politics, Tolomeo found means to satisfy himself. 'It is true,' he says, ' that the transference of the empire, as the Glossa on the Decretal asserts, was rendered necessary by the malignant heresy of the Emperors Leo and Constantine Copronymus, and was brought about by Pope Stephen; but he only decided upon and defined it, and the empire of the Greeks was not put an end to by order of the church until the time of Charles;'—many, he adds, are misled by Bernhard's Glossa. He himself has not the slightest doubt that, in accordance with his theory, the order of transference was passed against heretical emperors, but carried out against orthodox emperors forty and odd years later.[6]

This idea, that the transference was the act of the pope, had now practically become of the highest importance. It served as a basis for Germano-Italian political law as well as for that of the whole of Europe. It is instructive to mark how this fact affected the writing of history, and how the literature of public law, which developed after the 14th century, transformed it to its own advantage.

The first German prince who formally recognised the transference theory was *Rudolf of Habsburg* (A.D. 1279).[7] In

---

[5] Muratori, xi. 987-995. [Simson, 315³, tries to justify Tolomeo o Lucca against Döllinger's reproaches.]

[6] Muratori, *ibid.* p. 975.

[7] In many German histories Adrian IV. is named as the pope who, in the year 1159, first asserted the transference, and even maintained that the empire had passed to Pope Zacharias. The only source for this is *Aventin*, *Annal.* 6, 5, 10, p. 607 [*Werke*, iii. 2178], who quotes word for word a pretended work to this effect. Pütter, *Specimen de instaur. Imp. Rom.*,

the letter to Pope Nicolas III. by which he formally ratified the pope's claim to the whole district forming the States of the Church, from Radicofani to Ceperano, he declared that the Germans were under a perpetual obligation to the Roman Church, because the church had heaped blessings upon them, and had made them what they were, by transferring the Imperium from the Greeks to them.[8] Following this precedent, *King Albrecht* (A.D. 1303), when desirous of winning the favour and assistance of Boniface VIII. against the German archbishops, did not hesitate to acknowledge that the Roman Empire had been transferred from the Greeks to the Germans by the pope.[9] With this transference was coupled, in Albert's time and ever after, the assurance that the pope had bestowed upon certain German princes the right of electing the emperor. In the encyclical issued in the year 1314, in which Clement V. declared that the oath which it was customary for the emperor to take before the pope was undoubtedly an oath of fealty—he means the oath of a vassal—this assertion is supported upon two facts, the transference of the empire from the Greeks to the Germans and the bestowal upon the princes of the right of election.[1] A few years later Pope John XXII. in like manner turned the transference of the imperium to account in his suit against the Emperor Ludwig.[2]

In France, whilst the papal throne was occupied by French popes, the value of the transference theory was appreciated to the full extent. *Peter Dubois*, a publicist under Philip the Fair, demonstrates to the king, in a memorial of the year 1308, how easy it would now be for him to acquire the empire, with all that it implied, for himself and his heirs. The pope (who indeed was entirely

---

p. 68, has allowed himself to be misled by this. The work is nevertheless, like so many others, a fiction of Aventin. Pope Innocent was the first to set up the transference theory.

[8] Raynald, a. 1279, §4.   [9] Pertz, iv. [*Mon. G. LL.* ii. 1], 483.
[1] Clementin, 2, 9, in *Corp. jur. can.*   [2] Martene, *Thesaurus*, ii. 644.

devoted to the king) had only to say to the assembled
German princes: The empire was transferred in the person
of Charles from the Greeks to the Germans and the right
of election conferred upon you, because the emperor in
Constantinople, although many times warned, neglected to
defend the church; you in your turn have deserved to lose
this right, by your choice of emperors hostile to the church,
and I could withdraw it from you; you are to elect, therefore, him whom I shall point out to you, . . . and so on.[3]
It is well known that if Philip's plan, founded upon the
submissiveness of the pope, had been carried out, Charles
of Valois, the king's brother, would have become German
king and emperor.[4] The subject need not here be pursued. Nevertheless, to the Italian, French, and German
publicists from that time forward the transference was a
question of the highest importance; they wrote special
works to discuss it in its historical and legal bearings.
Jordan, Canon of Osnabrück,[5] and *Raoul de Coloumelle,
Canon of Chartres*, were the first to employ themselves thus.[6]
Marsilius of Padua (c. 1330), the Minorite, followed their

[3] The memorial is to be found in *Notices et Extraits*, t. xx., p. 186 s.

[4] Giovanni Villani, viii. 101, actually says that Philip, when demanding
from the pope the elevation of his brother, had introduced in favour of his
demand the fact that the pope and the Church 'altre volte per antica avea
rimossa la elezione de' Greci nei Franceschi e de' Franceschi ne' Taliani, e
delli Italiani nelli Alamanni.' Another transference might now all the more
reasonably be made. However, Villani connects the matter with his fable
of the six conditions by which Clement purchased the pontificate from
Philip, and that throws suspicion upon his statement.

[5] The pamphlet is to be found in Schard, *Syntagma Basil.*, 1566, p. 297 s.
That it was composed as early as I have stated is conclusive from the contents and from the dedication with which Cardinal James Colonna sent it
to the pope. The pope must have been Honorius IV. The dedication is
given by Denis, *Catal. MSS. Vindobon.* i. 1231.

[6] *Rudolphus de Columna de Translatione Imperii*, Schard, p. 284 s. If
the author, as we learn from a couple of MSS., was really Canon of Chartres,
then his name was most probably de Coloumelle, and under this name a
notice is given of him in the *Histoire littéraire de France*, t. xxi., 151.
Yet he is likewise described as Canon of Siena, and Marsilius, who has the
pamphlet before him, calls him *Satrapa Romanus*, under the supposition
that he belonged to the powerful Colonna family.

example, and wrote in the interests of the Emperor Ludwig,[7] and so did *Lupold of Babenburg*, Bishop of Bamberg, somewhat later (1353-1363).[8] They only gather the facts from confused and falsified later chronicles, particularly those of *Richard of Cluny*, *Martinus Polonus*, and others of the kind; and it is curious to observe that the German Jordanus first makes Charles the Great a blood relation of the Greek emperor, and then maintains that he sprang from a Greek, Roman, and German race in a direct line (meaning, of course, from the ancient emperors and kings); so that, in fact, the pope only transferred the imperial dignity to another branch of the imperial house. The view that the transference had taken place on account of the iconoclast heresy, and of the refusal of help, when once adopted continued to be held; what Stephen had ordered, Leo had accomplished. Why Leo should, forty years later, have carried out Stephen's project, at a time when the reasons which had influenced Stephen were obsolete, is not discussed. Marsilius, indeed, considers the papal conduct in the matter as altogether unjustifiable, and explains it by motives of ambition, but the other writers entertain no doubt of the validity and justice of the act.[9]

[7] Schard, p. 225. It was not composed till later than his great work, *Defensor Pacis*.

[8] *De Jure Regum et Imp. Rom.*, Schard, 328 s. Just at the same time, under Charles IV., *Conrad of Magdeburg*, parish priest of Regensburg, wrote thereon: 'Disputavi de translatione imperii in Germanos, an scilicet Papa iure humano an divino potuerit imperium transferre.' Struvii *Acta lit. ex MSS.*, iv. 86.

[9] Marsilius seems to have been unacquainted with any writings save those that ascribed the transference to Pope Stephen. Thus about fifty years had sufficed to bring so clumsy and transparent a falsification of history to a sort of established authority. For at p. 231 he says: 'Sic scripturæ omnes recitantes quod tempore huius Stephani Papæ translatum sit Imperium a Græcis in Francos, debent intelligi, scilicet quod tempore suo fuerit ordinata translatio.' In the *Defensor Pacis*, p. 150, ed. Goldast, Marsilius makes Leo the Isaurian come to Italy to take certain pictures to Constantinople, whereupon Pope Gregory excommunicates him. It is instructive to notice how so learned and acute a thinker, as Marsilius certainly was, struggles, as though taken in a net, with the web of historical fables, which, nevertheless, had only recently been put in circulation.

The confusion of ideas, the antagonism to history and to truth, the dilemmas and contradictions which arose out of this theory of the papal transference, are all clearly reflected in the writings of Lupold of Babenburg. He alleges that the jurist *Lanfrank* (c. 1220) declared the transference to have resulted from the refusal of the Greeks to recognise the Roman primacy, and he has thus fallen into a grievous anachronism. He mentions another legal expert, *Bernhardus Hispanus* (probably Bernard of Compostella (c. 1219), the author of the third collection of decretals), who declares the Greek emperor to be the true Roman emperor, and thus rejects the transference altogether. Now, Lupold sticks fast to the transference upon the ground of canon law (that is to say, of the decretal of Innocent III.), and several chronicles affirm that it took place; yet he sees that it cannot be ascribed to Stephen, but rather to Leo III. He, moreover, combines the idea of imperial government of the world with that of the papal transference; but he will not allow the deduction drawn by the papal theologians and canonists, that the supreme government of the world belonged properly to the pope; consequently he falls into a labyrinth, out of which he seeks to find a way by adopting the opinion that the transference was a matter of necessity, because the Greek emperors had abandoned the empire in the West, and had especially neglected to protect the clergy, whereas Charles had amply fulfilled all imperial obligations. The Romans, as a mere fraction of the empire, could not have undertaken the transference; they could only be said to have done so, if by Romans the entire population of the empire were understood. Thus, by an accidental necessity, in the absence of any higher power, the task fell to the pope.

Very different is the version of the matter given in a refined and scholarly work composed somewhat later (c. 1730), called *Songe du Vergier*. The author was probably Philip de Maizières.[1] Undoubtedly, he says, the right of transfer-

---

[1] So a good judge, Paulin Paris, thinks. *Manuscrits Français de la Biblioth. du Roi*, iv. 328.

ence pertained to the Romans as the founders of the empire; the pope and clergy formed but a part of the people of Rome, who were the principals in the transaction; such an interference in temporal concerns would not benefit the pope. The decretal of Innocent he manages to set aside by declaring that the pope only acted on the strength of the authority conferred upon him by the Roman people.[2]

About twenty years earlier Cardinal *Nicolas Rosselli*, a Dominican from Tarragona, had taken up the question of the empire,[3] and had, as might be expected, solved it in the opposite sense. 'Seeing,' he says, 'that, to give the pope disposal over all secular powers and governments, nothing further is required than for a sin to be committed by a prince, Stephen was fully justified in undertaking the transference in the year 756; for a sin, at least one of omission, had been committed, for the Glossa bears witness that the Greek emperors had failed to render the help which at that time Rome had solicited.'

The chroniclers of this later period (c. 1290-1450) usually write under the double influence of Martinus Polonus and of the Decretal, together with the Glossa. *Siffrid*, a priest of Meissen about the end of the thirteenth century, explained the event by a treaty concluded between the pope, the German princes, and the Romans, which stipulated that after the conquest of the Lombards and other invaders the empire should be transferred to the Teutons; whereupon Pipin, in accordance with the treaty, conquered Aistulf, but Charles received the *imperium* as had been stipulated.[4] Siffrid's contemporary, *Martin* the Minorite, at first refers to the papal decretal which ascribes the transference to Stephen, although afterwards, following a later authority, he makes out that all was due to Charles himself.[5]

[2] *Traités des droits et libertés de l'Eglise Gall.*, ed. 1731, ii. 99.
[3] In the document *De iurisdictione Ecclesiæ super regnum Apuliæ* in the *Miscellanea of Baluze*, ed. Mansi, i. 469 s.
[4] Pistorius-Struv. i. 1030.
[5] Eccard, *Corp. Hist. Med.* i. 1606.

Martin, Monk of Fulda (c. 1378), takes the Glossa as an indisputable historical authority; he remarks that the transference by Pope Stephen must be adhered to, for only thus can the Glossa be saved.[6] He also brings into his narrative the very popular and widely credited fable of Charles's expedition to Jerusalem, and of the relics given to him in Constantinople on his return journey.

The chronicler *Heinrich of Herrord* (A.D. 1370)[7] narrates the occurrence first in the words of Ekkehard and of Sigebert, but adds that Charles, having with a strong hand wrested the empire from the Greeks, was crowned by Leo with the consent and co-operation of the Romans; the imperium of the Greeks in Rome being by this means extinguished, and the government of the world devolving upon the Germans. All this he gives upon the authority of the well-known Decretal, together with the Glossa. Heinrich's further remark, that the empire no longer remained with the Greeks even though the monarchs in the East were called emperor in the wider sense, occurs frequently in a different form.

The *annals of Speier* (c. 1272) are content with a most superficial justification of the occurrence, viz. that Charles availed himself of the illness of the Emperor Michael, about the year 768, under the Popes Zacharias and Leo, to seize upon the Roman Empire.[8] More serious and dignified is the representation of the matter by *James Twinger* of Königshofen (c. 1410): according to his account the Greek emperors neither thought nor cared about the defence of the Christian faith or the protection of widows and orphans, and the government had fallen into the hands of a woman. Thereupon the pope and the Romans unanimously appealed to Charles that he should become Roman Emperor and accept the title of Augustus, so that the Roman Empire should no longer be under the Greeks. The Greeks, nevertheless, amongst themselves

[6] Eccard, *Corp. Hist. Med.* i. 651.   [7] Ed. Potthast, p. 39.
[8] Pertz [*Mon. G. SS.*], xvii. 81.

made another emperor,—'but,' says Twinger, 'the power of their emperor is but small compared with that of the German emperor.' It is evident that Twinger troubles himself neither about the Decretal nor the Glossa.[9]

The chronicle of the Abbot of S. Bertin, *John of Ypres*,[1] the chronicle of the Monastery of St. Egidius in Brunswick,[2] and that of Osnabrück[3] hold fast to the transference of the empire by Stephen. John of Ypres in particular betrays the confusion of ideas into which the conflict between the Decretal and his own historical knowledge had thrown him; first of all, he says that the Romans, who had long ago fallen away from their loyalty to the Greek Empire, used the occasion which was offered by the reign of a woman to proclaim Charles emperor; but immediately afterwards he feels himself compelled, upon the authority of Pope Innocent, to assert that Pope Stephen in the last years of his pontificate had already transferred the Roman Imperium from the Greeks to the Germans, and then that Charles, having been previously elected emperor, proceeded in company with Pope Leo to Rome, where he restored the pope to his throne, and thereupon was crowned.

A chronicler of *Malmesbury Abbey* (A.D. 1366) briefly remarks that Charles the Great at the request of Pope Stephen took the Empire of the Romans for himself.[4]

Meanwhile new embellishments had been added; an eclipse is said to have followed the blinding of the last Greek emperor, Constantine, and the darkness to have been so complete and to have lasted so many days that ships drifted about helplessly at sea. This is reported by the presbyter *Andreas* (A.D. 1431),[5] the chronicle of Lüneburg,[6] and *Bernard Witte*.[7] By this time it had also

---

[9] *Chronicle of Elsass*, published by Schilter, 1698, p. 101. [*Chroniken der deutschen Städte*, viii. 404.]

[1] Martene, *Thes.*, iii. 1499.   [2] Pistorius, i. 1084.

[3] Meibom. ii. 196.   [4] *Eulogium historiarum*, Londin. 1858, i. 367.

[5] Pez, *Thesaurus*, iv., iii. 421.

[6] Eccard, i. 1318.   [7] *Historia Saxoniæ*, p. 139.

been discovered that Pope Leo was a brother of Charles, as the chronicler of Lüneburg has found in 'several books.' 'At any rate,' says *Rolewink*, 'he was a German, a brother of the Count of Calw, so it is easy to see how it came to pass that he transferred the imperial dignity and the government of the world to the Germans,' which it was thought in the fifteenth century an Italian pope would hardly have done. The same Rolewink (end of the fifteenth century) also tells us that the church had long borne patiently with the Greeks and waited for their amendment, but at length, when they had altogether fallen away from their earlier piety, they were 'forsaken,' and the transference was decided on, with the unanimous consent of the Romans.

But the national Italian, or more properly the Latin, view of the occurrence still had its representatives both in Italy and in Germany. *Benvenuto Rambaldi* of Imola (A.D. 1350),[8] *Poggio* (A.D. 1405),[9] *Flavio Biondo*, secretary of Pope Eugenius IV., and *Æneas Silvius*[1] regard the Roman people as the acting and deciding authority, and introduce a partition or division of the empire in place of a transference, but in such wise, as Rambaldi says, that the Western Empire henceforth alone bore the name of the Roman, and the Eastern that of the Greek, Empire. Still later we find *Sabellico* and *Platina* adopting the idea of the Roman plebiscite confirmed by the pope. Matthew *Palmieri* (A.D. 1440), the author of a dry chronicle, deserves mention, because he first again mentions the name, unknown throughout the Middle Ages, of Augustulus, whose successor Charles became. Hitherto it had been always understood that the transference of the empire had taken place under Constantine the Great.

The German bishop, *Dietrich of Niem*, tries to harmonize the transference by Stephen with the Roman popular vote, and therefore maintains that the people had already

---

[8] *Liber Augustalis*, Freher, ii. 13.   [9] Muratori, xx. 382.
[1] *Dialogi de autorit. Concil.*, Kollar, ii. 371.

proclaimed Charles as Augustus in the year 774, and as it was not possible to assemble themselves again on every particular occasion, the people transferred their rights and powers to Charles.[2]

Æneas Silvius, on the question of the empire, as in other things, took, as Pope Pius II., different views from those he had formerly advocated. In a speech delivered in 1459, in which he enumerates all the gifts and privileges that the papal chair had made over to the Franks, he asserts that Pope Leo had transferred the imperial office in consequence of his indignation against the iconoclasm of the Emperor Leo IV. (A.D. 775-780). He seems to have been unaware of the fact that Irene and her son Constantine, who favoured the worship of images, had come to the throne in 780, that is to say, sixteen years before the elevation of Pope Leo. Pius further says: 'It was not a divided empire, as ye assert, which was conferred upon the Franks; there were not made two empires, one of the Greeks and the other of the Latins; a pope would never have committed such an absurdity as to leave the sword in the hands of the enemy of the faith—that is, the iconoclast emperor. The whole undivided imperium was transferred, but Charles divided what he had received entire, first with Irene, and then with Nicephorus, and kept only the half for himself.'[3]

In this instance it is not myth but theory which has prevailed over history. Yet the power of the popular myth is to be seen in the chronicle of the Milanese writer, *Donato Bossi* (c. 1480).[4] Here, instead of Charles, King Desiderius is the hero selected by the Lombard popular imagination, whose history is adorned with fable. Desiderius is victorious in a great battle over 300,000 Saracens, who were besieging Rome and the castle in which the pope and Charles were shut up. For this deed

[2] Schard, 788.
[3] The speech is given by d'Achery, *Spicileg.* iii. 813, ed. 1723
[4] *Chronica Bossiana* Mediolani, 1492, fol. 63.

the grateful pope grants extraordinary powers to Desiderius over all the Lombards and Italians (Italici), together with imperial rule over the whole of Italy. But soon afterwards Desiderius oppresses and robs the pope, who takes refuge with Charles. The latter says to him: 'If thou wilt give to me the kingdom of Italy, I will come and rescue the church out of the hand of the Lombards.' The pope naturally accepts the offer, and Charles thus attains the dignity of emperor, which Desiderius would not otherwise have forfeited. Side by side with this, however, in traditional deference to the Decretal, it is asserted that the transference of the empire by Stephen to Charles took place in the year 766.

In Germany, as well, the most wonderful distortions of fact were occasionally resorted to by historians who wished to render the web of circumstances which led to the creation of the empire comprehensible. Thus the *Chronicle of Hameln* (A.D. 1370) relates that Charles, having been appointed patricius in the year 800, conquered the last Roman Emperor who came from Greece, whereupon Leo consecrated him emperor. Thereupon the Roman Senate sought to appropriate the imperial rights, and mutilated the pope who attempted to oppose them. On account of this sacrilegious deed, the Greeks broke off religious communion with the Romans, and in this state of schism the empire passed to Charles and the Franks.[5] The chronicler *Meisterlin* of Nürnberg (c. 1480) gives a simpler account. Since the Greek emperors, he says, had given themselves up to luxury and did not care about the Germans, the transference was begun by Pope Stephen, was continued by Leo, and was finally carried out by Adrian.[6]

It is easy to understand how, amid such confusion and distortion of the facts, a man like Cardinal *Nicolas Cusa* finally came to conjecture that the whole empire of Charles the Great was a fiction. He had read, he says, the correspondence between Charles and Adrian, and had found

[5] *Ludewig. Reliquiæ MS.* x. 8, 9.   [6] *Ibid.* viii. 22.

no trace in it of the supposed transference; Charles can never have been more than patricius.[7] Cusa's contemporary, the highly esteemed jurist *Antonio Roselli*, of Padua,[8] contented himself, on the other hand, with accepting the transference as having been accomplished in the year 756 or 766; the Greek emperor was deposed from the imperial throne in proper judicial form, and on account of a crime—to wit, persistent neglect of duty—for which even the pope himself might be deposed.

The German lawyer, *Peter of Andlau* (c. 1460), who published the first attempt at codifying German political law, is unable to free himself from the story of the translation by Stephen, so he also takes refuge in the idea that Stephen only decided upon the transference, and being overtaken by death, was unable to carry it out. It was brought about because the strength of the Greeks was almost broken, whilst the Germans, on the contrary, were strong, energetic, loyal, eager for battle, and powerful, and therefore more fitted than any other nation to administer the Christian imperium. For this reason, and also to acquit herself of a debt of gratitude to the Frankish king, the Roman Church took the Roman Empire from the Greeks and conferred it upon the noble race of Germans. Peter of Andlau, who otherwise is a faithful disciple of the author of the Glossa, is convinced that in Charles Greek, Roman, and German blood were mingled.[9]

What conclusions the Italians of about the middle of the sixteenth century still further extracted from the transference theory, we may learn from the Perugian jurist, *Ristoro Castaldo*, in his great work on the emperors, which, the author assures us, was written for the glorification of the empire and of Charles V. 'It is,' he says, 'a true and Catholic assertion that by the authority of the pope, a transference of all kingdoms and of the imperial dignity was made to the Romans, from these to the Greeks, and

---

[7] *Concord. cathol.*, Schard, p. 613.   [8] Goldast, *Monarchia*, i. 290.
[9] *De Imperio Romano*, in the *Tractatus varii*. Norimb. 1657, pp. 49, 52.

from the Greeks to the Germans.' *Agostino Trionfo* (1320) had already expatiated upon this idea, and also declared in agreement with Castaldo that the pope might again, if he chose, transfer the empire to any other people. He further asserts that all monarchs and states not subject to the Roman emperor—for example, France and Spain—are only exempted by a special papal privilege, and that the pope, if he pleased, could nominate the emperor, as he alone had the right to depose him.'

¹ *Amplissimus Tractatus de Imperatore*, 1539. The work appears to have been printed in Rome.

IV
ANAGNI[1]

WE are in possession of three accounts by eye-witnesses of the events that rendered Anagni famous in history. The first is that of *Nogaret*, who in his defence, composed during the pontificates of Benedict XI. and Clement V., relates with great fulness of detail what took place at Anagni during the three days of September 7–9, 1303. His tone is naturally apologetic, yet upon all cardinal points his account is faithful and true. He was indeed bound to be accurate, because there were still several witnesses at the papal court who had participated in the transactions related. Moreover, in his own interest he would take care not to weaken the effect of his defence by making statements the inaccuracies of which could be proved against him. That he should represent himself as having played the principal part, first as the accuser, and then as the protector of the pope, is but natural.[2]

The second, and earliest, account—composed before the death of the pope—which is also the best and most instructive, is that of a man who describes himself as a '*Curtisan*,'[3] from Cesena, and so must have belonged to the papal

[1] This lecture, which was delivered before the historical class of the Academy January 5, 1878, is thus headed in Döllinger's MS.

[2] [Dupuy, *Histoire du différend d'entre le pape Boniface VIII et Philippes le Bel, roy de France*: Paris, 1655, 2°. Comp. the treatise by Ernest Renan, already made use of by Döllinger, upon *Guillaume de Nogaret, légiste*, in the 27th vol. of the *Histoire littéraire de la France*, Paris, 1877, pp. 233, 371.]

[3] This may be the first instance of the use of the word to describe an individual belonging to the Roman Curia; the next, as far as I am aware, is in a bull of Benedict XIII., consequently a hundred years later.

Curia, either officially as secretary or agent for others, or as an aspirant to a benefice.[4]

The third account is by an unknown person, an eyewitness, the author of a Life of Boniface VIII. in the collection of Onofrio Panvinio[5] (which has not hitherto been printed). Panvinio took it out of a chronicle at Orvieto, which, although perhaps it now no longer exists, must have been in existence as late as 1642, for Christopher Gaetano of Anagni, who died Bishop of Foligno in that year, and who wrote a Life (unprinted) of Boniface VIII. for the people of Anagni, made use of it, as I gather from an allusion to it by Renan, for the circumstance he relates is only mentioned in this account.[6] The author does not, indeed, like the Curtisan of Cesena, affirm that he had witnessed the whole affair; but the tone of his narrative, the introduction of facts which would otherwise not have been thought of, the absence of any sign of partisanship, all lead us to conclude that he was either himself present, or that he had copied the record of a witness.

The most distinguished person made use of by King Philip the Fair in his assault upon Pope Boniface was William of Nogaret, formerly Professor of Law at Montpellier, who had been in the king's service since the year 1296, and had been employed in important and difficult undertakings. He had been ennobled in the year 1299, and now styled himself *Chevalier-ès-loix*, '*miles*.' He belonged to a class which first took its rise in Philip's reign—the *noblesse de robe* of later time—a class which, though non-clerical, raised itself by learning and industry,

[4] [The best edition at present (1888) is published by F. Liebermann, *Mon. G. SS.* xxviii., 621 ff, in which the earlier editions are also noted. Liebermann makes it appear probable that the writer of the letter addressed to friends in England was not by birth an Italian, but a Frenchman, and, moreover, an opponent of the French party and of the Colonnas. From whence Döllinger has drawn the statement that this Curtisan came from Cesena I do not know.]

[5] [Now printed in Döllinger's *Beitr. zur Gesch. der sechs letzten Jahrhunderte*, vol. iii. Vienna, 1882, pp. 347, 353.]

[6] [*Hist. Litt.* p. 260.]

and brought legal skill and discernment as well as statesmanship into the management of affairs, and so became indispensable to kings, especially to those to whom clerical authority was becoming more and more of an oppressive yoke.

In March, 1303, Nogaret was sent by King Philip to Italy, with secret orders to apprehend the pope and convey him to France, that he might be deposed by a General Council. With him, in a subordinate position, went two men described as Magistri, Thierry d'Hiricon and Jacques de Gesserin, who must have been intended to be employed as secretaries, preparers of manifestoes, and copyists. The principal personage next to Nogaret was a Florentine, Musciatto Guidi dei Franzesi [7]—a banker, and, together with his brother Biccio, a trusted agent much employed by the king in financial affairs. He had already been deputed the year before, in December 1302, to assist the Bishop of Auxerre, the Count of St. Pol, and the Sire d'Harcourt, who were sent by Philip to the Pope, but, being refused admittance by the latter, had returned without having accomplished anything. The preparations and deliberations were to take place at Guidi's fortress of Staggia. He had already given shelter there in 1301 to the king's brother, Charles of Valois, and had rendered essential service to that prince on the occasion of the complications in which he had been involved in Florence.

We know from Gregorovius [8] that by a profuse expenditure of money Pope Boniface had raised his family in the course of a few years to a position of great wealth and importance. He had created a magnificent baronial estate in the Latin district, reaching from Ceprano to Subiaco, in order to bestow it upon his nephew, Peter Gaetano, and had founded it upon the ruins of the great house of Colonna, which he had doomed to destruction, just as his predecessor had annihilated the family of the Staufer. His design in creating

---

[7] In the French sources of reference he is called Mouchet [comp. *Hist. littér.* pp. 243 and 246].

[8] *Geschichte der Stadt Rom*, 2 ed., vol. v. 567 ff.

it was to oppress and to cripple the local nobility. The latter, united with the Colonnas, eagerly grasped Nogaret's proffered hand, partly for the sake of avenging themselves upon the pope, but chiefly with the hope of overthrowing the new barony conferred on the pope's nephew. The Italians, however, who had no desire to set about this rash undertaking in their own name, well knowing that it must inevitably entangle them in the net of ecclesiastical censure, made it a condition that Nogaret, the representative and envoy of the French king, should place himself at their head, and should cause the royal banner with the arms of France to be borne in front of them.[9] Nogaret, on his part, took care that the banner of the Roman Church should be given the precedence; for, as he often afterwards emphatically declared, it was an act of faith and of necessity in which he was engaging, not merely for the protection of France and of the king, but also for the rescue of the church from the destruction with which it was threatened by Boniface.

On September 7, 1303, the little army appeared before Anagni, just at the decisive moment, for on the following day, a festival of the Virgin Mary, the bull was to have been solemnly published which was to dissolve the bond between the oft-excommunicated king and the French nation, and was to release every French subject from his allegiance, thus giving up the country a prey to the wildest anarchy. The citizens of Anagni had been already won; the gates stood open. So detested was Boniface, or so powerful was French gold, that not only his most intimate officials and confidential friends, but even some cardinals, amongst them Richard of Siena and Napoleon Orsini, had been induced to join in the attack, and, next to them in importance, Giffrid Bussa, the commander (marshal) of the papal troops. The citizens of Anagni were straightway summoned by the great bell of the town, and the most powerful man in the Campagna, Adenulf Papareschi, a noble citizen of Anagni, who was known to be an implacable enemy of the pope,

[9] Dupuy, p. 441 [comp. *Hist. littér.*, p. 248].

was elected commandant. The chief men of the town at once swore fealty and obedience to Adenulf.

Sciarra Colonna, meanwhile, began the assault upon the two palaces of the pope and his nephews. Three other mansions—those of Cardinal Gentile, of the pope's nephew Francis Gaetani, and of Cardinal Peter Ispani—were quickly taken by assault and plundered, whilst the palace of the pope and that of his nephew, Count Peter Gaetani, were gallantly defended for a time. However, the armed citizens now making their appearance under Adenulf's leadership, and being joined by Rainulf of Supino and the sons and followers of John of Ceccano, whom Boniface had imprisoned, the assault was renewed with redoubled energy.[10] Boniface, perceiving that the palace would shortly be in the hands of the enemy, desired a truce, which Sciarra granted to him and his nephews until three o'clock. During the interval the pope secretly sent to petition the citizens of Anagni to save his life, promising to make them so rich that they would be happy all their lives long. But the townspeople referred him to their leader Adenulf, without whom they would do nothing. Boniface now turned to Sciarra; he requested him to state the special acts of injustice done to him and his house, for he (the pope) was ready, with the advice of the cardinals, to make satisfaction. Sciarra laid down three conditions under which the pope's life should be spared: first, the reinstatement of all the Colonnas; secondly, his own resignation; thirdly, that the pope's person should remain in his, Sciarra's, power. Thereupon, the Curtisan reports, the pope ejaculated, ' Woe is me, that is a hard saying.'

At three o'clock, when the interval had elapsed, the assault upon the two palaces was renewed. That of the pope was partly protected by the church against which it

[10] In a document composed a few years later by an apologist for Pope Boniface [Dupuy, p. 472] a prelate is named who lost his life in this tumult, George of Kratupani, Archbishop of Gran, of whom elsewhere also it is remarked that he came by his death whilst attending at the Curia in this year (1303) [comp. Gams, *Ser. Episcoporum*, p. 380].

was built. The door of the church was set on fire and burnt, and the people and merchandise found in it were plundered. Thereupon Count Gaetani gave himself up to the two leaders, Sciarra and Adenulf, upon condition that his life and that of his sons should be spared; but the latter on attempting to make their escape were thrown into a dungeon. On hearing of this the pope shed bitter tears.[1] At length, after battering in the gate and setting fire to some portion of the building, the attacking party broke into the papal palace from two sides.[2] All the pope's people, clergy and laity, had fled: Cardinal Peter the Spaniard alone remained faithful to him, the other cardinals having either hidden themselves or taken flight.

The chronicler of Orvieto mentions only Nogaret and Rainald of Supino as the two intruders who, entering the pope's chamber, found him lying on the bed holding a cross in his hands, and adds that Boniface reproached them severely, declaring that he was a Catholic and would die for the faith. The Curtisan, however, mentions Sciarra Colonna as well, and asserts that to the reproaches and accusations brought against him by those who had pressed into the room the pope answered not a word, but on the question being put to him whether he would resign the papal dignity he declared that he would rather lose his head, and added (*in suo vulgari*) '*Ee le col, ee le cape.*' Then Sciarra wanted to kill the pope, but was hindered by the others—by Nogaret, according to his own account. No bodily harm was done to the pope. The blow which Sciarra is said to have given him is a fable. Also the statement of Villani, that the pope received those who entered sitting on his throne in his robes of state, is incorrect.

Boniface and his nephews remained in prison until the third day. From the pope's chamber itself nothing was carried off, but all the rest of the palace, with the enormous

---

[1] *Lacrimatus est amare,* writes the Curtisan.

[2] According to the narrative of Orvieto the guard surrendered the gate to the assailants.

riches and costly treasures amassed in it, was ransacked and plundered, as was also the palace of the count. The same writer adds: 'If all the kings of the world were to collect treasures for a year together, the whole would not be worth the amount that was carried off out of those two palaces in a single day.' Boniface, as he looked on, only said, 'The Lord gave, the Lord hath taken away.' Simon Gerard, the pope's banker, was also plundered. The treasure of the Roman Church, says the witness from Orvieto, which it had been amassing for centuries—*a tempore Constantini*—became all in one day the spoil of Italian mercenaries and of brigands. The relics that were found were carried off for the sake of their silver setting. A chronicler of Pistoja[3] especially mentions a vessel containing the milk of the Blessed Virgin, which was then emptied.

Meanwhile Sciarra and his followers were deliberating whether to slay the pope or to hand him over alive to the French king. But in the meantime opinion in Anagni had veered round. The inhabitants were forced to look on whilst the treasures, which they had doubtless coveted for themselves, were carried off for the most part by foreign soldiers and brigands. This enraged the citizens, who, it was asserted, could have set in array 10,000 armed men, whereas the foreign intruders amounted only to a few hundreds. Secret deliberations took place, of which Adenulf, Sciarra, and the others who guarded the pope knew nothing. By the third day men were saying that though the pope truly has done much evil in his lifetime, nevertheless his life must not be taken. If this were to happen in our town, they said, the whole of Christendom would rise against us, the town would be put under an interdict, and Mass would never again be said amongst us; we should be rooted out. Thereupon the whole commune proceeded to the papal palace; the guard was overpowered, several of the soldiers were killed, and Rainuld of Supino and his son were taken

[3] [*Istorie Pistolesi*, Prato, 1835, p. 488.]

prisoners. Nogaret himself was wounded, but not being recognised, he managed to slip away.

This is the account given by the witness from Orvieto. In the better and fuller account by the writer from Cesena Nogaret is not even mentioned. Sciarra, Adenulf, and Supino are the principal and responsible actors. In fact, throughout almost the whole of Italy the occurrence was regarded as the work of the Colonnas and their friends, supported by the money and advice of the French king. This is the view of the chroniclers. The great Italian poet of the time takes, as usual, his own line, and, as we know, makes Philip, the cruel modern Pilate, answerable for all, without noticing the Colonnas, nor yet the many Italians and papal vassals who were their fellow-culprits.[4]

Nogaret's plan, in accordance with the terms of his mission, was to make himself master of the person of the pope, and to bring him to Lyons, where he would be kept in confinement until the assembly of the council. But he had no French troops, and only a couple of his own countrymen with him in Anagni,[5] and was consequently obliged to let the Italians act as they chose, whilst they, of course, thought only of the interests of the house of Colonna and of the rest of the barons of the Campagna. How could it be possible with only a hundred men-at-arms

[4] Perchè men paia il mal futuro e il fatto,
Veggio in Alagna entrar lo fiordaliso,
E nel vicario suo Cristo esser catto.

Veggiolo un' altra volta esser deriso;
Veggio rinnovellar l' aceto e il fele,
E tra vivi ladroni esser anciso.

Veggio il nuovo Pilato sì crudele,
Che ciò nol sazia, ma, senza decreto,
Porta nel tempio le cupide vele.
Purg. xx. 85.

[5] Nogaret says that he had only two French attendants (*duos solum scutiferos seu domicellos de sua patria*) with him. Dupuy, 246. [His companions, Musciatto, d'Hiricon, and Gesserin, who had been with him at first, could have been so no longer at the time of the attack on Anagni. Comp. *Hist. littér.* p. 251.]

to convey the captive pope of eighty-six years of age across the long distance to the French frontier? Attempts to liberate the pope were only to be expected. The Italian mercenaries were now satiated with the superabundant spoil, and were only thinking how best to place it in safety and to enjoy it. This explains why the victors let almost three days slip by without anything being done, and why Nogaret's plot failed in its principal object. In the defence which he afterwards wrote Nogaret is silent as to the plan regarding the pope's person; he represents himself as the envoy of the king, whose only mission was to give notice to the pope of the indictment brought against him, and of the consequent necessity of his answering for himself before a council. Nogaret affirms that he did everything that he could to protect the pope's person, although unable, denuded as he was of French assistance, to prevent the plundering of the treasure.

When all the foreigners had been turned out of the town the banner of the fleur de lis fell into the hands of the populace of Anagni, by whom it was torn and ignominiously trailed through the mud in the streets. Boniface and his sons suddenly found themselves safe and free. The people of Anagni assured the pope that they would watch over his person until the storm should have passed over. Thereupon they brought him out of the palace into the principal street of the town, where Boniface lamented to the people how he had been despoiled, declaring to them at the same time that if they would bring him the necessaries of life, bread and wine, he would absolve them from their sins, *a pœna et a culpa*. Then all shouted, 'Long live the Holy Father!' and the women collected and brought so much bread, wine, and water that his room was full in a twinkling; so much so that, there being no vessels at hand, the wine was poured on the floor of the chamber.

After this Boniface took his seat on the landing at the top of the great stairs of the palace, and from thence addressed the assembled crowd, thanking God and the people for his rescue. 'Yesterday,' he said, ' I was as poor as Job ; to-day I have bread, wine, and water.' Forthwith he absolved them all from guilt and punishment, with the exception of those who had robbed the church treasure or the cardinals and officials of the Curia, if they did not within three days make restitution of the goods ; on the other hand, he unconditionally absolved all who had taken his own personal property. As to the Colonnas and the rest of his enemies, he was ready to make peace with them, and was prepared to reinstate them in their spiritual dignities as well as in their secular possessions. This he caused to be proclaimed in the streets of Anagni. Some of the spoil was now really brought back, but only some ; the greater part of the church treasure, says the witness from Orvieto, was lost. According to Nogaret, Boniface said that what had happened was ordained by God, and that he therefore forgave all who had had a share in it, absolving them from any punishment *ab homine vel a jure* in his own name and that of the church. It became apparent afterwards, however, that he was not sincere in what he said.[6] Even Nogaret himself does not say that the Pope included the French king in the general absolution. According to the reports of the two Italian eye-witnesses, Boniface only mentioned the Colonnas and the people of Anagni.

Meanwhile the proceedings in Anagni had become known in Rome. A few days afterwards Roman senators appeared with a retinue of armed men, and Boniface suddenly and unexpectedly, as the Curtisan says, left Anagni and proceeded to Rome (September 13–18). This record was composed only a few days later, in the end of September or beginning of October. 'Boniface,' he says, ' is at present in Rome very much cast down ; for it seems that he can remain in no other town than Rome without risk to his life. His enemies are so numerous that no town in Tuscany or in Campania would be able to protect

[6] Dupuy, 312.

him against the power of the Colonnas; and if the Roman populace does not stand by the pope, it is to be feared that he will soon perish. The Orsini, indeed, are entirely on the side of the pope, but many other Romans have joined the Colonnas against the popular party.' 'We of the Curia,' he concludes, 'live in great suspense, expecting from day to day that we shall be robbed of our horses and other possessions. We cannot leave Rome, for the environs of the town swarm with banditti and robbers who lie in wait for every traveller, and are so numerous that even sixty well-armed men would be overcome by them. The Roman senators have consequently resigned, and utter anarchy prevails.'

Immediately after Boniface's death things came, as the Orvietan reports, to an open struggle between the Gaetani and the Colonnas; the whole of Campania became a battle-field. The Gaetani took a band of Catalonian mercenaries from Apulia into their service, and were victorious over their opponents throughout the whole of Campania.

Nogaret, much incensed against the people of Anagni, who, he said, had cruelly attempted to kill him and his followers, had gone to Ferentino, where he entered into an agreement with Rainald of Supino,[7] by which the latter, with the promise of subsidies and reinforcements, and the assurance of the king's protection, engaged to take vengeance upon the town of Anagni and upon the Gaetani for the outrage offered to the royal banner. The matter, however, went no further; the assistance of men and money, promised in the king's name, in all probability was never sent. Philip at that time needed all his resources for his struggle with the Flemings, and in his financial distress he even went so far as to utter false coin. It was not until the year 1312 that Rainald was paid in Paris 10,000 Florentine dollars in compensation for the expenditure which he and the commune of Ferentino

[7] Oct. 1303. Dupuy, 174.

had been put to on the king's account. The receipt for the payment is still preserved.⁸

The common testimony of all who wrote at that time is that Boniface died of grief, or in despair, or madness, either in Rome or its vicinity. '*Extra mentem positus*,' says the writer who continues the account of Tolomeo of Lucca; 'Boniface lives in Rome in great sadness,' writes the Curtisan of Cesena before the death of the pope; '*ex tristitia, senectute et infirmitate*' Boniface was in his eighty-sixth year—says the biographer from Orvieto; '*in lecto doloris et amaritudinis positus, inter angustias spiritus, cum esset corde magnanimus*,' is the expression of Petrus Lodovensis.⁹

Boniface, after regaining his freedom, lived thirty-two days, partly in Anagni and partly in Rome (Sept. 9 –Oct. 11), and not a single document remains of this period signed by his hand, which, considering the great number that he had been wont to issue, is astonishing.

According to Ferreto of Vicenza,[1] whose statement is confirmed by the Chronicle of Parma and the brief record of the Italian Chronicle at Mansi, the pope was subjected in Rome to a mortification even more grievous and degrading than that which he had experienced in Anagni. The two cardinals of the house of Orsini, Matteo Rosso and Jacopo, had not been without some knowledge of and share in the conspiracy against Boniface and the Gaetani. Boniface had withdrawn his confidence from them, and they, taught by the experience of the Colonnas, were prepared for the worst. Determined therefore to be beforehand with the pope, they caused him to be watched in the Vatican—the power possessed by their house in Rome made this feasible; and when the pope was on the point of

---

⁸ Dupuy, 608.

⁹ Duchesne, *Hist. Franc.*, SS. v. 788. [The passage quoted is out of *Guidonis flores chronicorum*; see *Recueil des Historiens*, tome xxi. 1855, p. 713.]

[1] [Muratori, *Script*. ix. 1002 ss.]

leaving St. Peter's for the Lateran, Matteo declared to him in the name of the cardinals, at any rate of the majority of them, that he was no longer free, but a prisoner. This was more than the haughty old man could endure.

The chronicler of Orvieto says nothing of all this. But John of Winterthur [2] declares that Boniface was brought from Anagni to Rome, and there kept in close custody; though the act, which is ascribed by Ferreto to the Orsini, is imputed by the Minorite to the Colonnas acting under the instigation of King Philip.

Boniface now found himself in a situation from which no escape could be made without incurring deep humiliation and much loss to the papal authority, which in all its struggles had hitherto proved victorious. In all previous conflicts the popes had gained the upper hand when, in alliance with the kings, they repressed the clergy, or, in union with the clergy, opposed the monarchs, or, again, when they menaced the latter with the power of other princes more submissive to the papal authority, and with their help compelled even monarchs to yield. None of these three means of defence was now available, for in France the king, the church, and the nation were combined, and Philip was too powerful to fear any external foe. There was not, throughout the whole of Europe, a single prince who for the sake of the pope would have cared to plunge into a war with France. The one weapon which yet remained to the pope—to place the whole of France under an interdict—had, owing to the unity of king, clergy, and people, lost its edge. Moreover, Boniface had only a very few of the cardinals on his side. If then the majority of the cardinals were to urge the pope to do what his successor soon found himself compelled to do, viz., step by step to recall the bulls issued against the French king, how could he refuse to do so? Philip, on the other hand, had also

[2] Ed. of G. v. Wyss: Zürich, 1856 (*Archiv für Schweizer Gesch.* vol. ii. 45).

already gone so far that he could neither return nor remain where he was. Boniface might, therefore, feel assured that the king would hold fast to his accusations against him and to his plan for the assembly of a council; he had not, as his predecessors had, the strong sword of the Norman at his disposal. Such a knot as Boniface had tied could only be loosed by his own retirement from the theatre of the world.

If we glance through the reports given by Italian, French, English, and German contemporaries of the events at Anagni, we shall perceive, even in their most brief and superficial notices, a national colouring and a partisanship for either the Guelph or the Ghibelline side, although as with Dante, the prevailing impression is that at Anagni an unheard-of outrage, a crime without example, had been committed.

Whenever the contemporary writers go beyond the mere outline of the incidents and allow themselves to pass on to details, their untrustworthiness betrays itself even in the case of the Italians. Giovanni Villani's account, for which the moderns Kopp, for instance, and Wattenbach, Reumont, Weber, and more recently von Sybel—have shown a decided preference, is fanciful and inaccurate throughout. Relying upon it, Kopp, for instance, says,[3] 'He caused himself to be arrayed in the mantle of St. Peter, the crown of Constantine to be placed on his head, took the keys and the cross in his hand;' and Wattenbach:[4] 'He assumed the papal mantle, placed the triple crown upon his head, took the cross and the keys in his hands, and sat thus, an old man of over eighty years, upon the papal throne.' Renan[5] quite recently has written in a similar style. In opposition to these accounts I will now point out the incorrectness of the following statements in Villani: First, he seems to have thought that amongst the papal treasure there was still in

---

[3] *Gesch. der eidgenöss. Bünde*, iii. 6. 185.
[4] *Gesch. des römischen Papstthums*, 1876, p. 225.
[5] *Hist. littér.* p. 254.

existence a mantle worn by St. Peter. This was not the case; the pope wore a pallium on great festivals like other prelates; at his election the *cappa rubra*, a red mantle that had nothing to do with St. Peter, was put round him. Secondly, the crown of Constantine, spoken of by Villani, is most likely a reminiscence of a clause in the fabulous Donation of Constantine, according to which the emperor had destined a golden crown, like that he wore himself, for Pope Sylvester, who, however, refused to wear it and preferred the Phrygian cap. Innocent III. certainly says that the pope in token of his imperium wore the regnum (a gold circlet), and in token of his priesthood a mitre. But a crown named after Constantine, as his gift, never existed. The third crown was first added under Clement V. On the tomb of Boniface VIII., the mitre upon the pope's head, as Gregorovius in the *Grabmäler der Päpste* remarks, has only two crowns. Thirdly, the cross keys formed, and, as is well known, still form, the papal arms; but real keys— of gold, silver, or iron, not merely pictured, and such as Boniface could have taken in his hand—belong only to the realm of fancy.

Amongst the more exact accounts is that of Tolomeo of Lucca, or, according to the Paduan MS., that of a writer who continued his history. He says not a word about the demeanour of the pope when he found himself in the power of his opponents, differs entirely from the description given by Villani, and agrees as to the facts with the reports of the two eye-witnesses, the writers from Cesena and from Orvieto. The actual perpetrators of the outrage he also considers to have been, not Nogaret, but the party of the Colonnas and the nobles of the Campagna.

The report, given in a couple of sentences, of the Ambrosian MS. differs from the last, and is certainly not by an eye-witness, nor even by any one who was well informed. Had the writer known more about the occurrence, which must have appeared to contemporary Italians as the most extraordinary and remarkable of their time, he would have said more about it. He certainly does say, *Pontificalibus indui voluit, tenens in manibus crucifixum*, but as he continues his history down to the year 1337, he was not even exactly a contemporary, and probably on this subject he followed Villani.

To the Italian contemporary writers belongs Jordanus, who probably lived in Venice or in its neighbourhood. He also⁶ makes Boniface assume the pontifical robes, and says that he afterwards died in Rome, *ex tremore cordis*, in a fit of insanity, in which he tried to scratch the faces and eyes of every one that entered the apartment.

In the short Florentine annals published by Alfonso Huber, of which this part must be contemporary, there is nothing further than the correct statement that the arrest of the pope was effected by Sciarra Colonna, with the consent of the people of Anagni.

In the Chronicle of Este,[7] in which the author describes himself as an eye-witness of the events of the year 1305, and therefore in the truest sense a contemporary, the state of Boniface after his release is described in more detail than by Jordanus. Boniface is represented as having become quite frantic and delirious, expressing doubts as to the existence of God. Of the proceedings at Anagni this chronicler gives no account. The chronicler of Siena,[8] on the contrary, makes Ungharelli—so he calls Nogaret— accomplish the *coup de main* against the pope with an army of 4,000 French horsemen, whereupon Italian courage shines forth brilliantly, for the men of Anagni suddenly fall upon this magnificent French army, routing and putting it to flight.

Independent of Villani's narrative, and upon the whole better, is a notice that occurs as an isolated fragment in the manuscript of the *Istorie Pistolesi*,[9] which contains one

---

[6] Muratori, *Antiq. Ital.* iv. 1020.
[7] Muratori, *Script. Rer. Ital.* xv. 350.
[8] Muratori, xv. 44.
[9] *Istorie Pistolesi*, Prato, 1835, p. 488.

or two touches and particulars that might proceed from the pen of an eye-witness. Much of importance is, however, here passed over in silence, and the writer proves himself to have been by no means so well informed as the Curtisan of Cesena. Of the share taken by the French in the affair he has no more to say than that King Philip had commissioned William of Nogaret, whom the writer transforms into a captain of the pontifical Curia, to kill the pope. Thereupon William allies himself with Sciarra Colonna and other gentlemen, and they win over the Cardinal Napoleon Orsini. According to this account also Boniface robes himself, when the conspirators force their way into the palace, in the mantle of St. Peter, and seats himself with the cross in his hand on a chair. Summoned to abdicate, like his predecessor Celestin he answers, 'Never! I am pope, and I will die pope.' Boniface is liberated by a knight of Anagni, who rides through the town and calls upon the citizens to rescue the Holy Father and to kill the traitors. In conclusion the writer points out, as other chroniclers have done, that in Boniface the prediction of his predecessor was fulfilled : *Intravit ut vulpes, regnabit ut Leo, morietur ut canis;* for, frantic with grief at that which had befallen him, he died like a dog.

The 'Annals of Parma,'[1] the work of a contemporary, also ignore the part taken by the French, representing the occurrence as the act of the Colonnas and of their Roman and Campanian friends. All the adherents and friends of the pope, it is asserted, were driven out of the town, and many were killed—which is certainly not true, since not a single name of any one who was killed on the papal side, excepting that of the Archbishop of Gran, is mentioned by the best-informed witnesses. The Cardinal Fiesco is mentioned as having, with the help of the people of Anagni, liberated the pope. Thus the writer appears not to have understood that the inhabitants of the town themselves had taken part in the assault upon the palace.

[1] *Mon. G. SS.* xviii. 729.

Pipin and Ferreto[2] are also silent upon the participation of the people of Anagni in the attack made by the French and Campanians. Ferreto has it that the Cardinal Napoleon Orsini treacherously possessed himself of the keys; according to Pipin, it was by the help of some nobles of Anagni that the enemies of the pope forced their way in. The inhabitants of Anagni, says Pipin, were in the greatest consternation when they found that their town was in the power of foreigners. He contradicts himself, however, immediately afterwards by saying that the inhabitants flocked to assist the nobles in the assault upon the palaces of the cardinals and the pope. Pipin makes the pope say when the strangers rush in: 'Open the doors, for I will suffer martyrdom for the Church of Christ.' The invaders find him lying with outstretched neck upon the cross.

Pipin's version appears to have made its way, by being passed on from one cloister to another, even into North Germany: for the annals written by a Minorite of Lübeck about the year 1324[3] relate that the invaders found the pope stretched upon the floor, with a cross, in which a piece of the true cross was enshrined, fastened upon his breast. But to the first fable another is now added, namely, that his enemies were unable to carry the pope from the chamber, and therefore ill-treated and beat him, and left him lying there half dead, so that Boniface died shortly afterwards in Rome in consequence.

Eberhard of Altaich[4] knows nothing of King Philip and of Nogaret; the actors he supposes to have been only Sciarra Colonna and his fellow-conspirators. The Chronicle of Osterhofen,[5] on the contrary, mentions as a rumour

---

[2] [*Chron. fratris Francisci Pipini o. P.*, written after 1320 (Muratori, *Script.* ix. 740). *Ferreti Vicentini Historia*, composed about 1330 (the same, 1002 ss.)]

[3] *Mon. G. SS.* xvi. 418 ad a. 1302.

[4] Böhmer, *Fontes*, ii. 526 [*M. G. SS.*, xvii. 592].

[5] Böhmer, ii. 560 [*M. G. SS.*, xvii. 538].

that the king of France was the originator of the deed accomplished by Sciarra and the friends of the Colonnas. The most extraordinary account is that given by John of Viktring,[6] who, nevertheless, was a contemporary. According to him, the French did all, the Italians nothing. Five hundred French warriors are said to have come by sea to Anagni for the sole purpose of demanding absolution of the pope. Boniface appears as a prophet, and as knowing beforehand all that is about to befall him; he prophesies the early death of the king and the extinction of his race. The ill-treatment of the pope amounts to this, that one of his enemies crushed him against the wall with the door through which he was just about to pass. The author of the Chronicle of Leoben has only copied the narrative of the Abbot of Viktring.[7]

In striking contrast with these Austrian narratives are some of the chronicles composed by Dominican and Franciscan monks. The Franciscan reader Detmar of Lübeck, who, it is true, wrote his chronicle ninety years afterwards,[8] supposes that Boniface was so severely beaten by the intruders that he was left for dead, but that he afterwards returned to consciousness. The ill-treatment said to have been suffered by the pope is depicted at greater length in the chronicle of the Dominican Henry of Hervord,[9] who compiled his learned work some sixty years after the death of Pope Boniface, and who, without copying any other writer, betrays unmistakable satisfaction in describing the deep humiliation and disgrace of the pope. He represents him as bound hand and foot, raving mad, and tearing his own flesh. The Minorite Hermann Gigas [1]

---

[6] Böhmer, i. 271.
[7] Pez, *SS. Austr.* i. 883. [The supposed prophecy of Boniface VIII., as well as the statement about his ill-treatment, is similarly given in a chronicle written after the year 1368. *Recueil des Historiens*, ascribed to Jean Desnouelles, tom. xxi. Paris 1855, p. 195.]
[8] [Ed. of Grantoff, 1859.]
[9] [Ed. of Potthast, 1859.]
[1] [Eccard, *Corp. hist.* i.]

says merely that Boniface died after five days, in consequence of being crushed between the door and the wall.

More correct representations of the affair than are given by Germans and by many Italians are to be found in a few English chronicles like those of Hemmingford and Rishanger —in Rishanger for the good reason that he made use of the account of the Curtisan of Cesena. In other English chronicles, on the contrary, like that of Walsingham and the Chronicle of Osney,[2] we come upon gross fictions, the product of monkish fancy, such as that Nogaret and the Colonnas put the captive pontiff upon a donkey with the tail in his hands, led him about till he was at the last gasp (*usque ad novissimum halitum*), and finally allowed him to die of hunger.[3]

It is not difficult to understand how such contradictory representations of the catastrophe came to be made. Villani, like most Italian writers, sees the affair in the light of a Divine judgment upon the pope in consequence of his many and great sins; but as a Guelph and an Italian he has also before his eyes the estrangement of the papacy from Italy, and the fact that it had by that time become entirely French, which to him and his nation was most offensive : he sees in Boniface the last genuine Italian and Guelph pope who defended the majesty of his chair and the prerogative of his nation against the presumption of the French. Villani, therefore, makes Boniface act and speak as, in his opinion, a pope imbued with the feeling of his own indefeasible dignity would in such a position have acted and spoken ; he makes him—*come magnanimo e valente*—say what has been so often repeated by later popes : 'Since I have been betrayed and taken captive like Christ, and since I must die, I will

---

[2] *Annales Monastici*, iv. 339.

[3] [In Döllinger's notebook there are also some brief passages from French chronicles in the lecture upon Anagni, but these are altogether wanting in the finished MS.]

at least die as pope.' Villani wrote this at a time when the acquiescence of the popes in French policy and their servile submission to mandates issued from Paris had become the rule; he therefore welcomed an opportunity of bringing into prominence the courage and self-possession of the last energetic Italian who filled the Roman chair, in contrast with the cowardly subservience which afterwards prevailed. Those contemporaries, however, who had experienced the haughtiness, the implacable hardness, and the despotic character of the pope, or who, like the Franciscans and Dominicans, had felt the irksome pressure of his rule, pictured to themselves the man's state of mind when suddenly hurled from the height of his supremacy and rudely awakened from his delusion of universal sovereignty when he, who was accustomed to see all worshipping at his feet, was himself insulted and threatened; and as it was generally known that Boniface had ended his life in misery and despair, it was easy to conclude that his mind had given way, and that madness had led to frenzy and self-inflicted injury.

The great fault of the chroniclers of the middle ages is that they readily represent and colour events that excite their sympathy and imagination in accordance with their own preconceived idea of the way the persons concerned were likely to have acted under the given circumstances.

V

THE SUPPRESSION OF THE KNIGHTS TEMPLARS [1]

In the last exhibition of pictures here [in Munich] a painting by a French artist attracted much attention, owing both to its value as a work of art, and to the interest of the subject portrayed. It represented a scene in the year 1308; the Templars at Poitiers before their judges, the king and the pope. The question must have arisen in the minds of many who looked at it, What is the real truth as regards this great tragedy? On which side was right or wrong, innocence or guilt? Were these men really criminals worthy of death? Did this great society, which extended over almost the whole of central and southern Europe, really deserve such a fate as extermination, and to be held up to ignominy on the testimony of historians not contemporary, but of later generations? To the solution of this question I wish to contribute a few remarks, which may possibly help to throw light upon its obscurity.

All that is most substantial and trustworthy in church and state bears witness to the guilt of the Order. The pope, the cardinals, the entire French episcopate, and on a lower grade the Inquisition, the whole of the Dominican Order and

[1] [Döllinger's last Academical lecture, given at the public sitting, Nov. 15,. 1889, printed partly from the stenographic notes of the report for the *Augsb. Abendzeitung*, partly from Döllinger's MS., as to which something is said in the preface. In an appendix are added particular passages of the enlarged text, which Döllinger wrote down in the interval between giving the lecture and his last illness, and which he intended should appear first in the *Allgem. Zeitung*, and then in a third vol. of his Academical lectures.]

the University of Paris, all are, or appear to be, convinced, all adhere to the conclusion, that this band of men stand convicted of the most abominable errors and offences. It was the same with the secular world of that day. The king, his ministers and legal advisers, his officials, the whole of secular France, represented in the assembly at Tours, gave judgment to the same effect. In addition to all this, at the close of the great tragedy, we have the weight of a church council ratifying the papal sentence of annihilation without a dissentient voice.

Turning to the voluminous literature of recent times concerning this question, I may mention at once that the latest work on the Templars, that of Hans Prutz, following two others by the same author, contains an unmitigated condemnation of the Order.[2] It therefore stands in strong contrast with the writings of apologists, particularly with the lately published work of Conrad Schottmüller.[3] To this must be added the high authority of Ranke, who in the eighth volume of his 'Universal History,' published since his death, has expressed himself in the same sense as Hammer-Purgstall with regard to the apostasy of the Order from the Christian faith.[4] The fact that Weber's great 'Universal History' takes the same line is also not without weight, and it may therefore be supposed that a very considerable number of educated readers amongst us believe in the guilt of the Order.

The opinion of Ranke, as the latest word of the great master, will long continue to be of great weight in Germany. Yet his representation of the subject is vague and cautious, hinting at much, and passing much over in silence. He seems not to have been acquainted with the newly discovered sources of information, or, at any rate, not to have used them. His comparison of the Templars to the Emperor Frederick and King Manfred certainly shows

[2] [*Entwicklung und Untergang des Tempelherrenordens*, Berlin, 1888.]
[3] [*Der Untergang des Templer-Ordens*, 2 vols., Berlin, 1887.]
[4] [*Weltgeschichte*, 8th Part, 1887, p. 621 ff.]

that he credited the report of the diffusion amongst the
Order of some mysterious occult learning imported from
the East through intercourse with Islam, and therefore
that he believed in the truth of the principal accusations
against it.

In France, England, and Italy this is hardly the case,
notwithstanding the high esteem which Ranke enjoys in
those countries. In France the historians of highest rank,
above all, those who have most carefully investigated the
new sources of information, are, with the exception of
Michelet and Dareste, convinced of the untruth of the accusations, and of the innocence of the Order. I allude to
Mignet, Guizot, Renan, Boutaric, as most thoroughly acquainted with that period of French history; also Lavocat
and Bonnechose. A number of older students preceded
these, whose opinion was discernible even from the middle
of the eighteenth century, in spite of the censorship of the
press, and became by degrees more and more plainly outspoken. This was the case with Vaissette and Villaret, and
most clearly in the detailed work of the monk Le Jeune,
published just at the outbreak of the French Revolution.[5]

In Italy the opinion of Dante[6] and Villani, both contemporaries, continued in spite of ecclesiastical authority
to be also the opinion of that and of succeeding generations,
and this is enough to show that the Templars were regarded
as having been the innocent victims of the avarice of the
French king. It made a great impression in the country
that so holy a man as Antoninus, Archbishop of Florence, canonised by the church, and much esteemed as a
theologian, should, although he belonged to the Dominican
order, have represented the matter in just the same way
as Villani.[7]

[5] [The brilliant defence of the Templars written by Raynouard in 1813 ought especially to have been mentioned here.]
[6] Comp. *Purg.* xx. 92 f.
[7] [A flysheet of an earlier date has the following remarks by Döllinger upon recent Italian literature: 'In Italy also opinions are divided.

In England, torture was not employed in criminal trials, and was never regularly introduced, so that the necessary instruments and appliances were unknown. Yet the pope finally succeeded, after long resistance, in enforcing its use against the Order, by an admonitory bull especially addressed to the king. Even then only a couple of Templars who had left the Order succumbed. At this day in England, so far as I am aware, almost every authority on English history regards the acts of the trial, which have been fully preserved, as bearing weighty testimony to the innocence of the whole Order.*

It is most astonishing that in modern German literature we almost universally meet with the assertion that the Templars had long been a corrupt association, unfaithful both in spirit and in letter to their rule, dissolute in life, and consequently standing very low in the popular

Fumagalli, as a Cistercian, has already asserted the innocence of the Order in his *Antichità Longobardico-Milanesi*. Cantù and Cibrario have expressed themselves on the same side. The former, in his *Storia d'Italia*, does not in actual words declare the innocence of the Order, but relates the proceedings taken against them in such a manner that he leaves no doubt as to his opinion. Cibrario, with the help of the first volume of Michelet's *Procès des Templiers*, published in 1841, has attempted to prove the same. Vini, on the contrary, in a treatise styled *Dei Templieri e dal loro processo in Toscana*, hitherto little noticed in Germany, and contained in the *Atte dell' Accademia Lucchese*, vol. xiii. (1843), has sought to prove its guilt. One must, he says, reflect that everywhere outside of France the proceedings against the Order were conducted with great moderation! The man who says this caused the acts of the trial in Florence to be printed from a Vatican MS., from which it appears certain that the rack was employed.]

* [The Editor refers to a recent work—*The History of the Inquisition of the Middle Ages*, vol. iii., by an American author, Henry Charles Lea—in which the same view of the innocence of the Templars is upheld. Dr. Döllinger does not, however, appear to have made use of the book for his lecture.—TRANSL.] ' It is not too much to say that the very idea could not have suggested itself, but for the facilities which the Inquisitorial process placed in able and unscrupulous hands to accomplish any purpose of violence under the form of law. If I have dwelt on the tragedy at a length that may seem disproportionate, my apology is that it affords so perfect an illustration of the helplessness of the victim, no matter how high placed, when once the fatal charge of heresy was preferred against him, and was pressed through the agency of the Inquisition.' *A History of the Inquisition of the Middle Ages*, by Henry Charles Lea, London, 1888. Vol. iii. p. 334.

estimation. This belief has been confidently handed down from one writer to another. Yet any one who examines into the matter more carefully is everywhere met with strong evidence to the contrary, even amongst the enemies and destroyers of the Order. Previously to October 13, 1307, the day on which the great blow was dealt, no mention had been made of this assumed corruption and degeneracy of the society. I find, on the contrary, in the literature of the time and of the period immediately following, even until as late as the beginning of the fourteenth century, that authors who sharply condemn the degeneracy of the ecclesiastical communities of the day, give evidence in favour of the Order of Knights Templars, either negatively, by omitting any mention of them in the enumeration of degenerate orders and monastic bodies, or positively, by holding them up as a pattern to others.

Let us now first turn our attention to the author of that fearful tragedy, Philip IV., or the Fair, of France. Philip as an historical personage appears, as a French writer has expressed it, wrapped in an impenetrable disguise. He combined an ostentatious display of piety with the acts of a Tiberius; rapacity with a prodigality usually guided by political motives. Philip's wish and line of policy was to govern in the spirit of his grandfather St. Louis, to whose reign his own forms the most striking contrast. Whatever he did was undertaken in the name of God, ostensibly for the protection and in the service of the faith, of the church, and of freedom.[9] . . .

What, then, was the motive which led the king to the ruthless annihilation of an order devoted to the defence of Christendom and to the struggle with the infidel?

First and foremost, the distressful condition of his finances. Everything was exhausted; not a single resource

* [Evidently a sentence was here omitted, both in the lecture itself and from the MS. It would have referred to the contrast between Philip's actions and words, especially with regard to the deed of violence at Anagni.]

for obtaining money was to be found. Especially in consequence of the unlucky war in Flanders, Philip found himself threatened with the shameful collapse of his political designs and undertakings. He had already despoiled the Lombard brokers and bankers, pillaged and banished the French Jews, given the last turn to the screw of taxation, when the riches of the Templars suggested to him a way of escape. He was tempted also by the desire to possess the fine and strong fortress of the Order in Paris, the Temple which but shortly before had offered him an asylum during a popular tumult. It was the general opinion of the time that a covetous desire for the property of the Order formed the king's chief motive, as all contemporary chronicles in Germany, in Italy, and, above all, in France itself openly or covertly express this conviction, which is confirmed by the whole course of events. But other motives were indubitably at work. A remarkable document, which has only of late become known, gives an insight into one of these. William of Nogaret, the king's keeper of the seal, who next to Philip was most actively instrumental in the destruction of the Templars, presented a document to the king just before the withdrawal of the ecclesiastical censures suspended by Boniface VIII. over Philip, which, in view of Nogaret's position, affords an insight into the king's views and projects.[1]

'From of old,' begins Nogaret, 'the kings of France have been pillars of the faith, the foremost defenders and champions of the church, so that they have the prayers of all believers. The danger is that this glory and fame will now become obscured, for Boniface has left behind

[1] [Published by Boutaric in the *Notices et Extraits des Manuscrits de la Bibl. Impér.* xx. 2, Paris, 1862, p. 149 ; comp. Schwab's treatise in the *Tübinger theolog. Quartalschrift*, 1866 (vol. xlviii. p. 23). Döllinger appears to have adopted Schwab's view of the meaning of Nogaret's document. Comp. also Schottmüller, *Der Untergang des Templer-Ordens*, i. 32. Renan (*Hist. littér. de la France*, xxvi., 1873, p. 499 s.) considers that another influential legal adviser of Philip, Peter du Bois, was the author of the document.]

him a powerful party composed of high prelates and princes, learned and respected ecclesiastics, and numerous members of the monastic orders. Whatever may be brought forward in defence of the king, the fact still remains that the outrage of Anagni, whether committed for the sake of the king or in obedience to him, was a disastrous and atrocious proceeding, an insult offered to God's vicegerent upon earth. The conscience of many, even amongst the king's own friends, is perplexed and troubled; they think that neither the king nor I can have quiet or peace of conscience before God, because hitherto there has been no sign of any sufficient satisfaction being offered to the church. The royal conscience will not be free from reproach nor the king's good name be re-established, nor will the murmurs even of the good cease, until something fresh comes to light, or, at least, until something more is done with regard to the matter itself. It will be well, then, to look up documents which will convict the opposite party and reinstate the king in the opinion of all men as the conscientious son and protector of the church. If a regular search be made, [not only may such a document perhaps be found, but something besides, much greater and more surprising, with regard to the situation of this and other kingdoms, even though there may be no occasion to give any reasons for this conjecture. More might be said . . . but enough for the present.'

What Nogaret was aiming at in this document, which breaks off in such a striking manner and was intended only for the king, is evident from the events which followed.²]

Let us recall the situation.

The French kingdom was at that time subject to the Inquisition. The laws prepared by the popes for that

---

² [Döllinger's manuscript breaks off before the passage marked by the parenthesis. Probably he had not sufficient time to put the whole of this passage into German before November 15, 1889; but added the sense of it upon delivering the lecture.]

ecclesiastical tribunal were in full political force; all who held office were bound to facilitate the execution of the judgments passed. Now the foremost of these laws, the one most severely enforced, was that every one was bound in conscience, under pain of excommunication, to give information of anything whatsoever of an heretical nature, in word or deed, that came under his notice, even if the circumstances were such as merely to rouse suspicion. For a man to neglect to do so was at once to draw suspicion upon himself and to render himself liable to examination. This was also the case in Italy and Spain—in short, in all countries where the Inquisition existed as an institution. I will here at once remark that the Templars did not by any means live in an exclusive or retired manner, as though they were a secret society, but that their way of life was well known to people of every rank. Philip the Fair put himself forward as the patron and protector of the inquisitors and the Dominicans as no other monarch before or after him, not even Philip II. of Spain.

The inquisitor-general, William of Paris, was his confessor; Imbert, another inquisitor, the confessor of his children.[3] The inquisitors were in the pay of the king; but, as the Inquisition was already generally treated as a source of income, they were pledged to pay over the amount of the confiscations into the royal coffers. The annihilation of the Templars could never have been accomplished but with the help of the Inquisition and of the statutory powers at its disposal.

The statutes most serviceable for the purpose were the following:—

1. The names of the witnesses before the tribunal of the holy office are not to be mentioned in presence of the accused;

2. The witnesses may be of any kind—criminals, perjured, excommunicate, in fact the basest villains;

[3] [According to Schottmüller, William of Paris and William Imbert appear to be the same person.]

3. As soon as any testimony has been obtained which the accused disavows, the rack is to be applied, repeatedly if needful, and with increasing severity;

4. Whosoever attempts to render legal assistance, or to give any other sort of counsel to the accused, is liable to excommunication;

5. Everything that falls under the definition of the *Fautaria*, *i.e.* favouring or in support of the accused, will be visited with the severest canonical penalties;

6. Those of the accused who recant, and declare themselves willing to do penance, are sentenced to imprisonment for life; finally—

7. (And this article worked most effectually of all)— Whosoever recalls his confession will be treated as a backslider and burnt.

It was in accordance with these statutes that Philip's counsellors and lawyers, their tools, the officers of the Crown, and their ready coadjutors, the Dominican inquisitors, began the work which they carried on for seven years.

Next to King Philip, the originator of the tragedy, we must make mention of his fellow-criminal, Pope Clement V.

Bertrand de Got, Archbishop of Bordeaux, was elected pope (June 5, 1305) at the king's desire and through the influence of his agents in Perugia, but, as is well known, took up his residence permanently in France, or close to the French frontier. According to the narrative of the Florentine chronicler, Giovanni Villani, before the election of Bertrand de Got a secret meeting had taken place between him and the king, and a compact made, one condition of which was the co-operation of the pope in the destruction of the Knights Templars. No such meeting took place, as has been recently proved; but before the election King Philip sent his chancellor, the Archbishop of Narbonne, Gilles Aycelin, to De Got, with whom a compact of some kind was made. Yet the question of the Templars seems to have formed no part of the understanding, for Pope Clement subsequently asserts very positively that the king first mentioned the affairs of the Order when he met him at Lyons upon the occasion of the pope's coronation (Nov. 14, 1305), and that he then declared not so much his intention of instituting proceedings against it, as his belief in the Order being so far corrupt that there was gross misconduct amongst its members.

The complete subservience of Pope Clement V. to the French king is proved not only by all contemporary authorities, but also by all that occurred at the time. From the first the pope allowed Philip to load him with favours and to bestow rich benefactions upon his nearest kinsmen.

But Philip had a special means of putting pressure upon the pope, which he was able, whenever he saw fit, to apply most effectually. Even in the earliest period of their friendship and alliance Philip put forward a demand which must have caused the greatest anguish of mind to Clement, and must have tested his wonted compliance to the utmost. The king, in agreement with some of the cardinals, asserted that Boniface VIII., the last predecessor but one of the pope, had been in word, as well as deed, an unbeliever and a heretic, who had pillaged the church and caused untold scandals. It therefore devolved upon the king, as the divinely chosen champion of the faith and guardian of the church, to look to it, and to insist that atonement be made in some degree for this great scandal. [This could only be done by formal proceedings being instituted against the late pope, by taking evidence of the host of witnesses that would be forthcoming, and then by the present pope, or rather by a general synod to be assembled by him, pronouncing a sentence of condemnation upon Boniface; it must be publicly pronounced that Boniface was an illegal intruder. To Clement this was a fearful proposition, for it would cut the ground, so to speak, from under his own feet. If such a declaration were made, then all that had taken place under Boniface VIII., and even after him, the appointment of cardinals, the publication of ecclesiastical laws, was rendered invalid. The demand was all the more terrible to Clement in that some of the cardinals sided with the king. We still possess the minutes of a judicial enquiry which the pope, at the king's desire, was forced to undertake with the assistance of the cardinals, and in which they openly declared that the king's accusations against Boniface were assuredly well founded, that Boniface was manifestly an unbeliever in word and deed, nay, even a scoffer at the faith of which he ought to have been the chief defender. Now as often as Pope Clement showed signs of hesitation or delay in the matter of the destruction of the Templars, as often as he betrayed any scruples, or showed even an inclination to grant the Templars a hearing, so often did Philip and his legal advisers apply this special means of pressure, and always with unfailing result.][1]

Even at his first meeting with Clement V. at Lyons in the year 1305, King Philip had announced in presence of the pope that the Order of the Knights Templars was utterly corrupted by abuses of the worst kind. He felt himself secure in his statement, for he had already entrusted four men, thoroughly pledged to his interests and possessing his entire confidence, amongst whom was William of Nogaret, with the unprecedented power of setting at liberty certain criminals from the prisons in various parts of the country, and of guaranteeing to them restitution of all their possessions ecclesiastical and secular, not only in his own name, but in that of his successors.[5] It is evident that the object was to find plaintiffs and witnesses against the Order. Of course they were to be found; two men

---

[1] [The whole passage marked in the text by [ ] is, like many others, wanting in Döllinger's manuscript, and was therefore spoken extempore.]

[5] [Deed of authorisation granted on Ash Wednesday 1304, published by Boutaric in *Notices et Extraits*, xx. p. 152. Boutaric assumes that the granting of this license, as well as the warrant also issued about the same time for granting exemptions from the general prohibition to leave the country, could only have been designed to fill the exhausted coffers of the king.]

imprisoned for grave offences, Squin, com-Prior of Montfaucon, and a Florentine of the name of Noffo Dei, seemed to be suited to the task of conducting the preliminary accusation, and of obtaining a speedy confession of guilt by the application of torture.[6]

Pope Clement at first gave neither credence nor weight to the assertion made by the king, first in Lyons, and again in the spring of 1307 at Poitiers. The thing, he said and wrote, was quite incredible; the Order enjoyed everywhere the best reputation and the highest esteem. Nothing but a frivolous, confused murmur of the populace, probably unworthy of notice, had penetrated to the ears of the pope. Had not his immediate predecessor, Pope Benedict XI., quite recently confirmed all the rights and privileges of the Order?

[But Philip the Fair would not allow himself to be deterred from carrying out his plan.] As is well known, on one day, October 13, 1307, all the Templars throughout France were seized and thrown into prison by the king's secret orders, and their interrogation by torture was forthwith begun.

As a preliminary it was ordered by the Grand Inquisitor, William of Paris, that the Templars should be interrogated, first by the king's officials, and then by the inquisitors; that the denials of guilt by the accused were not to be reported, but that the rack was to be applied, and the extorted confessions alone recorded in the protocols.

At this point we should observe that at no time, nor anywhere in the whole of Christendom, did a Templar make any confession, except when it was wrung from him by the infliction or through the fear of torture.[7] The descriptions given not only by the Templars themselves, but by other contemporaries, of the mode of procedure are fearful.

[6] [Lea (*History of the Inquisition*, iii. 255) considers the account of the two denunciators to be an invention of a chronicler. Schottmüller takes it for a popular tale.]
[7] [With this statement of Döllinger's compare Lea, iii. 260*.]

In Paris alone thirty-six Templars died under torture. Ingenious refinements of the most horrible torments were called into requisition; these, occasionally, were utterly shameless, and any one acquainted with modern French writers knows that they have not concealed the feelings of shame excited by the deeds of degrading and inhuman infamy then perpetrated by their forefathers.

This leads us on to the point which has hitherto been most obscure in the history of the fall of the Templars—What is the truth about the confession made, according to contemporary testimony, by the Grand Master, Jacques de Molay?

That Molay really confessed to the denial of Christ and to spitting on the cross is an undeniable fact, and the most recent advocate for the Order, Schottmüller,* has vainly attempted to weaken the evidence respecting this. Evidence destructive to his moral reputation had been procured by the usual means, not only from one, but from three persons who were intimate with him. Besides the denial of Christ, spitting upon the cross, and other indecencies, the gravest accusation against the Order was that it had not only formally introduced abominable vice amongst its members, but had to a certain extent made it obligatory upon them. A fellow who asserted that he had been in Molay's personal service gave evidence against his master on this head. The offence was one which even according to the civil law would be punishable with death. It might be possible to wring confession from Molay by the rack, and he would then, even if his life were spared, be marked with an indelible brand of shame. But the chief point with his judges was that he should confess to the denial of Christ, because such a confession would necessarily implicate the whole Order, whereas the other sin left the Order untouched. Therefore it was contrived that the Grand Master should declare himself ready to confess to the denial and to the spitting, if only he might be spared the other and more

* i. 617.

personal accusation. And this is what happened. Molay, however, soon after the scene in Paris retracted his confession. In the document preserved in the royal archives in which this is reported, it is said that he must be made to keep to his first confession, as it tallies with the depositions of the other Templars.

[Within the last few years an important document has come into our hands, which throws considerable light upon the subject. The origin of the document was as follows. During the year 1308 King Philip came twice to Poitiers, where the pope then was; on the second occasion, at the head of a retinue consisting of the most notable men in church and state, and in the name of a large popular assembly lately held at Tours, he declared the prosecution of the Templars to be an affair of national importance for France. On this occasion, by the application of the means of pressure already mentioned—the threat of the condemnation of Boniface VIII.—the pope was induced to overcome his scruples, and submitted without reserve to the demands of the king. Philip insisted that the imprisoned Templars should be delivered into the power of the pope, and that the pope should conduct the trial—which, indeed, in appearance he did—but also that the pope should then empower a confidant of the king, the Cardinal Bishop Taillefer of Palestrina, to deal with the Templars—as his representative—as he should see fit. Taillefer at once turned over the prisoners again to the king, on the ground that he, and he alone, was able to guard them securely. The unfortunate Templars consequently remained uninterruptedly in the power of their tormentor.

At the same time the pope sent instructions to the French bishops and inquisitors as to how they were to deal with the Templars who were still living. These, the pope declared, ought to be fed upon bread and water and other slight refreshments (*et aliquibus paucis refectionibus*). If they still did not 'turn to the truth'—the pope here uses just the same phrases as the lawyers and the inquisitors—that is to say, if they did not confess to the principal accusations, and if they be not otherwise convicted, they were to be informed that great numbers of the brothers of the Order, and, above all, the Grand Master himself, had confessed. If one amongst the Templars were *bene perseverans*, i.e. if he abided by the confession which he made upon the rack, he was to be allowed to converse with the others that have not yet confessed, in order that they might be persuaded by him. Should that prove useless, they are to be threatened with torture; the instruments of torture are to be displayed before them, and gradually applied by a *tortor clericus idoneus*, that is, by a priestly executioner or gaoler. To the obstinate the sacraments are to be refused; they are, indeed, to be admitted to confession, but not to absolution. The father-confessor is to terrify them thoroughly, yet to assure them that the church shows mercy to such as are converted. The means of working through terror were simple enough; the rule of the Inquisition was that any backslider, i.e., any one retracting his previous confession, should be punished by death at the stake. Only those who confess and persevere in their confession are to be, after abjuring their heresy, admitted to absolution, and henceforth to receive milder treatment as to lodging and food.[9]

It was now no longer the king, but the bishops who enhanced the cruelty of these dreadful transactions. Philip had also extorted from the pope the recommendation that the bishops should always be present with the inquisitors at the examination, that is, that they should attend in the interests of the king, lest the proceedings should take too mild a form.

So far did the pope go in his submission to the king's will, that he now even ordered the numerous articles of accusation, 132 (127 ?) altogether in number, which the

[9] [In Döllinger's notes there is the following obscure reference: '*Modus procedendi* p. 446 im liber *Guil. Majoris*.' Comp. Boutaric, *La France sous Philippe le Bel*, Paris, 1861, p. 136 s.]

lawyers and inquisitors had collected as the basis for the judicial examinations and trials, not only by the bishops and inquisitors in France, but in other countries as well.]¹

Amongst the principal articles which were thus formally confirmed by the pope was that relating to the devil worship, to which it was affirmed the Templars were addicted. Satan had appeared in their chapter meetings in the form of a great tom-cat, had made them swear allegiance to him, and had given them advice and instruction. In Bologna he had once caused all the members in a house of the Order to worship him for the space of an hour, and had told them many things. The pope himself, not the king only and his inquisitors, now commanded that the men of the Order, in Italy first, and afterwards everywhere, should be interrogated on this point, and by the application of the usual means confessions were extorted. In Southern France, besides the tom-cat, beautiful female devils had appeared amongst the Templars, and had, as they confessed under torture, seduced them into sin. But the majority of depositions went upon the whole to prove that the Order had set up two gods, whom the brothers worshipped after denying and scoffing at Christ.

Their second god was, it was said, an idol's head to which they ascribed unlimited power. To it was imputed the fertility and fruitfulness of the fields and trees. Whether the fields and trees of the Order only, or those of the whole world, seems to have been an open question. This head must have been a Proteus, for it was seen under the most diverse forms; it was sometimes a painted board, sometimes a human skull; was sometimes bearded, at other times clean shaven. The brilliant eyes illuminated the whole convent. Yet in spite of the most diligent search, and although the Templars, as we know, had been com-

---

¹ [For the passage enclosed within [ ] Döllinger's MS. contains only a few short notes and unfinished sentences. It must therefore have been delivered almost entirely from memory.]

pletely unprepared when they were suddenly arrested, it was never found.

The same fate must have overtaken the idol's head as has befallen the secret statutes of the Order, for which even to the present time diligent search has been made, but which have never been found. There are even now literary men in Germany who think that these pretended secret statutes, containing all the imputed abominations, must still be hidden somewhere, and who diligently rummage the libraries for them.

Time will not allow me to follow out the course of this drama, which stands alone in history, but I should like in conclusion to point out *three* consequences involved by the annihilation of the Order of the Knights Templars.

The first is as follows :—The Templars, as is well known, made the island of Cyprus their headquarters. It was there that the flower of their force was maintained; most of the members were always to be found there, whilst in the West, in France, in Germany, etc., they were only quartered temporarily. They went thither, as occasion offered, on business, to incite people to fresh crusades, or to collect arms and money; their real home was always in the East. In Cyprus the Templars, had they not been destroyed, would have become what the Hospitallers were in Rhodes, a bulwark for Christendom against Islam. Their destruction was of great advantage to the future growth of the Turkish power.

The second consequence was the introduction or strengthening of the harshness and senseless cruelty of the French criminal law, which lasted down to the Revolution.

The third consequence, of which we have already had a glimpse, was that the popular belief in witches' sabbaths, in personal intercourse with the devil, and in short in every form of black art, could claim from henceforth the sanction of the highest authority both spiritual and secular, and thus became unassailable. What incalculable results this brought about I need hardly say.[2] The use of the rack to extort the desired confessions was recommended and authorised. History relates how the Inquisition provided for the improvement of education and morality in general.

Were I to select a single day in the whole course of history which in my opinion might most emphatically be described as a *dies nefastus*, it would be none other than Oct. 13, 1307.

APPENDIX.

PASSAGES FROM THE ELABORATED TEXT OF THE LECTURE UPON THE ORDER OF THE KNIGHTS TEMPLARS.[3]

Foundation and Rule of the Order.

The Order of the Knights Templars was founded in Jerusalem in the year 1119 by nine French knights, who besides taking the three vows of chastity, poverty, and obedience, laid themselves under an obligation to escort pilgrims, and to defend the Holy Land against the attacks of the Moslem foe. Hugh des Payens [de Payns] was chosen as the first Master. The lodging which the king appointed for him, a part of the royal palace covering the

---

[2] [Lea expressly points to the intimate connection between the belief in the guilt of the Templars and belief in the reality of witchcraft, iii. 267.j 'Riding through the air on a broomstick, and commerce with incubi and succubi, rest upon evidence of precisely the same character, and of much greater weight than that upon which the Templars were convicted, for the witch was sure of burning if she confessed, and had a chance of escaping if she could endure the torture, while the Templar was threatened with death for obstinacy, and was promised immunity as a reward for confession. If we accept the evidence against the Templar we cannot reject it in the case of the witch.' Lea, p. 267, vol. iii. Sampson Low, &c., London, 1888.

[3] [Döllinger's MS. consists of detached leaves, mostly unnumbered, which I have endeavoured to arrange in the order in which he would probably have used them. As to two of the leaves, I was uncertain whether they were not of an earlier date; but the greater number of them were undoubtedly written during the weeks immediately preceding his death, *i.e.* between the middle of November and the end of December, 1889.]

site of Solomon's Temple, gave the name to the Order. As voluntary paupers the Templars depended at first for support upon the alms they received.

This knightly brotherhood developed and strengthened with wonderful rapidity. The favour of the world assisted it with valuable donations. Legacies in money, in revenue, and in landed estates poured in upon it in increasing amount. Papal privileges facilitated the acquisition and secured the possession of wealth. Nevertheless, along with collective riches, the rule of poverty as regards the individual was adhered to.

At the Synod of Troyes in the year 1128 the Order obtained the papal sanction, and the outline of a rule conceived in the spirit of St. Bernard of Clairvaux, if not actually designed by him. In its later form, with which alone we are acquainted, it almost entirely corresponds with the Benedictine rule, so far as this could be made to harmonise with the knightly vocation and with military exploits.

Constitution.

With regard to the constitution of the Order, only so much will be given as is needful for the comprehension and appreciation of the tragedy. It was under the direction of a hierarchy consisting of various gradations.

The power of the elected Grand Master was very limited. He was bound by oath to obey the decrees of the Convent. Without its sanction he could undertake no affair of importance; he could make no official appointments, nor had he at his disposal more than the very limited sum of a hundred Byzantine dollars. He was unable to change one of the statutes of the brotherhood. If, besides this, the diversity of nationality and of language amongst the members of the Order is taken into consideration, it will not be possible to imagine that a Grand Master, either alone or with the assistance of a few like-minded with himself, could have effected any important change of teaching or practice. The very first attempt would infallibly have led to his deposition. The errors imputed to the Order were, moreover, not of a kind that could be imagined as gradually creeping in and insidiously taking root.

Admission into the Order and Withdrawal from it.

A promise was made by each new member on admission that he would not transfer himself to another order, but permission to do so could be obtained from the Master. Dismissal from the Order for grave offences was not altogether infrequent; and amongst the first informers and torturers of the Templars there was at least one such defaulter. Sentence of death was never passed in the Order, certainly never carried out. The statutes contain no mention of capital punishment, which is contrary to the principles of all religious associations. Dismissal followed in cases of simoniacal purchase or bestowal of the dress of the Order, or upon a breach of silence with regard to the deliberations of the Chapter, or in punishment of heresy, murder, and unnatural offences—of which latter crimes the rule expresses particular abhorrence. Besides this, flight in the battlefield, embezzlement of goods belonging to the Order, gaining admission upon false pretences, were requited with dismissal.

Voluntary withdrawal from the Order was often allowed, in spite of the promise given on entrance, but it was necessary to obtain the consent of the Master. The statutes defined what the departing member might be allowed to take with him and what he must leave behind. According to the statutes transference to another order could only take place if the Templar was received into a stricter, that is to say, a more monastic order, and not another knightly one. A knight after his dismissal might at his request remain as a lay brother or be re-admitted. Whoever after leaving the Order petitioned for re-admission had to submit to the performance of some penance, but this was sometimes remitted. A knight who was condemned to do penance was usually scourged by the hand of the chaplain of the house after prayers had been offered up for him.

Rule of Life.

The desire to lead a life of comfort or of self-indulgence could have induced no one to join the Order. The ascetic severity of the rule would have been more likely to act as a deterrent. The fare was simple, meat was eaten only three times in the week,[4] and the fasts imposed were many and long. Every tenth loaf

---

[4] [H. de Curzon (*La Règle du Temple*, Paris, 1886, p. xxvi) supposes that the strict fasts enjoined by the first rule were soon discontinued.]

was given over to the almoner. The Templar, bound by his vow of poverty, had no possessions, and could neither procure luxuries for his own enjoyment, nor accept presents except for the Order. He received his clothes from the convent store. His bed consisted only of a sack of straw and a coverlet. If he travelled over the sea, he first begged forgiveness of all the brothers of the house for any annoyance that he might have caused them. He might never allow himself to be served by a woman, nor might he write a letter without the permission of the Grand Master.

Different Ranks of the Order.

The composition and constitution of the Order rendered it impossible that a smaller secret association, differing in practice and with a mysterious cultus, should be formed within it. All the various ranks and callings in the Order—office-bearers, simple knights, temporary members, priests, attendants, workmen, labourers—all were constantly under reciprocal supervision, shared the same board, and attended Divine service together four times daily. In the houses of the Order there was no space for secret apartments cut off from the rest. Any attempt at exclusiveness would at once have aroused suspicion and called for stricter supervision. Owing to the great number of estates and dependencies secular clergy were often engaged for a time to assist the priests belonging to the Order, and were then witnesses of all that went on in the house.

When, by a bull issued by Pope Alexander in the year 1179,[a] members in priest's orders were introduced among the Templars, the constitution of the Order was already fully established. When secular clergy entered the Order they became monks with the three vows, renounced all earnings and possessions, and bound themselves to obedience even to the lay superiors of the Order. They were certainly treated with the respect and reverence due to their office, but there could have been nothing attractive in the Order to the average priest of that period. Their numbers, consequently, were never sufficient for the wants of the Order, and that is why we find that the Templars often engaged other ecclesiastics for a certain time to help them and admitted them to a share of board and lodging.

As a rule the Templar was allowed to confess only to a priest

[a] [Comp. H. de Curzon, § 637.]

of the Order—a regulation which existed also amongst the Hospitallers and the Knights of the Teutonic Order. Yet if, as often happened, a priest of the Order was not within reach, the Templar was allowed to make his confession to a strange priest. One especial reason for giving the preference to a brother of the Order was in the fact that by papal licence he possessed far wider powers of absolution than an ordinary priest.

The numerous ranks of lay brothers included various callings. Frequently they were masters of single houses or priors of a commandery; in which cases they could hold chapters and admit brothers, and had a seat and a voice in the General Chapter. Even amongst the thirteen who were charged with the election of the Master, some were civil and lay brothers. In the Temple at Paris itself the treasurer of the Order was a lay brother. The working brothers belonged to the same rank, whether those employed in the workshops of the Order, or [in kitchen, stall, or field, and other meaner duties of the household].

Alleged Wealth of the Order.

The wealth of the Order in France has been immensely exaggerated. The constant endeavour to add to its gains, and the employment of every permissible and honourable means of increasing its revenues is not surprising in a belligerent association. The rule that to carry on war money must be forthcoming again and again held good for the Templars as for others. That which they acquired was not their personal property; they remained poor and without possessions—the reproach of breaking their vow of poverty was never levelled against them. They were continually having to send men, arms, equipments of every sort, horses and ships by Marseilles to Cyprus, as their army and fleet had to be maintained and reinforced.

The accusation of avarice which even Münter brings against the Templars seems to me to be wholly undeserved. If they amassed and saved money it was not for themselves, but to defray the expenses of the whole Order. On Asiatic soil everything had been lost, through no fault of theirs, and yet they had to be always fully prepared for war, furnished with money and mercenary troops, and ready forthwith to act at once on the offensive, whenever the great expedition of the crusaders, continually promised and announced for the next spring, should really be undertaken. They had to be ready to pay the papal tithes, to assist with advances or loans princes who were arming, and they employed considerable sums in redeeming Christians from Moslem captivity.[6]

As to the amount of their wealth in France we can arrive at a pretty accurate conclusion. Cardinal Simon, who came as papal legate to France about the year 1300, for the purpose of collecting a tithe with which the clergy had been charged, and who was remarkably acute in estimating the exact amount of all the ecclesiastical property and revenues, charged the Templars in those days with exactly the same sum— 6,000 *livres tournois* — as the Hospitallers, and the Cistercians with double, *i.e.* 12,000 *livres*. This proves that the Templars were not richer than the Hospitallers, and were only half as rich as the Cistercians. But the latter order lived and cared only for itself, and occupied itself neither with the care of souls nor with preaching, neither with nursing the sick nor with the instruction and education of the young. Philip the Fair, partly to punish the Cistercians for their devotion to Boniface VIII., partly because they were rich, levied the heaviest tax in money on them, and they declared it was almost impossible to raise it, and complained of it bitterly. But he suppressed none of their monasteries; they were left unmolested and they quickly recovered themselves. Had the king required it, the popes would willingly have allowed him to tax the Templars by exacting a tithe from them, and the ever-obedient brothers would have paid it.

That their existence and wealth were any real obstacle to the plan for the centralisation of the administration, which Philip had already partly carried out, does not appear. Their rule enjoined obedience to the king ; no transgression of the laws of the state nor revolt against the secular authorities was laid to their charge ; on these points they stood in exactly the same position as the Hospitallers, whom the king left entirely unmolested. Such conflicts as were of daily occurrence between the bishops and their followers on one side and the royal officials and judges on the other were unknown in the history of the Templars. The latter never aspired to exercise jurisdiction over any one but the members of their own Order. They were not permitted to take part in any war between Christians, their prowess was only to be displayed against the infidel Moham-

⁎ [This paragraph, which partly repeats the preceding one, would doubtless have been absorbed into it by Döllinger in preparing for the press.]

medan. Consequently they were no hindrance to Philip's system of centralisation. No instance ever occurred of a Templar taking part in an act of rebellion against the state or in a popular disturbance. They were an element of order and tranquillity in the community, which could not fail to be welcome to statesmen.

Observations on the Trial of the Templars.

There were at the time not a few Templars who had passed from their own Order into others. Justice would have required that their evidence should have been heard first, but neither pope nor king would have that --they could not have been put to the torture.

In the latter days of the Order, the Templars, for some unknown reason, had departed from their original rule of admitting only adults. We find a considerable number of boys and youths who were admitted at the early ages of from twelve to seventeen to take the vows. According to the assertion of the opponents of the Order, they had all been obliged to deny God, to spit upon the cross, and to promise to conform to vice. One of these was the unfortunate Prince Guido, son of the Dauphin of Auvergne, who was afterwards burnt together with Molay.

Any one of noble birth must have been knighted before he could be admitted as a Templar. It is well known that this was formerly an entirely religious ceremony, preparation for which was made by ascetic exercises and the reception of the sacraments of the church. The knight first swore to fight for the faith and to suffer death a thousand times rather than deny it, and never to break his word.

That there were in reality unbelievers amongst the Order who had allowed their sentiments to become known seems not to have been admitted by any one who was examined. It was always said : Just as I, in spite of denials made against my will, am a simple, believing Christian, so is this the case also with the other brethren of the Order. In those days for an unbeliever to belong to a religious order would have been an inconceivable incongruity.

According to Prutz the Order was formally organized as an heretical community in the year 1220,[7] in such a way that only a small but continually increasing number of members were

---

[7] [Comp. Prutz, *Geheimlehren und Geheimstatuten des Tempelherrenordens*, Berlin, 1879, p. 99.]

initiated into the secret. Those whose office it was to admit fresh members varied their practice upon such occasions, sometimes initiating the candidate into the secret, and at other times not. What was taught was a combination of the Waldensian, Albigensian, and Luciferian heresies. Now this discovery was never made at the time : there is nothing about it in the records of the trials in the different countries; not a single inquisitor had knowledge of it, though his daily practice would make him intimately acquainted with these questionable doctrines.

At the papal court in Poitiers, which was not entirely composed of the servile partisans of Philip, it was thought suspicious that, although the king publicly declared that he had long been informed by trustworthy persons of the scandalous behaviour of some of the Templars, he had never named any one such person to the pope. Everything that had preceded the general order to torture the Templars remained wrapped in impenetrable obscurity. The people were told that a special Divine illumination had revealed the whole matter to the king. The king's tutor, the famous theologian .Egidius Colonna, Archbishop of Bourges, said that the discovery had been made through the astuteness (*astutia*) of the king. The same astuteness, he supposed, had succeeded in discovering the secret of the worship of the black and oracular tom-cat.

The Dominican, Peter de la Palu (de Palude), next to .Egidius Colonna the most esteemed theologian of the time, solemnly stated before the papal commission that he himself had taken part in the examination of a number of the Templars, and his impression was that those who denied, and not those who confessed, were speaking the truth.

The security which the Templars felt as to their safety, the firm confidence in their rights and liberties, in the protection of the church and in the favour of public opinion, was such that Molay, with several of the heads of the Order, came to Paris somewhere about September, 1307, although they had been previously warned. The pope, on their repeated and urgent petition, had promised to institute an investigation himself. The thought had not entered their minds that the king, who appeared to be upon the best of terms with Clement V., would nullify this intention, and wrest the conduct of the trial into his own hands by an unparalleled exercise of authority. He had hitherto shown them so much favour and confidence that he had even entrusted them with the education of his sons. . . .

Clement V. repeatedly declared, after November 1307, that this matter of the Templars, which involved so much that was incredible and apparently impossible, placed him in a very painful position; he could scarcely breathe for anxiety and sorrow. The confidence with which Molay had solicited an investigation, and his subsequent public confession of guilt in Paris, must have seemed to him an insoluble enigma. But instead of wishing for a personal interview, which Molay earnestly desired, Clement now managed, under various frivolous pretexts, to keep him at a distance, and caused him to be interrogated only through the cardinals -the special friends of Philip. He never once during the following five years saw Molay, nor showed the slightest token of interest in the man's fate. Instead of that, he did not hesitate to base his condemnatory bull upon [the confession that had been wrung by torture from the Grand Master].

In a letter addressed to the imprisoned Templars by the Provost Vohet- who, together with the torturer Jamville, was entrusted with the guardianship of their persons and the direction of their treatment—it is written: 'Hold fast to the good confession which we have left with you.' There was then a form of words that had been given them, which they had to commit to memory and to repeat. This form contained, of course, the chief points, upon the avowal of which those in authority laid most stress—viz., the denial, the spitting, and the immoralities.

These men, who everywhere enjoyed the reputation of courage and dauntless valour, confess themselves to have been weak and spiritless cowards [in that at their admission into the Order they consented against their will to deny Christ, and to insult the holy cross when required to do so]. . . . And the same men afterwards again display the most heroic contempt of death, not before the enemy, but before the vigilant, sharp-sighted inquisitors who surrounded them. They knew, and again and again wer reminded by the sight of frequent executions and public recantations, that they [were accused of having] committed things which were reckoned in those days as crimes worthy of death; they knew that a single unpremeditated word, or indiscretion on the part of a youthful member—many were only fifteen, sixteen, or seven een years old—imperilled their honour and their freedom; that their life depended upon the discreet silence and prudence of the meanest attendant or workman of the Order. Finally, they knew that the denunciation of any single word that could rouse the slightest suspicion of heresy, was reckoned a conscientious duty that could not be neglected without personal risk. . . .

That those Templars who perished by crowds in the royal prisons one and all asseverated their innocence to their last breath is the testimony even of their enemy, the Provost Volict of Poitiers. The Templars who appeared before the papal commission earnestly begged that these dying utterances might be placed on record. Naturally the request was refused.

VI

THE HISTORY OF RELIGIOUS FREEDOM[1]

THE persecutions of the early Christians by the imperial power of Rome and by the heathen populace, differed entirely both in origin and character from the coercion and violence practised by Christians upon their fellow-Christians in later times, although outwardly the two resembled each other.

According to the conception prevalent amongst the Romans, the weal or woe of their empire, and of each community comprised in it, depended essentially upon reverence for the gods of the state, and upon observance of the legal forms of worship. All prosperity, physical and political; all military success, as well as immunity from public disaster, was connected with general and assiduous attention to the worship of the Græco-Roman gods. The Christians were enemies to both gods and men, their existence was an evil, injurious alike to the community and to the individual. The fact that enemies of the gods were present in a city aroused apprehension lest the guardian divinities might desert it, or take vengeance upon it. It was thus not so much for the sake of old laws, but rather in self-defence, that the state armed itself against the Christians, and the Christian religion seemed all the more dangerous in proportion as it became evident that it was destined to become the faith and practice of the masses. Frequently the governing power only yielded to the popular

[1] Lecture delivered at the meeting of the Academy of Science at Munich, March 28, 1888. Upon the fragment added as an appendix, see preface.

clamour for blood, though statesmen on their part felt themselves bound not to tolerate a secret association, the existence of which, as an *hetairia*, was already legally prohibited.

If the popular paganism had not already begun to yield to the process of corruption and dissolution, the persecutions of the Christians would without doubt have been carried on with far greater severity, and in a more thorough and systematic manner. As it is, we find long intervals of rest and peace for the Christians, interrupted only now and then by acts of violence on the part of the heathen populace. The Emperor Gallienus (cir. A.D. 265) recognised Christianity as a lawful religion, and thereby ushered in a period of forty years' repose, after which Diocletian set on foot the last and most terrible of all the persecutions. This was the first instance of a persecution of which the avowed object was the extirpation of Christianity throughout the whole extent of the empire; but it came much too late, and consequently brought about exactly the opposite effect, namely, the establishment and purification of the Christian Church.

When the rulers had recognised that it was impossible wholly to root out Christianity, a reaction set in. From edicts of toleration, the advance was rapid to favourable enactments, and from thence to the triumph of Christianity. The edict of Galerius, A.D. 311, granted simple toleration; two years later, Constantine and Licinius proclaimed religious liberty throughout the empire, and freedom to embrace the Christian faith. Henceforth, with various and increasing privileges, Christianity advanced until it became the religion of the Roman state, although the Emperor Constantine treated heathen forms of religion with great consideration, keeping, so to speak, one foot in the polytheistic state *cultus*, the other in Christianity, and remaining unbaptized even until the end.

Constantine's three sons, who divided the empire, at once assumed an attitude hostile to heathenism. After a few years, laws were passed which threatened the offering of Pagan sacrifices and the veneration of the images of the gods with the punishment of death. Adherence to heathenism had already become a state offence. Nevertheless no actual compulsion was as yet used to enforce baptism, so that immense numbers of persons who professed to be Christians remained unbaptized, and consequently outside the church to the end of their lives. The Emperors Jovian and Valentinian I. still pronounced themselves in favour of general religious freedom. When, subsequently, the attempt on the part of the Emperor Julian to restore the heathen religion in its ancient splendour and with its political prerogatives had failed, without leaving any lasting results, there began, under Theodosius I., the first systematic attempt to uproot heathenism.

The prohibition of sacrifices, and the closing and destruction of the temples were the means employed; actual compulsion to embrace the Christian creed was not yet exercised. Yet since the mass of the people could not exist without religion, the stream of those who still remained wholly or partially heathen at heart discharged itself into the church, so that as early as the year 423 the Emperor Theodosius II. could describe heathenism as extinct.

It was inevitable after this that the Christian Church should, as time went on, experience great and profound internal changes. The Roman Empire received fresh vigour from the church, but the church itself, into which the mass of the heathen were only outwardly and formally, and in many cases compulsorily, incorporated, had admitted within her pale elements of heathen superstition and moral corruption, destined to produce very dangerous fruit.

That same Theodosius I., who was not himself baptized until he had become emperor, brought about a decisive change in the temper of Christianity by issuing a decree establishing the Catholic religion as the exclusive religion of the state, to which all Christians under severe penalties must adhere. Heresy, or deviation from the prevalent doctrine, became henceforth an offence, to be dealt with by the civil law. Succeeding emperors down to Justinian, following the precedent set by Theodosius, passed increasingly severe laws, and there arose in this way a copious code of punishment for heresy. The evil spirit of heathenism seemed to have found a home in the imperial council-chamber. Even capital punishment was decreed against certain sects.

The first instance of an execution for heresy took place on German soil, at Trèves, when the Emperor Maximus caused Priscillian, the founder of a new sect, and his followers to be beheaded. At the time this act met everywhere with most decided disapproval. The most notable dignitaries and teachers of the church abstained from any intercourse with the two bishops who, as the accusers of the victims, had been the cause of the catastrophe, for hitherto amongst Christians coercion in matters of religion had been regarded as altogether reprehensible.

A new power, not exactly unknown to the ancients but not understood by them, had been brought to light by Christianity — the power of conscience. The classically educated Greeks and Romans either regarded the enigma as insoluble or, failing to solve it, chose to explain it in the most unfavourable manner. The constancy of the Christians appeared to them as a blind and unreasonable obstinacy, which, if not blind and unreasonable, betrayed a vanity that courted notice and applause. The Christians, on the other hand, perceived in the inner voice of command, or of prohibition, a law which for them was paramount to any human power or authority. To obey this was, in all moral and religious questions, the duty as well as the inherent indefeasible right of every human being.

Thus the early church, until far on into the fourth century, unanimously taught that coercion in religious matters was an act of violence to conscience, and that every Christian was in duty bound to withstand it to the utmost, even unto death. ['If religious freedom be taken from me,' said Tertullian, 'and the choice of a deity be forbidden, so that I be forced to worship any one against my will, this is contrary to the essence of religion.'] Again, at the close of the fourth century, the most distinguished teacher of the Eastern Church, John Chrysostom, wrote— ' Not by force or of compulsion, but only by persuasion, reasoning, and the evidence of love, is a Christian permitted to combat error.' Chrysostom [2] may have been expressing the opinion of most of his contemporaries. Yet shortly afterwards a sudden change set in, which may well be called a falling away from the ancient precept, and which looks as if the emperors had become the teachers of the bishops.

This change was principally brought about by the great master of the Latin Church, Augustine, Bishop of Hippo. He had formerly thought and taught as Chrysostom did; but he now affirmed that, through the experience he had gained from the compulsory conversion of the Donatists, he had arrived at more correct views. These views he sought to establish by such palpable sophisms and such gross perversion of the utterances of Christ and of the Apostles, that we seem to recognise no longer the acute theologian faithful to tradition, but rather the disciple

[2] As Dr. Döllinger paraphrases rather than translates these passages, we give the original, with an exact English rendering. Tertullian, *Apology*, 124:

' Videte enim, ne et hoc ad irreligiositatis elogium concurrat, adimere libertatem religionis et interdicere optionem divinitatis, ut non liceat mihi colere quem velim, sed cogar colere quem nolim. Nemo se ab invito coli volet; ne homo quidem.'

' For beware lest this also contribute to the charge of irreligion, to take away the liberty of religion and to forbid the choice of a God, so that I am not allowed to worship whom I will, but am compelled to worship whom I will not. No one, not even a mortal, desires to be worshipped by any one against his will.'

St. Chrysostom, 'De Sancto Babyla contra Julianum et Gentiles.' *Opera*, t. ii. p. 540:—

' οὐδὲ γὰρ θέμις χριστιανοῖς ἀνάγκῃ καὶ βίᾳ καταστρέφειν τὴν πλάνην, ἀλλὰ καὶ πειθοῖ καὶ λόγῳ καὶ προσηνείᾳ τὴν τῶν ἀνθρώπων ἐργάζεσθαι σωτηρίαν.'

' For neither is it lawful for Christians to overthrow error by compulsion and force; but rather by persuasion, reasoning (or argument), and gentleness, to work out the salvation of men.'—*Translator's Note*.

of heathen sophists and rhetoricians. Nevertheless his opinion gradually, though slowly, made its way. His teaching was pregnant of results for Western Christianity. From the middle of the twelfth century it became incorporated in a series of test words in the general manual of law and instruction, the 'Decretal' of Gratian.

Augustine indeed condemned the use of capital punishment for errors of faith; but there was nothing to hinder the drawing of this conclusion from his theory of coercion. The great Synods of 1179 and 1215 sanctioned it, and the law of the Decretals established it as the prevalent practice. It was a victory won over the Germanic mind by the imperial law of ancient Rome as it had been developed and codified by Theodosius and Justinian.

Amongst the Germanic tribes, during the earlier period of their history as a nation, religious coercion was unknown. The christianized Germanic races who had been brought by tribal migration to settle in the countries of the Western Roman Empire were not inclined to persecution. Although mostly Arians, they left the Catholics who were subject to them in the free practice of their faith, and, unless required by them to do so, did not meddle in religious matters. This was true of the Ostrogoths, and afterwards of the Lombards in Italy, as well as of the Arian kings of the Burgundians and Visigoths in Gaul. The Catholic Franks also treated their Arian subjects with consideration.

The Vandals formed an exception to the rule after their conquest of Roman Africa. They also were Arians. Sensible of their numerical weakness in presence of a population differing from them in faith, and setting their hopes upon a revival of strength in the Eastern Roman Empire, the Vandals set to work seriously to uproot Catholicism—more from fear than from fanaticism. They failed in their endeavour, and hastened their own downfall.

The extension of the church through the conversion of the heathen tribes of the north is sufficient to show the sort of spirit which had become prevalent in Western Christendom. Charles the Great's treatment of the Saxons was only too readily imitated. The genuine race of evangelically minded missionaries, such as had been the bishops Anskar of Bremen, Otto of Bamberg, and Vicelin of Altenburg, had died out since the middle of the twelfth century. Crusades took the place of missions, and by them whole tribes were exterminated rather than converted, and their countries devastated. Next, armed with the same weapons, came the knightly orders, the Knights of the Order of the Sword, and the Teutonic Order, who transformed Prussia into a wilderness, so that the aboriginal population disappeared, and was only gradually replaced by German colonists.

The chief means employed in combating sects and divergencies of doctrine, whenever these had obtained a numerous following, were crusades. Then came the Inquisition! I pass willingly with hurried steps over a period in which religious feeling was so greatly intermixed and interpenetrated with terror and hypocrisy. Men could not in those days perceive that a church supported by such forces, however much it might possess the external symbols of power, was not manifesting its strength, but rather its internal weakness and incapacity.

From time to time—but at long intervals—a courageous though solitary voice was uplifted to advocate the rights of conscience, and to denounce the perversion and injustice of the church's system of coercion and punishment; one such was that of Abbot Rupert of Deutz, the most learned of German theologians in the twelfth century; another, 160 years later, relying upon the protection of the Emperor Ludwig the Bavarian, was that of the bold Marsiglio of Padua. Going further than Rupert of Deutz, Marsiglio denied to the priesthood all coercive authority, saying that its influence upon human conduct ought only to be enforced by teaching, counsel, and warning. But there was no place in Europe at that time for such views, and immediately afterwards (A.D. 1327) the papal anathema was issued, in which the right of the pope to use coercive and penal measures was declared to be an article of faith. Thus all contrary opinion was silenced.

When, after the long years in which it was maturing, the Reformation at length broke out, and Europe was forthwith divided between two hostile camps, it seemed as though the recognition of the rights of conscience must be the prime issue, the first-fruits of the intense intellectual struggle. But so deeply had the old doctrine of coercion sunk into the minds of the people, so rooted had it become in the ideas of all ranks and classes, that the reformers themselves were incapable of grasping the conception of religious freedom. In defiance of logic and of the Bible, they thought it just and fair to deny to others what they claimed for themselves.

Luther, by his doctrine of Christian liberty and of the common universal priesthood, came nearer to the right conception, and during the first years of his labours he preached that the word, as the true sword, ought to be allowed to take effect, and that force should be used neither against conscience nor for the truth. But all that occurred after the year 1525—the springing up of new sects, and the schism on the doctrine of the Eucharist—combined to change his views, and made him no longer willing to concede liberty of worship and of teaching to Catholic, or Protestant, or Anabaptist. Only the news that men for their faith were rendered liable to capital punishment wrung from him once more the declaration that every man should be allowed to believe what he pleases, and that false doctrine can only be arrested and withstood by God's word, and not by fire. He, nevertheless, soon relapsed into the old doctrine of persecution, and preached to the authorities the use of the sword against sectarians and disturbers of the peace of the church.

How widely prevalent this opinion was, even in the Protestant world, was strikingly shown soon after Luther's death, when Calvin (A.D. 1553) caused the Spaniard Servetus to be burned in Geneva for denying the doctrine of the Trinity.

Calvin, as well as his friend Theodore Beza, wrote in defence of the employment of capital punishment against false doctrine, and found universal approval. Capito alone, the reformer of Strasburg, formed an exception. That a man, otherwise so mild and conciliating as Melancthon, should approve the deed done at Geneva, shows what a firm hold the conceptions of the Middle Ages still had upon men's minds.

The religious peace of the year 1555 revealed how far both sides, Protestant as well as Catholic, were still removed from the thought of introducing real religious freedom. A certain equality between the two denominations was indeed agreed to; every prince or state of the empire was free to decide either for the Confession of Augsburg or for the Catholic creed. But their subjects were given no choice; their religion depended upon the opinions of those in authority. *Cuius est regio, illius est religio*, was the political principle of the Germans. The only mitigation obtained by the people was that, in place of the old punishments for heresy, emigration was allowed. This led to whole countries being obliged, sometimes more than once, like the Palatinate, to change their creed, whilst ministers of religion were ejected wholesale and driven to seek refuge abroad.

Soon the Catholic counter-reformation began in Germany, in France, on the Lower Rhine, and in Westphalia. In Austria the younger Styrian line, which combined effort to establish absolute government with Jesuitical proselytizing zeal, replaced the elder and more moderate branch of the House of Habsburg, so that here also a Catholic counter-reformation was quickly set on foot. The Protestants were forced to emigrate or to profess Catholicism; former promises and privileges were withdrawn; resistance was drowned in streams of blood. Outwardly and officially all the various countries of the Austrian dominions again became Catholic; but hundreds of thousands still clung secretly to their Protestant faith. This fact became apparent when, after 186 years of oppression, the Patent of Toleration issued by the Emperor Joseph threw open the gates of the prisons, A.D. 1781, and granted to the Protestants not only liberty of faith and worship, but the right to educate their own congregations.

The Thirty Years' War, the flames of which were kindled by the Bohemian insurrection, was undoubtedly — although the question has often been disputed — a religious war. The Protestants fought for liberty of faith and worship, of which they had been already partly deprived, or with the loss of which they were threatened. Had this been secured to them, peace would at once have been attainable, and the difficulty of arriving at an understanding would have existed only in the necessity of satisfying the claims of France and of Sweden, the two foreign nations who had assisted in the war.

To Germany the actual result of the Peace of Westphalia was altogether disastrous. The principle of equality between the two confessions had been fought out, but the goal of practical religious liberty, for subjects as well as princes, was as far off as ever. The stipulations respecting the right to belong to the reformed religion contained fruitful germs of fresh discord and trouble. The unsatisfactory character of these provisions in the treaty was so keenly felt that a clause was inserted requiring that negotiations for religious unity should be diligently carried on, *donec de religione convenerit*. Against the coercion of subjects by their rulers, except so far as the Normal Year [3] afforded them protection, nothing but the right of emigration was secured to the people. The gain which the house of Austria reaped after

---

[3] The ecclesiastical *status quo* of January 1, 1624 — the Normal Year — was to be the standard according to which both Catholics and Protestants were to be permitted the exercise of their religion under a ruler of another denomination.

innumerable sacrifices and exertions was the permanent suppression in its hereditary dominions of the Protestant religion, and the continued banishment of those who had been driven out or had emigrated. But in Vienna the remnants of the ancient imperial power had been forfeited; nothing remained but the shadow, in the shape of a few honorary rights and forms. In fact, France, as the guarantor of the treaty, now became more influential in Germany than the imperial house.

The particular effect of the religious persecutions of those days upon our own time is still felt in the results of the extensive emigrations and colonisations which they occasioned. Since the migration of the barbarian tribes a thousand years before, nothing like it had occurred. Without dwelling here upon the psychological changes effected in the character of nations, I would emphatically call attention to the great shifting of political vigour and consequently of the balance of power which in course of time made itself felt. The state that expels its subjects makes over to the state that admits them flesh of its flesh and blood of its blood, and that too of the healthiest and morally best type. The men who are ready to sacrifice so much that is dear to us all, rather than be forced into lying, deceit, and hypocrisy, are as a rule better and more useful citizens than those who, for want of courage and energy, submit to the constraint, and wear the mask of an authorised faith. England and the Netherlands were strengthened in this way, and Brandenburg-Prussia thus rose step by step to greater power. French refugees flying from before the dragonades of Louis XIV. were willingly received, and brought manifold advantages to the Margravate of Brandenburg. Then came also Protestants from the Palatinate, Waldenses, Mennonites, all seeking an asylum, and liberty for the exercise of their faith. Even in the 18th century Salzburgers, compelled by their ecclesiastical princes to emigrate, found a hospitable reception in Brandenburg. In the year 1780 it was calculated that of the three million inhabitants of the Prussian kingdom one million consisted of the descendants of immigrants.

Never, it may be affirmed, was a country rendered so miserable by the dissensions of religious party strife as Bohemia. National hatred betwixt Czech and German aggravated the religious schism and made it irremediable. The mischief began with the disastrous burning of the two theologians Huss and Jerome of Prague by order of the Council of Constance. Five crusades followed one upon another from Germany against Bohemia, all ending unhappily and even shamefully for the Germans. The attempt to arrive at peace or at least at mutual toleration upon the basis of the compact of Basle (A.D. 1433) was frustrated by a papal edict. After streams of blood had been shed by Germans and Bohemians over the question of the chalice in the Lord's Supper, we turn over a new page of their history. The reformer of Wittenberg adopts the Hussite tenets and develops them. The Bohemians engraft German Protestantism upon their previous faith, and it soon becomes apparent that, except a very small minority, the whole nation, German as well as Czech, has become Lutheran. But the battle on the Weissenberg (A.D. 1620) brought ruin alike to Bohemian Protestantism and Czech nationality. A third of the nation, it is reckoned, emigrated at that time. Whole towns were devastated, Czech literature and education were suppressed, even their books were destroyed. In fifteen years, at the death of the Emperor Ferdinand II., Bohemia had been transformed ostensibly from a Protestant into a Catholic country. What is going on there at the present time is the effect of the deeds then done.

Less unfortunate than Bohemia, which might well be called the Job of nations, was Hungary, and yet she also suffered unutterably from religious oppression and persecution, especially in the 17th century, so that at times Turkish rule was reckoned more tolerable than Austrian. A plan for the religious conquest of Hungary had been devised in Vienna and Buda-Pesth. To allow of this being carried out, Hungary was forced to remain for many years an open door to the Turkish armies, and Germany forfeited her rights and her honour on the Rhine. The news of the Bloody Assize in Eperies (A.D. 1687) resounded throughout Europe and earned for the monarch the hatred of millions; — the Emperor Joseph I. who strove to heal the grievous wound by mildness and justice reaped, in the war of the Austrian Succession, the bitter fruits of those deeds of violence.

Hungary in those days cast envious glances at the neighbouring country of Transylvania, where five denominations—Catholic, Lutheran, Calvinist, Greek, and Unitarian—although obliged to pay tribute to the Turks, or perhaps for that very reason, lived in religious peace.

One of the most instructive instances, showing how a nation can be ruined by religious intolerance and oppression, is that of Poland, once a powerful country with twenty million inhabitants. In consequence of the union with Lithuania and of conquests in the East, some millions of members of the Greek Church were included among them. In the middle of the 16th century, at the high tide of Protestant conversions, multitudes adopted the evangelical doctrines, partly of the Lutheran and partly of the Calvinist denomination, so that at one time a large majority of the Polish Diet consisted of non-Catholics. But Cardinal Hosius and other bishops invited into the kingdom Jesuits, who forthwith usurped the direction of the upper-class schools and of the whole intellectual life of the nation. King and nobles suffered themselves to be guided by them; and thus fanatical hatred against all sectarians was instilled into the minds of the people. In the towns the popular fury was turned against the persons of the Dissenters, as well as against their churches and presbyteries, and these were burned or pulled down. The compulsory union (A.D. 1595) was a permanent source of vexation and oppression to the adherents of the Eastern Church, and led to bloody wars with the Cossacks. Naturally the sects turned for protection and defence to the neighbouring powers; some to

Russia, others first to Sweden, then to Prussia. These powers concluded treaties by which the governing class was bound to observe the chartered rights of their subjects in future; but under ecclesiastical influence the treaties were speedily broken. So things went on for nearly two hundred years. The foreign powers were drawn more and more deeply into Polish affairs. The result is well known; a kingdom and a nation, from which all political vigour had departed, incapable any longer of standing alone, was partitioned amongst others.

With regard to Italy, it is sufficient to say that, according to the acknowledgment of the popes themselves, it was only the Inquisition which saved the Catholic religion there in the 16th century. Yet even this mighty institution was powerless against the little band of Waldenses in Savoy. They have now existed for seven centuries, and their history is a true martyrology. The widespread opinion, that by the persistent application of the well-known means of coercion and extermination every strange doctrine can be rooted out, has been brilliantly refuted by this little people. Countless times have the iron blows of the Holy Office fallen upon this anvil. Villages were burnt, the people themselves slaughtered in heaps, or driven into the inaccessible fastnesses of the mountains, where they perished of hunger or sickness. Assaults were made upon them from all quarters, by secular as well as by ecclesiastical authorities, and by the members of all orders; even princesses showed themselves not the least cruel of their persecutors. The weapon of slander was unsparingly used against them. Whenever they could, they emigrated, and settled wherever a ray of hope for liberty of conscience rested on them,—in Germany, in the Netherlands, or in Switzerland. To-day they are free in their home and throughout Italy; they have formed congregations in the towns, and enjoy the full protection of the law.

We must turn our eyes westwards if we would discover

the working centres in which religious freedom was at last so fashioned that it could be appropriated by the rest of Christendom as a precious acquisition and a salutary possession for all. These were England, the Netherlands, and North America.

England took the lead. Yet even here the end was not attained without a struggle which lasted two hundred years, a struggle carried on with unexampled perseverance and devoted self-sacrifice. A bloody civil war lasting for years, the upsetting of a throne, and the overthrow of a dynasty, had to intervene before the principle of liberty of conscience became a national conviction penetrating all civil and political life. Not until then did all parties recognise that without liberty of conscience men cannot attain to civil freedom, or maintain it for any length of time.

England under the Tudors had given her adherence to an Episcopal State Church, which, according to the design of the founders, was destined, in strict alliance with the monarchy, and as the chief support of it, to attain to exclusive authority in the land. But it was just this deviation from the constitution of the Reformed churches on the continent—the supremacy of the king and the hierarchy of bishops, together with the fact that much out of the ritual of the older church had been retained—that was offensive and intolerable to the numerous followers of a purer Calvinism. So the Puritans formed themselves into a sect in opposition to the church, and in the course of the seventeenth century divided into three denominations—Presbyterians, Independents, and Baptists.

After the year 1640 and through the Long Parliament (1649-1653) the Presbyterians, who had found their chief support in Scotland, got the upper hand in church government. They were as exclusive and intolerant towards other denominations as the Episcopal Church had been. When Cromwell by means of his army, chiefly composed of Independents, rose at length to power, and shortly afterwards to sole government, he, with the assistance of his friend, the poet Milton, and of Goodwin, the theologian, drew up a plan for the friendly union and legal equality of all Protestant parties and communities, but of them only; for the Catholics were excluded, and, in reality, this union found its strongest support in an offensive and defensive alliance against the threatening power of the old church. At a later time, when King William III. embodied Cromwell's plan in his Act of Toleration (A.D. 1689), Catholics were again excluded.

In districts where Protestants had won the upper hand, whenever the question of religious toleration arose, the position of the Roman Catholics formed the greatest difficulty. Even the friends of general toleration found themselves at fault where Catholics were concerned. How could complete freedom be accorded to those who declared the principle itself to be heresy, and advocated coercion, suppression, and extermination of all who differed from them, as a sacred obligation, from the fulfilment of which they could only be absolved by its practical impossibility? Every bishop had to swear to his supreme head in Rome to persecute heretics to the best of his power; and was it not generally taught that any promise of toleration was only binding so long as the necessity for it lasted?

After the Gunpowder Plot (A.D. 1605), and the disclosures to which it led, had proved that, as a result of the doctrines so widely diffused amongst the Catholics, the life of the king was continually threatened, James I. endeavoured to secure himself by prescribing to the Catholics, as a condition of toleration, the taking of an oath of fealty. The form of oath required that, in spite of any possible sentence of deposition, they should remain faithful to their king, and that they should reject as godless and heretical the doctrine which set forth that princes, excommunicated or deposed by the pope, ought to be deposed and murdered by their subjects. The pope at once prohibited the taking of this oath.

Subsequently, when the toleration to be granted to

those who were separated from the Established Church had become a vital question of government policy, an attempt was again made to render the Catholics politically harmless in the eyes of their Protestant fellow-citizens. They were to subscribe to three points—first, that the pope could not absolve English subjects from their allegiance to the governing power; secondly, that an oath sworn to a heretic was binding; and, thirdly, that it was not permissible to take the life of a heretic, or excommunicated person. Many priests had already declared that these points contained nothing contrary to the Catholic faith, when a papal prohibition again interposed, coupled with the command that ecclesiastics of any order who had given in their adhesion to the oath in this form were to be punished and banished from England.

Thus it came about that not only England, but the whole of Protestant Europe, long held fast to the opinion that the safety of monarchs and of states was incompatible with the concession of full religious liberty and political equality to the Catholics. Even before this time, when the English Catholics had been hoping through Charles I. and his French wife, Henrietta, for an amelioration of their position, Holden, an English theologian attached to the University of Paris, had declared his opinion that the Jesuits must first be induced to leave England, for as long as they remained in the country the Catholics would be suspected and hated.

Next to England the Republic of the Netherlands, now freed from Spanish rule, became a nursery of religious freedom. During eighty years of incessant warfare this little state, a mere handful of men vastly outnumbered by the Spaniards, preserved its self-reliance and political independence amid constant sacrifices for faith and freedom. By the Peace of Münster the exhausted and humiliated Spaniards were forced to acknowledge this, and to cede to the new Republic, which by this time had become a naval power of the first rank, their acquisitions in the East and West Indies.

The majority of the population of the Netherlands had adopted the teaching of Calvin, and a firmly organized church had grown up there, as in Geneva and in Scotland. It was natural at that time that its clergy, strong in the favour and confidence of their congregations, should endeavour to make this reformed church supreme. At the Synod of Dort (A.D. 1618–1619) the victory seemed to be secured for exclusive, intolerant Calvinism. But with political freedom granted, religious freedom could not long be withheld. The Netherlands became the asylum for all the persecuted from other places, and prudent councillors and statesmen soon recognised that, by guaranteeing the free exercise of religion, their country could not fail to gain in wealth and power.

The peaceful severely moral and law-abiding Mennonites or Baptists, had collected in considerable numbers in the Netherlands. In spite of the difference as regards the rite of baptism, their agreement with the common doctrines of Protestants was sufficient to win for them toleration. Lutherans from Germany had likewise formed congregations, which the States-General had good cause to treat not only with toleration but with favour.

The Catholics did not fare so well. They inspired the rulers of the state with constant fear, partly on account of their numbers, partly because they were secret adherents of the hereditary Spanish foe, or, at all events, were considered as such. It was known well enough that Spanish influence preponderated in Rome, and that the Catholic Netherlanders would, as far as in them lay, obey the mandates that issued from thence. Consequently in A.D. 1576 they had already been forbidden in Holland and Zealand to hold public worship, or to celebrate mass excepting in private houses. In other respects their position in the Netherlands was far better than that of the Protestants in Catholic countries.

It was principally religion which led to the establishment of the first colonies in North America. English Puritans, the so-called 'Pilgrim Fathers,' flying from the persecution of the Stuarts and their Episcopal Church, settled themselves in A.D. 1628 in Massachusetts. They gave themselves a theocratic constitution, so strictly organized with a view to excluding dissentients in religion, that in A.D. 1631 two-thirds of the population were debarred from the exercise of political rights. Having begun, in the spirit of Calvin, with the closest union of church and state, they passed through a course of natural development to the complete separation of the two, by the Act of Federation, A.D. 1783, and to the decision that all public offices could be held independently of religious creed. A year later it was determined that Congress, the highest power in the state, should on no account interfere with religious affairs.

But in the early days, when Puritanism so flourished in America that the popular regard for their own sect left no room for large-hearted toleration, persecution followed, and the Quakers especially had much to endure.

Meanwhile English Catholics, under the leadership of Lord Baltimore, founded the colony of Maryland, where equality for all denominations of Christians was at once proclaimed as a fundamental principle. Thus it happened that in North America, where Protestants were greatly in the majority, Catholics were the first, by the proclamation of the year 1649, to give practical effect to the principle of religious equality.

On the Protestant side the Baptists and the Quakers were the first to tread in the same path. The preacher, Roger Williams—a highly honoured name in American history—became in the little state of Rhode Island the apostle of liberty of belief. His book, 'The Bloody Tenet of Persecution,' written with glowing enthusiasm, opened the eyes and hearts of many. By the constitution of this state it is distinctly laid down that the principal object of its foundation was to give practical testimony to the fact that a flourishing community could be best

organized and upheld with complete religious freedom.
The Quaker state of Pennsylvania followed this example,
and here also Catholics were tolerated, although they had
been excluded from participation in religious freedom by
other states of North America.

Even in America it took a century and a half of struggle
and strife before full religious liberty was established in all
the states. During the century that has elapsed since the
separation from the mother-country, this liberty has been
maintained intact, and it now rules the popular conscience
to a degree hardly to be found elsewhere.

Throughout the Latin and German countries of Europe
and America freedom of conscience now exists, and if we
compare our own century with the 16th and 17th we perceive that a complete and irresistible change of opinion
has passed over the world; that incidents which in the
first and second period of the Reformation were still, so to
speak, of daily occurrence, have now become impossible.
The great church bodies are no longer satisfied with mere
reciprocal toleration, but claim and receive legal equality
in religious matters. The smaller sects enjoy a more or
less limited toleration, and, as a rule, desire nothing more.

Yet even at the present day theory is apt to be far removed from practice. The most numerous and influential
community in the Catholic world, the Order of the Jesuits,
has set itself the task of recommending and defending, as
being in full accordance with the true spirit of Christianity,
the system of coercion, of religious penalties, and of persecution even to extermination. According to the Jesuits the present is a condition of serious error, a falling away from right
teaching and practice. The application of capital punishment as formerly prescribed is, indeed, so far as I can see,
no longer insisted upon; but milder means, imprisonment,
deprivation of food, flogging, and the like, when practicable,
ought even now in these days to be employed. Those who
err from the true faith must be treated as insane. This is

the teaching to be found in the writings of the Cardinals Tarquini, Liberatore, Florian Riess, and others; and it is well known that, within the limits of the Order, no difference of opinion is tolerated.

With regard to such teaching, Count Montalembert said, shortly before his death, when speaking of the *Civiltà Cattolica*, the accredited organ of the Jesuits and of the Curia : 'They treat the church like one of those wild beasts that are led about in a menagerie. " Study it well," they seem to say, "and learn to understand its nature now that it is in its cage, subdued and tamed by force of circumstances; but remember it has claws and fangs, and when once it is let loose, then you will see what it can do ! " '

In the same spirit the present Duc de Broglie has pointed out how the anti-religious literature and daily press in France are completely in harmony with the church writers on this question of religious coercion. 'Both,' he says, 'agree in affirming that the practice of state intolerance is an article of faith for every Catholic, and that the assertion of religious liberty is heresy. The church exercises its penal authority over heretics whensoever and as far as she can. If, sometimes, she tolerates them here or there, she does so only as a temporary evil is endured, in the hope of getting rid of it on the first opportunity. But nowhere can she recognise religious liberty as a permanent principle of Christian society. Intolerance is justified so soon as it is possible.' De Broglie then proceeds to show how anti-religious newspapers and other publications assiduously give the widest publicity to such statements and opinions of the ecclesiastical organs, and how this fact in some measure accounts for the profound hatred with which a great part of the nation regards the clergy.

When, in the year 1863, Catholics of different countries, principally of France and Belgium, attended a congress at Mechlin, Count Montalembert, amid general applause, declared that of all kinds of liberty freedom of conscience was the most sacred, precious, legitimate, and indispensable. Whilst thus energetically testifying his abhorrence of religious coercion and of the penal system, Montalembert could only account for the past by gross perversion of historical facts. According to him, princes and governments had been to blame. Still further went Deschamps, the disciple of Liguori, afterwards Cardinal and Archbishop of Mechlin, by affirming that the rebellions so punished had never been anything but political.

Genuine, complete equality, as a sentiment prevailing over and penetrating the whole of society, is impossible so long as one church is continually threatening another and ceaselessly proclaiming, as the heathen did to the Christians of old : ' *Non licet esse vos;* your very existence is an evil ; whenever the time comes we shall again use all our endeavours for your extermination.' So long as such sentiments are entertained by one church, others will not lay aside their arms, and instead of true peace there can never be more than a truce.

Thus the question still confronts us which for 1800 years has remained unsolved ; the great dispute is still far from being at an end. In America, it is true, scarcely any one would think seriously of the possibility of a retrograde movement ; but it is otherwise in Europe. The tenacity of purpose in those master spirits who set before them the endeavour to bring practice once more into conformity with their theory must not be underrated. The final result cannot be doubtful to any one capable of understanding the unchanging laws of history.

APPENDIX.

FRAGMENTS from a proposed enlargement of the lecture upon religious freedom.

Liber Pontificalis.

The Pontifical Book (*Liber Pontificalis*, ed. Vignoli, i. 125), brought together in its present form towards the end of the seventh century, betrays the design of appropriating to the popes the right of exercising coercion against heretics. It records how in Rome Pope Siricius (A.D. 384–A.D. 398) punished the Manichæans with banishment. In reality at that period it would only have been possible for the emperor or the prefect representing him in the city to do so.

Missionaries of the Middle Ages.

The propagators of the faith in those days (about the time of Charles the Great and later, comp. above p. 235) were usually wanting in moderation, in subtle, adaptive insight into the thoughts and feelings of the heathen, in patient forbearance and consideration for their weaknesses, very frequently also in correct knowledge of their language. Those whom they aimed at converting were usually aware that the missionary would speedily be followed by his prince or king bringing servitude with him.

Laws against the Heretics.

Throughout the earlier Middle Ages—until the thirteenth century—no statutes are to be found either in the canons of synods, or in secular codes enacting corporal punishment for heretics. We meet with only a couple of isolated instances, in the tenth and eleventh centuries, when kings caused sentence of death to be carried out. These took place under King Robert in France and the Emperor Henry III. in Germany.

Christendom and Islam.

Between these two religions, essentially opposed as they are in character, there was one point of agreement, namely, that both declared bloodshed and extermination to be the easiest and surest means of ensuring the salvation of men. All that perished were martyrs—even those countless multitudes who fell victims to pestilence, want, hardship, or hunger. This was believed by Christians as well as Moslems. Both regarded war, as then carried on, with its accompanying miseries and devastations, as a Divine ordinance extending to all time, seeing that unbelievers and misbelievers would never cease to exist. To the Moslem, indeed, it was easy enough to bring this world and the next into accord. For the Moslem Paradise is but the prolongation and intensifying of sensual joys, with lovely women, exquisite viands and beverages. But how could such a conception be made to harmonize with that of Western Christendom, where it was preached that the blessedness of the next world was a condition of pure, untroubled love, an eternal contemplation of the Deity, and a complete union of the human with the Divine will, which in itself is only infinite love? . . . .

Thomas Aquinas.

Thomas says: 'Assuredly baptism is invalid when the rite is imposed upon a man by force. But if a man through terror, through threats, or ill-treatment is brought to submit to the rite being administered to him, then he really receives the sacrament ('In IV.' dist. 6, quæst. 1, art. 2). Hence it followed that if such a one betrayed any leaning towards his former faith and customs, he was looked upon as a schismatic, and was liable to be punished as a heretic.

The Inquisition.

One product of this new institution was the development of belief in possession and witchcraft. The clergy thought that the constancy with which unbelievers endured the most agonizing deaths, as well as their gift of winning proselytes, and of attracting multitudes to listen to their teaching, could only be explained by the supposition that they were in league with the powers of evil, and worked wonders through the help of Satan. That very constancy, out of admiration for which the veneration of martyrs and the whole system of worship of the saints had arisen, was now, to the astonishment of all observers, displayed by condemned heretics; this was an unheard-of scandal and danger, which could only be met by severer tortures and by confessions of Satanic intercourse wrung from the sufferers.

The Church of the Reformation.

It now came to pass that in the place of bishops, secular princes and the magistrates of the Imperial towns everywhere assumed the government of the reformed churches by the desire of the reformers, or at all events with their consent. Hence consistories, formed of spiritual and secular members, were organized with sovereign authority and entrusted with the direction of church affairs. At first, Luther thought that princes might act as makeshift bishops (*Nothbischöfe*) in rendering such services to the church; but soon afterwards he and Melanchthon devised a far more comprehensive theory—viz. that it was a religious obligation on the part of the governing power to provide for the due observance of the Divine law as contained in the ten commandments; and consequently, in accordance with the first table of the Law, to watch over the preaching of pure doctrine and the corresponding exercise of Divine worship, and if need be to enforce them. Rulers are also called upon to guard their subjects from 'dissensions, factions, and tumults.' In this way the government of the church by the rulers of the land was understood to be a necessary and permanent ordinance of Divine appointment. By this means the church again became a coercive institution. The consistories everywhere set up were composed, after the Saxon pattern, of jurists and theologians, and dealt with church discipline as if it were a police organization. Civil punishments were inflicted for spiritual offences, sins were treated as crimes, absence from Divine worship was punished with fine and imprisonment; communities had no rights, only obligations. Some mitigation of the position may be found in the fact that usually princes and states were in agreement in enforcing the Reformation and in setting up the new church organization. But, on the whole, both portions of the German nation, Catholic as well as Protestant . . .

The Edict of Nantes.

In France the denial of religious liberty had cost a forty years' civil war, carried on with the grossest cruelty, and only at intervals interrupted by a truce. The war was brought to a close (A.D. 1598) by the Edict of Nantes, which King Henry IV., in spite of great opposition, granted to his former co-religionists and companions in arms. The Protestants were permitted to hold all offices, and allowed the right of political organization and of holding secular assemblies, but their exercise of Divine worship was placed under many restrictions, and in the larger, and especially the cathedral towns, it was, if not altogether prohibited, confined to private houses; in Paris and its environs, as well as at the Court, their form of worship was not permitted. Mixed tribunals were, however, conceded to the Protestants, and a great number of places of refuge, with Protestant garrisons, given up to them. Thus they were given at once too little and too much, the latter to their detriment; for a state within a state could not be tolerated for any length of time by such a despotic monarchy as that of France, whilst the Huguenot nobility only relinquished the attempt to erect an independent republic in alliance with foreign governments after two bloody campaigns. From that time forth and after the fall of La Rochelle the Protestants remained peaceful and obedient subjects. The Edict was, nevertheless, a progressive step in civilisation. France thereby raised herself in power, and soon also in intellectual cultivation, above the other countries where religious strife was still rampant. It was proved to be possible that the two churches could live peacefully side by side, and Richelieu was enabled, in alliance with the Protestants of the Netherlands, Germany, and Scandinavia, to sustain a successful struggle with the double power of the Habsburgs.

The Spanish Netherlands.

When Belgium was brought back under Spanish rule, a great emigration of Protestants took place; those who remained behind were made Catholics by the use of the traditional means. With what success, and at what price, became apparent 120 years later, when part of the country passed temporarily under Dutch rule. People, as Fénelon reports to Pope Clement XI., streamed in crowds from the villages into the towns to attend the Protestant service, and felt themselves to be genuine Protestants, whose forefathers for more than a hundred years had deceived the clergy and passed their lives in a continual state of dissimulation.—(*Corresp. de Fénelon*, iii. 376.)

VII

VARIOUS ESTIMATES OF THE FRENCH REVOLUTION[1]

THAT highly gifted woman, the daughter of Necker, an eye-witness and participant in the drama of the Revolution, said in the year 1797, that foreign nations ought to abstain from forming a depreciatory estimate of the state of things brought about in France by the Revolution. A century must elapse before it would be possible to measure the height of greatness and dignity to which France might again attain.

Sixty years afterwards her grandson, the present Duc de Broglie, wrote:

Les doctrines de 1789, prises dans leur véritable acception, forment donc une sorte de foi publique qui survit aux faiblesses des apôtres et aux égarements des disciples. C'est une terre promise dont l'image ne périt pas. Beaucoup de nos pères ont pu mourir au désert en désespérant de l'atteindre ; moins excusables qu'eux, nous avons pu mériter de la perdre et de la pleurer dans l'exil. Cependant elle existe ; nous le savons, car nous avons goûté sa paix ; son souvenir vit au fond des cœurs et le malheur passe sans l'effacer.[2]

Under Napoleon III. this note of lamentation was all that was allowed expression.

Since then thirty years have passed away ; the empire

[1] [Fragments from a lecture delivered before the Academy of Munich, of which no consecutive manuscript has been found. Two versions of the preamble have come to hand, but of which of these Döllinger made use in his lecture I cannot remember, nor easily find out.]

[2] *Etudes morales et littéraires*, par Albert de Broglie, Paris, 1853, p. 93.

has fallen, de Broglie himself has for a short time been at the head of his country's government, but the land of promise—peaceful, constitutional monarchy is still as far off and unapproachable as ever. The most eminent Frenchmen are of opinion that the National Assembly of 1789 signally proved that the French nation was unfitted by its past for this form of government; and, moreover, the Assembly itself did everything to render it impossible, or, at any rate, untenable. All are agreed in recognising the benefits of the Revolution — liberation from a court, and the rule of a court like that of Versailles; civil equality; the reform of the administration of justice; the opening up of a career to every talent and every taste. Yet thoughtful men consider that some of the gifts of the revolution are the gifts of the Danai, and contain a germ of death — the abrogation, for instance, of the testamentary power of the parent. The historical glory of the Revolution will not survive the attacks of Taine. The illusion is destroyed. Still, I doubt whether many Frenchmen would readily endorse De Tocqueville's final verdict: 'The French people of to-day stand far below those of the eighteenth century. Seventy years of revolution have quenched our courage, our faith, our self-reliance, our public spirit, and, in the great majority of the upper classes, even our passions—excepting those of vanity and avarice.'

A blast of discouragement and sadness has evidently passed over the minds of the best and wisest thinkers on the banks of the Seine. Nevertheless, *sanabiles Deus fecit nationes!* So gifted a people, endowed with strong intellectual powers, still rich in the noblest productions of the mind, and foremost amongst the Latin nations, will and must rise again to political greatness. It would least of all become us Germans to doubt of the future of France. Germany after the Thirty Years' War was suffering more sorely from murderous, self-inflicted wounds, and had sunk far lower than has France at the present day.

In a few years France will celebrate the centenary of her first great revolution. It will be honoured as a great national festival, dedicated to the glorious memory of an event which raised France to be the political leader of Europe, and which procured for her a rich harvest of permanent advantages.

We all know that the fortunes of Germany have been largely affected by the occurrences of the year 1789. The French Revolution has some connexion, more or less close, with all that has happened to us during the last ninety years. The history of that political convulsion touches us so nearly, and is so remarkable as an event in the history of mankind, so full of instruction and warning, that we are forced to study it with the same interest, and in the same spirit of earnest investigation and criticism, with which we treat the great events of our own history. A thorough acquaintance with the origin and course of the great revolution is necessary before we can form a judgment upon it, or hazard a conjecture as to its issues in the future.

If, as is generally admitted, France is still in a state of revolution, must not every thoughtful man ask himself when and how the process of recovery from this century of political and social disease is likely, clearly and unmistakably, to set in? It is a question to which history alone can supply an answer, and even then only to the few who understand how to read and interpret her hieroglyphics.

The literature of the subject is overwhelming. German and French authors have vied with each other in depicting the great and fatal tragedy. Statesmen, far-famed scholars and brilliant masters of style, such as Thiers, Mignet, Michelet, Lamartine, Droz, Barante, and a long series of less honoured names, have applied themselves to the task in France. Germany contributes the works of celebrated historians like Wachsmuth, Niebuhr, Schlosser, Eduard Arnd, Zinkeisen, Häusser, Dahlmann, Von Sybel. England has Carlyle.

But many of the works of these authors bear only too strongly the impress of their time and of the political circumstances under which they were written. The strict censorship which existed under the first Napoleon forbade any honest presentation of recent facts, and in the works belonging to the period of the Restoration we are sensible of the combative spirit of the day. The political opposition and strife between Liberals and Royalists inevitably threw both parties back upon the history of the Revolution. The Liberals exerted themselves to establish a fundamental difference between the years 1789 and 1793. The Royalists contended, on the contrary, that the Reign of Terror was only the logical development of the principles and deeds of 1789, that Lafayette and Barnave were only the forerunners of Robespierre.

At a later period, after the revolution of 1830, a multitude of imitators followed along the path thus opened for them. There were some who, while admitting that there had been occasional errors, undertook to justify the whole revolution, especially the Convention and the party of the Mountain. Far from needing palliation and excuse, *la Terreur* was held up to admiration. Saint-Just and Robespierre became heroes, and Danton was justly punished for his subsequent attempt to check the bloodshed.

Auguste Thierry has laboured with wonderful acuteness and great expenditure of erudition to represent in the Revolution an occurrence which on historical grounds was as justifiable as it was needful. Under the designation of Jacques Bonhomme, he has represented the poor Gallic people as for centuries ill-treated and trampled upon by their Frankish conquerors, suffering the grossest oppression with inexhaustible patience, and always remaining entirely distinct from the dominant race. He maintains that the condition of the Gallico-Roman people under Frankish rule resembled that of the Greeks under the Turk. In the Revolution this struggle between two races burst out into a decisive conflict, which is to be regarded as the triumph of the

Romans over the Teutonic Franks. Auguste Thierry's brother, Amadée, who may also be reckoned amongst the most distinguished of French historians, once, after the Revolution of February, said to a German literary man that the historical consequence of this European convulsion could be no other than the entire liberation and severance of the Latin (*Romanenthum*) from the Teutonic (*Germanenthum*) element.

Foremost amongst the panegyrists of the Revolution of 1789 stand Mignet and Thiers, whose works met with immense success, and, besides making a profound impression upon the educated classes, were soon offered to the lower classes in a popular and less refined form. They are written in a spirit of fatalism; even the horrors and crimes recorded are regarded as the logical sequence of the advent of a new epoch in human life. Thiers is always on the side of the victor; the conquered, the despoiled, the beaten side has in his eyes no right to complain; the giant wheels of the Juggernaut-car of Revolution have passed over them simply because they were in the way.

The history of the Revolution thus revised to suit French taste had the effect of an intoxicating drink. The intoxication reached its height in the year 1847 with the appearance of Lamartine's 'Girondins,' in practical importance by far the most remarkable work that his pen produced. 'This romantic and sentimental rehabilitation of the Reign of Terror had at the time an immense effect. The work had an extraordinary and truly national success: when the crisis came (though certainly nobody then imagined it to be so near at hand) it marked the author of the book as the man of the time.' The conclusion was patent; he who was capable of such intelligent comprehension of the First Revolution, who had entered so sympathetically into its spirit, must be the statesman best fitted to guide the new revolution. And so it came to pass. Lamartine's book without doubt did much to eliminate that fear of the Republic which had survived in the public mind ever since the last decade of the eighteenth century.

The history of the Girondins appeals much less to the judgment and principles than to the imagination and nerves of the reader. It depicts the scenes of heroism and horror, the thrilling and stirring incidents of the Revolution, at one moment tragical, at another burlesque, with the detail and high colouring of an historical romance. The subject took possession of Lamartine's imagination; he became intoxicated with his own narrative. The horrors of the Revolution are, of course, neither praised nor justified, but their hideousness disappears under the dramatic charm of the skilful grouping and the flowing eloquence which mark the whole narrative. To a generation weary with the tedium of existence, and athirst for novelty at any price, the atrocious deeds and stirring fortunes of their fathers were brilliantly depicted in a work which combines the seductive charm of romance with the apparent trustworthiness of sober history. Involuntarily, the villainy of the Girondins was forgotten in admiration for their audacity and in sentimental pity for their downfall.[3]

In France at the present moment the First Revolution has still a numerous circle of worshippers. How far this idolatry is carried we know from Victor Hugo, the gifted poet, who places before the eyes of his countrymen their own thoughts, either in a poetic garb or else with rhetorical adornment. 'The French Revolution,' he says, 'is the greatest step in progress that humanity has made since the time of Christ. France has put forward the Encyclopædists, the Physiocratists, the Philosophers, and the Utopians—four noble armies, ready to do battle for suffering humanity.'

Henri Martin, the author of a copious and widely read history of France, which was more than once crowned by the Academy, has also within the last few years published a history of the time of the Revolution. In tendency this work is similar to those of Mignet and Thiers. His favourite heroes are the Girondins; the First Republic is a period of infinite glory: this Republic conquered the whole

[3] Comp. *Preuss. Jahrbücher*, viii. 1861, p. 113 f.

world; but as it knew not how to conquer its own passions it lacerated itself with its own hands and perished, choked by a military despotism. The Third Republic, that of to-day, exists under a more favourable star; it has regenerated France, and will revive her greatness and restore to her the Rhine frontier with all that belongs to it.

Martin cherished these hopes till the day of his death, and left behind him a school which aspires, by means of popular pamphlets, to inoculate the world with his views of history.

Our own Herman Grimm is a follower of Martin. He regards the French Revolution of the last hundred years as the upheaval of the Celtic subsoil out of the Roman stratum which formed the overlying arable land, and represented the intellect, the energy, and the wealth of the country. France, the country of the Celts, lying between the Meuse and the Pyrenees, fertilized for two thousand years by Teutonic and Latin blood, has again become the ancient Gaul. Worn, wearied, and exhausted in the noblest sense, the French race again makes way for the rabble of Celts, which, rising like the released dregs of the population, smothers with its scum the remains of the Roman element and drags it down to itself. We follow the course of this process as it advances by fits and starts, and we see how as the aggressive portion of the race becomes dominant, the weaker succumbs. The time must come when the last breath of opposition will be spent, and the pre-historic Gallic element under Druid leadership will celebrate its decisive victory. What manner of men this result may bring forth, let Cæsar, or recent French history, inform us.[4]

A salutary reaction against this idolizing of the Revolution set in under the Second Empire with the works of Granier, Mortimer Ternaux, and Barante. But the most decided advocates of this change of opinion were Tocqueville and Taine.

Taine tears to pieces the legend of 'the rosy dawn of the

[4] *Preuss. Jahrbücher*, 27, 1871, p. 588.

Revolution.' Malouet had already remarked, 'The Reign of Terror—*la Terreur*—begins with July 14' (1789). The date might be put even further back. Lawlessness began from the very first; there was no central power, nor security for life and property. It was hunger that caused riots and attacks on castles. It was the fatal destiny of the French Revolution to have famine for its forerunner, and want, misery, and bankruptcy for its companions, to which was soon added a double war.

Taine enumerates six '*Jacqueries*' in the time of the National Assembly. The Revolution caused them, for it exposed the prevailing injustice and abuses, proclaimed the rights of the people, and substituted, in the place of the old resignation, a spirit of revenge.

The old machinery of government came at once to a standstill. Justice, finance, administration, army, everything was unhinged. It was no longer revolution, says Taine, but dissolution. The old régime was convulsed in the agonies of death. The National Assembly especially loses most of its attraction in the light that Taine throws upon it; it was composed almost entirely of young men without experience and without political training. They were completely fettered in their undertakings; in Paris and in Versailles they already groaned under the 'yoke of popular control, beneath which their two predecessors had been crushed.'

Just at the moment when the art of government had become more than ever difficult, journalists and pamphleteers were busied in popularising it, and representing it as universally attainable, as though every one could understand and give an opinion upon it. 'Each one considered himself fitted to take part in the government of his country.' Even the king himself thought that the nation understood more about governing than he. Dumont aptly observed at that time that if any one in the two cities of London and Paris were to ask the passers-by in the street whether they were ready forthwith to undertake the government of the state, in London out of a hundred persons ninety-nine would answer 'No,' whilst in Paris ninety-nine would answer 'Yes.'

It is a much disputed question whether, in the year 1789, or even fifteen years earlier, on the accession of Louis XVI., it might still have been possible to avert the revolution, and through timely reforms undertaken by the government to save both throne and people.

Contemporaries would, for the most part, have answered the question affirmatively. Even now there are some who would do so. One of the best historians of the Revolution, Droz, has expressed this opinion even in the title of his book, for it professes to give a history of the years during which it would still have been possible to avert the revolution, or to direct it. Count Pontmartin [3] says that he suffers the torments of Tantalus when he sees in the documents and papers that have recently come to light how mistakes might have been avoided, and preventive measures adopted.

The student most thoroughly acquainted with the France of 1789 was of a different opinion. 'When,' says de Tocqueville, 'one recalls the incarnate abominations of that period with sufficient vividness to imagine oneself a contemporary spectator, one becomes convinced how impossible it would have been for the revolution not to break out.'

In the recognition of the fact that reform was impossible, and that with the first shock a convulsion became inevitable, lies, as it seems to me, the decided advance which our age has made towards the right understanding of history through the opening of fresh sources of information and through more careful examination of the older. For if a sick man is to recover, the organs which have not been attacked by the disease must, for the most part, be healthy; but if all of them, especially the most vital, are diseased, recovery is impossible.

A Conservative party, like that which almost every

[3] In his article on Malouet's Memoirs, *Nouveaux Samedis*, xi. 85.

country has produced in our own time, a party whose principle is to preserve and uphold that which exists, was not at that time to be found in France.

It is significant that Mably, the only man amongst the *literati* of that day who had studied French history, was not only entirely free from the hopeful delusions in which his contemporaries were apt to indulge, but was a decided pessimist. Whenever the government passed a good and useful measure, he said: 'So much the worse! That will give the old machine which we have got to overthrow another respite.'*

It is remarkable that Goethe, the careful and sympathetic student of the French literature of the eighteenth century, has observed such a strict, I might almost say such an anxious, silence upon this great event, although he, like all Germans, must have been both moved and shocked by its consequences. I can find amongst his writings only one passage on the subject, though this is certainly a striking one. After reading the history of Louis XVI. by Soulavie, he remarks: 'Looked at broadly, the impression left is similar to that produced when mountain torrents and streams, propelled by an irresistible impulse of Nature, pouring from the heights down many ravines and valleys, combine at last to cause the ruthless flood, which overwhelms alike him who foresaw its approach and him who never expected it. We can discern in this monstrous catastrophe nothing but an outbreak of relentless natural forces, no trace of that which we philosophers love to signalise as liberty.'

Goethe recognised that, in opposing this irresistible process of dissolution, all human thought and endeavour must fail, that no individual could break through this brazen chain of cause and effect, or check the disaster. When such a fate befalls a great people, it must necessarily impress the poet as would a catastrophe in Nature, a volcanic outburst, or a flood. But any one who studies the real history of this people, not merely the court history, and reflects upon

* *Supplément au Cours de Littérature*, par La Harpe, 1810, p.

the social and political conditions of the nation, perceives that assuredly here also we have to deal with a process which worked itself out in accordance with moral laws, and consequently with freedom. Yes, with freedom. For even in a whole people, or a class, or an order, there is, and abides, free will, and with it responsibility.

When we mark the influence exercised by a false view of ancient history on the general course of the French Revolution; when we find examples of Roman and Greek heroes cited to excuse every murder for which a political pretext could be found; every atrocity lauded as an act of virtue if a parallel for it could be gathered from the life of a so-called great man by some classic author, it becomes evident that not only the way in which, during the eighteenth century, ancient history was studied, was ruinous to taste, but that the line taken by the encyclopædists, to whom the thorough investigation of historical events appeared superfluous, and who purposely distorted facts for the sake of establishing certain theories, was in the highest degree pernicious, both to learning, and to the whole moral development of France.[7]

One cause of the Revolution hitherto but little noticed lay in the condition of the Universities, and in the multitude of their students. The number in proportion to the population was greater than it is at the present day. Before 1789 France had 562 colleges with more than 72,000 pupils, of whom about 40,000 were foundation scholars (*boursiers*) who received instruction and board and lodging gratuitously, either altogether or in part. In France at the present day there are only 4949 such scholars in 200 colleges or educational institutions, and therefore fewer by 35,000 than in 1789, although the population has increased from twenty-five to thirty-eight millions. Thus it was, that year by year an enormous flock of half-educated

[7] Comp. Eötvös, *Herrschende Ideen*, i., 1851, p. 408.

literary proletarians was turned out from the lecture-rooms into the world, with but slight prospect of winning a good position in life, since the whole of the public service, in consequence of the sale of offices, belonged to and was hereditary in certain families. The consequence was that a very large number of discontented young men were ready to become the tools of the leaders of the revolutionary movement and to fan the flame of discontent by pamphlets and newspaper articles. The country swarmed with lawyers far beyond the requisite number. We find in the National Assembly, besides 176 merchants and farmers, 279 lawyers, exclusive of sixty-two officials of the lower courts,—a majority therefore of at least 340 jurists, whose whole stock of learning was limited to an acquaintance with Latin, to reminiscences of Brutus Cassius and Cato, with perhaps a fragmentary knowledge of French history and of Roman law acquired in the unscientific fashion in which it was then studied. These were the people to whom the decision of every question was entrusted; in their hands lay the fate of France.

Quite the worst of the manifold diseases and infirmities from which the body politic in France then suffered was the court at Versailles. The letters of Louis XIV.'s sister-in-law, Elizabeth Charlotte, as well as those of Madame de Maintenon, give us a glimpse into the wicked corruption of the court in their day. During the orgies of the Regency and the sixty years of Louis XV.'s reign, things became even more hopeless. The court, with its dependencies, consisted of 60,000 persons, whose mission it was to serve and to entertain two persons; and these two, the king and his consort, were all the while submitting with reluctance to the burdensome constraint imposed upon them by court tradition.

From Versailles, the residence of the court and of the royal family, our eyes turn to another city in the immediate neighbourhood, maintaining the liveliest intercourse with Versailles—Paris, the centre of all the real or cultivated intelligence that then existed in France, the nursery of public opinion which the government had now called into being; the oracle of the provinces, where no one durst form an opinion until that of the capital was known; the focus of all the public offices, ever since the royal plan of centralisation had been carried out. Thither, now that famine had begun periodically to visit France, flocked a swarm of bread-seekers from all parts of the country. Those who had been poor when they arrived quickly sank down into the ranks of the already organized mob, swelling the numbers and strength of the rabble who paraded the streets, and whose occupation was to stir up tumult and riot, to which were soon added murder and plunder. This was the class which, directed by secret leaders, extolled by the daily press and the National Assembly, and hailed as the 'people,' rapidly rose to power. The Assembly which, with the help of this rabble, had overpowered the government, was forced to give way and to formulate decrees at its bidding;—within a few months France had passed from a monarchy to an ochlocracy.

It had become customary to speak of a revolution as of an event which might come to pass in any state in a perfectly natural and even orderly way. People had in their minds revolutions in the palace or the seraglio, or a change in the order of succession such as had been accomplished in the revolution which happened to be best known, that of England in the year 1688. The Abbé Vertot had narrated the history of the Portuguese and Swedish revolutions, and also that of the Roman Republic. But the catastrophe in France was the first to give to the word the meaning of a fundamental political transformation. With a wantonness which now seems to us incredible, and with unsuspecting confidence, the ship of the state was allowed to drift out into a stormy, shoreless ocean. All experience was utterly at fault; the world's history had never before produced a phenomenon of the kind.

It is certain that the suffering classes of the nation would have behaved very differently in the years of preparation before the outbreak of the Revolution if they had been acquainted with their own history and had drawn correct conclusions from it.

[In a review of the causes of the Revolution one item that must not be undervalued is the widespread hatred of the established church.] The church was formerly the most powerful body in the land, and possessed apparently every guarantee of security and durability. But the clergy had long since lost their influence, and had ceased to be trusted by the larger and more enterprising part of the nation; confidence had given place to bitter hatred.

[Let us hear what was said on the eve of the Revolution, by one well acquainted with the situation, as to the feeling that prevailed among the educated classes with regard to the church:]*

'On avait tant mêlé d'erreurs superstitieuses aux vérités de la religion; les écrivains du jour, en nous déroulant nos tristes annales, nous montraient tant de guerres civiles, tant de massacres inhumains, tant de persécutions, tant de princes déposés, tant de sorciers brûlés par le fanatisme, tant de peuples opprimés par les préjugés, par l'ignorance, et par la tyrannie du système féodal; l'expulsion et la spoliation d'un million de Français, pour cause d'hérésie, étaient si récentes; les querelles encore existantes contre les jansénistes et les molinistes, et celles des billets de confessions, nous semblaient si ridicules, qu'il nous était impossible de ne pas saisir, avec enthousiasme, l'espérance, peut-être trop illusoire, que des hommes de génie nous donnaient alors d'un avenir où la raison, l'humanité, la tolérance et la liberté devaient régner sur les derniers débris des erreurs, des folies et des préjugés qui avaient si longtemps asservi et ensanglanté le monde.'

* *Mémoires de Ségur*, 1859, i. p. 88.

269

LECTURE VIII

THE PART TAKEN BY NORTH AMERICA IN LITERATURE[1]

ONLY a few weeks ago an American Congress was holding its sittings in Berlin. Four hundred scholars, European and transatlantic, were assembled to discuss the antiquities of the American continent, the relics of the races that peopled it, and the state of civilisation existing at the time of its discovery, and previous to it. The idea thereupon occurred to me that it would be worth while to take into consideration another American subject, namely, the literature of the United States, the course of its development, and the relation that it bears to the literature of Europe.

The times are gone by when each nation was sufficient for itself, resting content, even in the intellectual world, with its own creations, and rarely overstepping the bounds of its own language and literature to enquire into the literary works of foreign lands, unless they happened to be written in Latin, the common language of the learned. Literature and science have become to an unforeseen degree international; all must supplement, reinforce, and rectify the productions of other civilised nations, and desire to use and to enjoy them. The interchange of ideas between all the nations of the world becomes each year more rapid, general, and comprehensive. The criticism which decides

[1] [Lecture delivered at the Festival of the Academy of Science in Munich December 27, 1888, enlarged from Döllinger's MS.]

upon the worth of eminent works is frequently the unanimous verdict of several nations.

The States of the Union, which now number 61,000,000 inhabitants, arose about two centuries and a half ago out of insignificant beginnings, and were scarcely noticed in their silent growth for a considerable time by the rest of the world.

The first colonists were Englishmen, who, fleeing from oppression at home in search of liberty of conscience, proposed to organize a community in accordance with their own religious principles. The Pilgrim Fathers, the first founders of the six states of New England, belonged to different sects, but of whatever denomination—Presbyterian, Congregationalist, or Baptist—all alike were imbued with the strict moral and religious principles of Calvinistic Puritanism. The Bible and a few religious books which they had brought with them were all they needed. Religion was the first concern of life, especially to their preachers, amongst whom were some learned men, educated at the English universities. Certain controversial questions were much discussed among them, above all that of toleration, which gave rise to Roger Williams's still famous and popular book, 'The Bloody Tenet of Persecution,' a book which struck out a new line, and worked like a fresh revelation, so that its appearance is still looked back upon as an honour to America.

It was fortunate for the Puritans, both English and American, that they possessed in Milton a classical poet qualified to enlarge the circle of their ideas, and to refine their deepest feelings. His 'Samson Agonistes,' that mighty hymn of the chosen champion of God, must have been read with enthusiasm and rapture in New England, so closely does the subject bear upon the fate of the colonists and their fathers. The historian of the earlier American literature[2] mentions a number of poets of the period from

[2] Moses Coit Tyler, *A History of American Literature*, vols. i. and ii. reaching down to 1765. London, 1879.

the end of the seventeenth to the beginning of the eighteenth century. They wrote chiefly on religious subjects, but none of them deserve to be mentioned by the side of Milton. They were rough, fanciful versifiers, rather than poets.

The social influence of the preachers was powerful and strongly marked in these colonies, so much so indeed that Tyler characterizes the Mather family as a dynasty. But the influence of these men was due to their personal qualities—in their writings they only echoed the ideas of European theologians.

The fact that no attempt was made to found an American newspaper before the year 1698 proves that the intellectual needs of the colonists and their families were but slight. The modest leaflet which then made its appearance in Boston was promptly suppressed. Six years later another attempt was made with better success, and for fifteen years a newspaper, issued weekly, and containing a bare record of events without any expression of opinion, remained the only periodical in the colonies. A strict censorship existed under the direction of an ecclesiastic, the president of Harvard College.

So, until far on in the eighteenth century, American literature was kept within very narrow limits. Works on the topography of the different colonies were composed, and narratives of the wars with the Indians and the French, but nothing appeared of lasting value, or likely to rouse the interest of a wider circle. But in theology a star of considerable magnitude arose in the person of the preacher Jonathan Edwards, 1703–1758. He has been described as a man in whom a Calvin and a Fénelon were combined. He was in fact an independent and acute thinker, and an exceedingly prolific writer. He became the founder of a school which exists to this day, and if there be, properly speaking, an American theology, it must exist mainly in connexion with Edwards and his disciples.

The first century, the infancy of the colony, had passed

away; the middle of the eighteenth century had been reached before any man whose name is worth recording in history, or any book fit to take a place in the world's literature, appeared. Then arose Benjamin Franklin, a man with whom few of the world's heroes can compare. He was, to use an English expression, a self-made man. With wonderful moral energy, this son of a tallow-chandler, this poor printer's apprentice, by the force of self-discipline and self-education, trained himself to become a most influential scholar and statesman in his time, an instructor of his countrymen in religion, and their leader in politics. His whole life was a series of successes. His autobiography, written for his son, might well be said to be written for the sons of all nations. The educational influence which this typical life and example has exercised, and still exercises, in the States can hardly be overrated.

This great career naturally brings to our minds a still greater name, held in the highest honour not only by the American nation, but by the whole civilised world—George Washington. Great alike as a soldier and a statesman, he was singularly high-minded and free from selfish ambition, and was actuated solely by patriotism and a sense of duty. He was highly favoured by fortune. The very existence of the new state was due pre-eminently to his creative genius. At the close of his career his loss was mourned by all nations. The most careful scrutiny of his life can discover no dark spot or stain sullying the lustre of his virtues. America must acknowledge herself peculiarly blessed in having the privilege of setting before the rising generation in their homes and in their schools the examples of two such men as Washington and Franklin. About a dozen biographies of Washington have appeared in the States; that by Marshall brought to the publishers a profit of 100,000 dollars.

At the conclusion of the peace of 1783, thirteen colonies, with a population of about three million souls, were inscribed on the roll of independent states. Was the severance from the mother country—the 'home country,' as it was still called—really unavoidable? The British Government in these colonies was by no means tyrannical or oppressive. The breach was principally due to temporary misunderstandings brought about by the fault of a few individuals, above all by the short-sighted obstinacy of the king, and the weakness of his minister, Lord North. Had the old maxim, 'No taxation without representation,' only been put in force, the separation might never have taken place. Relations might easily have been established between the colonies and 'Old England' similar to those at present existing between Canada and England, under which that colony continues prosperous and contented. England would then have been powerful enough to check the despotism of Napoleon on the continent of Europe. In America the monarchical principle would have been preserved in a very mild yet effectual and beneficial form, without depriving her of the power of self-government. The great question of slavery would then, as in other British colonies, have found a peaceful solution, and the four years' war of secession, with its immeasurable sacrifices and far-reaching evil consequences, would have been avoided. Only had such been the course of events, there would, of course, have been no such thing as a special American literature.

The forty or fifty years following the birth of the new republic continued unfruitful in literature. Political party struggles, connected with the gradual organization of the constitution, were productive indeed of much pamphleteering, but of no book of lasting importance. In Europe the opinion prevailed that anything printed in America must be too superficial to deserve the name of literature. As late as 1828 in the most widely read English magazine, the 'Edinburgh Review,' the question is contemptuously asked, 'Who reads an American book?' And even on the further side of the Atlantic the possibility of America taking any part in literature or science was spoken of with great diffidence. In the year 1837 Emerson in a speech observes:

'Perhaps the time is already come . . . when the sluggard intellect of this continent will look from under its iron lids, and fill the postponed expectation of the world with something better than the exertions of mechanical skill. Our day of dependence—our long apprenticeship to the learning of other lands, draws to a close. The millions that around us are rushing into life cannot always be fed on the sere remains of foreign harvests.'[3]

There were four men who at length attracted the attention of Europe to the productions of transatlantic intellect, and who awoke in Americans the idea that they were able and called upon to take an active share in the literary work of the world : Washington Irving, Fenimore Cooper, William Prescott, and William Ellery Channing.

Irving is still by far the most popular and widely read author in America, and deserves to hold a permanent place in the literature of the world. It has been calculated that 60,000 volumes of his works were sold during his lifetime in America alone, and that the yearly sale has since amounted to 30,000 volumes.

Prescott is a literary star of the first magnitude, and would have been an ornament to any nation. His two great historical works, on Ferdinand and Isabella, and on Philip II., the fruit of fifteen years' strenuous labour and preparatory study, stand alone on a par with the works of Ranke and Baumgarten as the best of the kind which this century has produced. His books on the Conquest of Mexico and the Conquest of Peru are not less excellent ; all belong to the literature of the world, and America may well be proud of her citizen who, in spite of a persistent weakness of the eyes, was able to accomplish such tasks.

Channing stands far lower in general importance. Outside the Union his memory is already half effaced, although in America the feeling still justly prevails that much gratitude is due to him. His influence in his time

[3] Emerson's *Works*, vol. ii. p. 174. Bohn's *Standard Library*. London, 1888.

was wide and beneficial. He is reckoned as the most indefatigable and successful opponent of that greatest of American evils, slavery; he prepared its downfall. Eloquently and persistently he enforced on the younger generation the need of independent thought and of the exercise of private judgment. What, to us, perhaps, is displeasing in him is there accounted to his credit; he belongs to the foster-fathers of American Chauvinism. 'In every other country,' says Channing, 'the individual is set aside; here he is recognised.' This, after all, is a modest statement compared with the expressions used in every school and from every platform in America on the yearly commemorative festival of the Constitution, July 4.[4]

In the main England is still the great preceptor of America. She expends in wages and plant at least ten times the amount that she receives from thence. Nevertheless it is apparent that the influence of America upon English national life is continually increasing. England has, indeed, not only kept free from some of the most serious evils in American political life, such as place-hunting and office-selling, but has struck into exactly the opposite path of free competition and examinations. None the less, England regards the great transatlantic republic with mingled feelings of admiration, fear, and envy. The same ideas and measures which, in their French form, act upon the island folk west of the Channel with a deterrent effect, assume so seductive a form in the garb in which America has clothed them that Englishmen are induced to copy them.

So far as literature is concerned America remained until towards the year 1845 much in the position of a young man who, having inherited a considerable fortune from his father, at first seeks only to enjoy it, instead of adding to it by his own enterprise. This remark, however, does not apply to the natural sciences—physics, chemistry, engineering, and mechanics; for these studies had long

[4] [Döllinger's MS. contains no further notice of Fenimore Cooper.]

been pursued with indefatigable zeal and with the happiest results. Libraries of natural science, collections, laboratories of every kind seem to have sprung like mushrooms from the ground. Only to mention one example, there are in America twenty-eight well-equipped astronomical observatories. Indeed, the recent discoveries of natural science have transformed the whole of modern life, and still further victories over the forces of Nature are to be expected. It is to this side of life and science that America with characteristic energy has devoted her powers of thought and investigation. In the sphere of literature, taken in the narrower sense, that is in classical and historical study, the advance towards creative effort has been comparatively slow. A continual and abundant influx of literary works of that kind from the old country has seemed to render the labour of original work superfluous. I must make an exception in favour of some of the articles in the 'Cyclopædia of American Biography' which has been compiled by German-American industry.[5]

It is not surprising that fresh editions of the Bible are yearly issued in the States. Next to the Bible, Bunyan's 'Pilgrim's Progress' appears to be the most popular religious book. This work of fiction, written in prison about the year 1680 by a religious enthusiast of humble origin, is highly prized by the whole Anglo-Saxon race; its deep psychological truth and magnificent well-sustained allegory are thoroughly adapted to the popular mind, and the book is seldom wanting on the shelves of any one calling himself a Christian.

In secular literature, Shakespeare stands first as a matter of course. Sixty editions of his dramatic works have been published in America. The fact that thirteen

[5] Appleton's *Cyclopædia of American Biography*. New York, 1888. Four vols. already published (completed in 1889 in six vols.). This fine work gives a number of illustrations, some of them of excellent quality, of famous or well-known persons, and even of their dwellings. It comprises the whole of America, including Canada, Spanish America, and Brazil; but the men and women of the Union occupy at least eleven twelfths of the space.

editions of Gibbon's great historical work have appeared is a sufficient indication to any one well acquainted with that author, of the current opinion amongst Americans regarding the history of the first ten centuries after Christ, and of their incapacity to appreciate the productions of the German historical school. It should also be mentioned that eight editions of Plutarch's 'Lives' have appeared, a proof that they are more read in America than in Germany.

It is a good sign, I think, of the healthiness of American taste that within the last few years four editions of old Chaucer, seven of Spenser's 'Fairy Queen,' and as many as forty-six of the poems of the Scotch peasant Burns have been published. Goldsmith's 'Vicar of Wakefield' has been printed ten times within eight years. Of the numerous works of fiction by Dickens, nineteen editions have been sold; and of Macaulay's 'History of England,' six. These figures point to the conclusion that the American, despite social and political differences, remains thoroughly Anglo-Saxon in intellectual thought and feeling, retaining all the characteristics of the race, and that the educated classes, at least, ought not to be judged from their newspapers. How very different is the impression we derive from a consideration of the books that have run through twenty or thirty editions among our western neighbours in the shortest space of time!

The rights of foreigners in literary property and copyright are not recognised in the States. England's proposal to conclude a treaty of equal rights in this matter was rejected. The consequence is that American booksellers are able to issue cheaper editions of English books and magazines, and thus to place within the reach of the poorest the means of satisfying their intellectual cravings.

In the general use of the older English literature there is no difference between America and England, and it may be taken as a matter of course that English classics form the foundation in all American schools. Their common literature is a strong and indestructible bond between America and England, and even in America it is not anticipated that the classical works of the old country will ever be superseded by transatlantic productions.

In order to form a correct appreciation of the quality, importance, and originality of American literature, a brief survey of the American national character, and of social conditions in the United States, is necessary.

One principal cause of the many mistakes and prejudices current with regard to the United States is due to disregard of local differences. Occurrences and characteristics which belong to a particular district or state are treated as universal, and general conclusions are drawn from personal idiosyncrasies or local peculiarities. Now there is no country on earth in which there are such marked and startling contrasts as in the American Union. There is, to begin with, the enormous contrast between the North and the South. It is true that since the close of the four years' civil war the union between the two has been firmly cemented, and that any serious fresh attempt at separation is altogether improbable within any conceivable period. But how divided are the interests, how different the standard of education and the combination of races, and consequently how unequal is the share taken by each in the production of literature! To judge only by the number of printing offices, the intellectual activity of the North— more particularly of the states of New England— is at least seven times greater and more productive than that of the South, with its twelve s'ates of four times greater area.

The whole structure of society in the States differs essentially from that on this side of the Atlantic. There no insurmountable barriers hinder the social progress of the citizen. Class prerogatives, a court, an aristocracy, a privileged hierarchy, titles, orders, a servile class, are unrecognised by the genuine American. Only the Irish, the Chinese, the negro, and now and then a German condescends to enter domestic service. All class distinctions are fluctuating; the portals of every profession stand open to all. The wheel of fortune revolves rapidly; a man may be to-day a minister, a senator, a governor; to-morrow a merchant, a manufacturer, a lawyer. Nowhere is there an impassable gulf. Even the contrasts between rich and poor, which are so difficult to obliterate or even to smooth over, lose much of their sharpness and bitterness—first, because, according to the general opinion, it is easier in America than elsewhere for an individual to work himself up from indigence to competence, and even to riches; and secondly, because the idle enjoyment of the gifts of fortune is held in contempt, and the wealthy assiduously court popularity by founding benevolent institutions. Such institutions, whether elementary or higher grade schools, art schools, or philanthropic institutions of various kinds, are more numerous and better endowed in America than elsewhere. Undoubtedly the founders are to a great extent influenced by the desire to immortalise their own names.

A mixture of many different qualities lies at the foundation of the American character. From the English the American has inherited his energy of will and tenacity of purpose, his receptivity and preference for what is practicable, measurable and financially profitable, and his indifference or distaste for all that does not give him the impression of immediate practical utility. Hence the American shares with the Englishman an aversion for speculative philosophy; metaphysics fail to interest him; he has no genius for abstract theories or ideal systems. If the English, the French, and the Germans are pre-eminent as the discoverers of natural laws and physical forces, to the Americans is due the honour of being richer in inventions, so much so that in the opinion even of a British critic⁶ America is twenty years ahead of England in technical inventions and in political and commercial undertakings. In Appleton's 'Nationa Biography' the title

⁶ *Nineteenth Century*, June, 189 p. 799.

'inventor' is fixed to the names of a number of men, as though it denoted a profession or calling. A writer in the 'Nineteenth Century' contends that England must gather up all her strength if she is to overtake her great rival and keep abreast of her ; but that if once she succeeds in doing so she need trouble herself no further about the possible progress of other states. America has been specially successful in inventions for the saving of time and human labour by mechanical contrivances, the necessity for this having been forced upon her by want of hands. For, as has already been remarked, persons of British extraction will not undertake household or domestic service, whilst Irishmen, who are ready to offer themselves, are not welcomed. The American, from his education and the moral atmosphere by which he is surrounded, is imbued with a sense of self-reliance. He far more frequently errs from an exaggerated self-confidence than from the opposite failing of diffidence as to his own powers. He readily believes himself capable of overcoming obstacles apparently insurmountable. He is a member and citizen of a state with a 'manifest destiny'— that is to say, he lives in the full assurance that his republic is destined by Providence, within a measurable period, to extend its rule over the whole continent, and even beyond it.

Strangers visiting America are astonished to find public opinion so unanimous, and the people so submissive to it that few venture to oppose its verdict. I find that even Americans resent this condition of things as a tyranny, though only anonymously, and in the British Press. The fact is explained by the dead level of the mass of the population, amongst whom no social gradations, no aristocracy, or privileged or learned classes can properly be said to exist, where one great middle class fuses all society into itself, and where each individual knows that, while the doors of every profession stand open to all, he must not by any openly expressed deviation from prevailing opinion create an obstacle to his own career. English observers have recently pointed out that in America there are none of the 'grumblers' so frequently met with in England. Yet no doubt they exist, and in no inconsiderable number, in that class especially who are best acquainted with the real state of things, and who are in a position to draw comparisons between matters at home and abroad. But the dread of the one almighty monarch, Public Opinion, closes their mouths, besides which, no one would wantonly choose to expose to a stranger the failings of his own nation. Emerson has remarked that the American Eagle very often closely resembles a peacock. An American boy leaves school in most cases too early, and before his mind is matured, in order that he may not be left behind in the great race of life. He finds himself forthwith in full possession of civil rights, and, as an elector, has to decide upon the weightiest political questions. His first real school is life; he begins with practice, he ends with theory. 'Help yourself' is almost the first precept inculcated in childhood, and it accompanies him in every stage of his career. This precept falls in with the prevailing optimism, the conviction that the political and social state of things around him is the best that exists on the earth.

Another noticeable feature in the American character is the love of travel. The countries of southern and central Europe have an irresistible attraction for Americans, many of whom either make a voluntary sojourn in foreign lands of some years' duration, or travel to and fro at intervals. What is the motive which impels them so frequently to cross the ocean? It has been said that it is the desire to foster the flattering conviction of the superiority of everything at home in contrast with the state of things in Europe:

Et quibus ipse malis careas quin cernere suave est.

Be this as it may, the better organs of the American Press give us to understand that the more educated are influenced by other and higher motives—the desire for self-culture by personal acquaintance with all those advantages which are to be found in Europe alone.

Attendance at lectures on instructive and even strictly scientific subjects has become with Americans a kind of necessity, and is now the universal custom even in villages as well as small towns, whilst in the large towns audiences of a thousand persons of both sexes are not unfrequent. To us it may appear astonishing to read of a travelling lecturer earning 10,000 dollars by lectures on Ethics. The most popular subject, however, is Natural Science.

A learned class, i.e. a class of men whose lifetime is devoted to the pursuit and extension of knowledge, does not exist in America. Specialists in physical science, mechanics, and technical knowledge abound; but there are few who would be reckoned by us as genuine scholars, and those who might be considered as such, have for the most part gained their information, not at home, but in Germany, France, or England. These are just the men who are seized periodically with the longing to breathe an intellectual atmosphere in Europe, although their frequent visits to this continent do not loosen their attachment to their fatherland.

In America there are no academies, no colleges with Fellows, such as the English universities have the good fortune to possess. Every man must depend upon his own resources, and if he possesses no private income, must make his livelihood by his literary work.

The wish, so earnestly expressed by Washington in his testament to the nation, that a central university should be founded in the United States, remains still unfulfilled. America has not a single college which can compare with even a third-rate German university. There is consequently a great deficiency in the means provided for the advancement of scientific education, or for granting facilities for higher intellectual pursuits. This is especially felt in classical learning, but also acts prejudicially on other special schools, such as law and medicine.

Amongst the things which fetter the progress of literature and learning in America must be reckoned the style of the newspapers. With few exceptions the tone is lower than it is in England. They vie with one another in setting forth the most insignificant matters with startling exaggeration, and spinning out trivialities in long-winded phrases so as to fill the largest possible space. Petty gossip, whole columns filled with the account of some ball, interspersed with vituperations against men even of the highest character, and sensational accounts of crimes or criminal trials—such is the kind of matter, abundant in quantity but poor in quality, which adorns the sheets of the daily Press. So the time for wholesome reading is wasted, the sense and taste for what is worth knowing are blunted and destroyed. It may be truly said that newspapers are the enemies of books, and that they cause many a good book to remain unwritten.

The last few decades have witnessed the development of another evil highly injurious to the constitution of the state, which also has a blighting effect upon literary progress. I refer to the form that the system of official life has taken. President Andrew Jackson and the democratic party that shared his triumph first formulated the watchword 'To the victors belong the spoils,' that is to say, the numerous and well-paid appointments in the president's gift. Upon Jackson's entry into office thousands of officials were ejected for the purpose of rewarding services rendered during the election, and satisfying the greed of party followers. There are in America no pensions for public officials who are anxious or forced to resign, or for widows and orphans. Herewith has grown up an organized body of men who make a livelihood of politics; these are a heavy burden upon society, and embitter the life of thousands of families by the dread of imminent starvation. In Europe the book-buying and reading public consists of that wide middle stratum of the educated and half-educated of which the backbone is the numerous class of government servants, the higher ranks of the army, the clergy, and the medical profession, living in the repose of an assured position. Next to and depending on them are the classes engaged in trade, manufacture, and the higher kinds of handicraft. But in America those social grades in which the readers and authors of standard literature are to be found are either absent or represented only in very small numbers. Whole departments of professional life are wanting of which the proper duties left to the care of individuals; there is no military class represented by officers in the army; the majority of the medical men lack the necessary training.

One capital fault in the American literature of the day may be expressed in a word : it is too democratic. The democratic spirit pervading politics penetrates and luxuriates in the organs of intellectual life. The opinion expressed in the fourth decade of this century by Professor Schaff, a competent and very favourable critic, that scarcely one in twenty of the literary productions of the Union deserves to see the light, would appear, to judge by the lamentations of the best reviews, to apply no less to the present time. It would be a literary task of the highest kind to counteract the consequences of this omnipotence of democracy. Things have already gone so far that in the Southern states one-half of those who are entitled, by the right of universal suffrage, to vote at the elections are unable to read. Every day the notion gathers strength amongst the great body of electors that nothing in the state is permanent or unassailable, that with this mass, and its ephemeral majorities, rests the ultimate decision of everything, and that in every department of life it alone has the power to make and unmake the laws.

For this reason serious and dispassionate observers do not regard the future without anxiety and gloomy foreboding. There are many difficulties and complications of which no one knows the solution. Undoubtedly the bulk of the nation is loyal to the Constitution; any attempt to change it would be met with universal and energetic resistance. Yet the Constitution itself contains internal contradictions; the limitations and barriers which it has set up seem to render impossible reforms that are not only pressing but universally desired. The enormous power which lies in the hands of the great railway companies is regarded in government circles as no slight danger.

There are, besides, two ever-present and pressing problems which baffle any attempt at solution. First, what is to become of the increasing millions of negroes and coloured people to whom full rights of citizenship have been granted without any possibility of their admission to the social life of the community? Secondly, what measures ought to be taken with respect to the ceaseless influx of European immigrants? For the scantily populated South fresh settlers are indispensable, and they meet there with hearty welcome and assistance; in the North they are daily becoming an intolerable and dangerous burden.

It was formerly supposed that America was strong and healthy enough to absorb all the elements of moral disease year by year imported into her by the immigration of so many outcasts of European society. This hope, however, has not been justified, and the prospect in the future is becoming more and more gloomy. The German immigrants, it is admitted, are as a rule moral, peaceable, and useful members of the community, or they soon become so. But all the stronger is the aversion felt for the Irish and to some extent for the English immigrants, many of whom are discharged convicts. They go to swell the proletariate in the large towns and crowd with criminals the American prisons and houses of correction.

Another difficult problem, which can only be solved if leading men will arouse and direct public opinion through the medium of the Press, especially in periodicals, is the marriage question, which for want of uniform legislation has fallen into sad disorder. The state legislatures, with whom has rested the responsibility, have in most cases treated the question carelessly and with arbitrary caprice;

divorce has become extraordinarily frequent. A general law based on Christian principles is urgently needed.

Such questions supply the chief topics in the current literature of the day on the other side of the ocean, and are warmly discussed not only there, but in England, Germany, and France also. For thoughtful men of all nations are strongly convinced that these subjects affect the whole of mankind more or less for weal or for woe.

Let us now take a brief glance at recent American literature, under the competent guidance of the still unfinished National Biography by James Grant Wilson and John Fiske, already mentioned. The meaning of democracy and its claims become clear from a glance at these pages.

Evidently it is far easier to become a celebrity in America than in Europe. Thousands of persons find a place in this biography whose history might be comprised in these words: he was born, became a lawyer, or a journalist, married and died. Still more surprising is the disproportionately large number of women who are all supposed to be famous, or, at any rate, interesting. The number of books mentioned in biographical works as written by women is ten times greater than that recorded in similar works of other nations. However, one must allow that the social position of women in America is very favourable to literature, if not exactly to learning, and in this respect the American nation differs from all others, certainly not to its disadvantage.

If we consider American literature from the religious, or rather denominational point of view, it appears to be like the English, and, in some ways, more essentially Protestant. For the spirit of the old Puritanism, although in thought and practice much weakened or softened, still survives. To it is due the rigorous rejection of any hierarchy or priesthood claiming to be the necessary intermediary and channel of grace between God and the believer. The Catholic Church in America numbers, indeed, six millions,[7] but the majority are Irish and Germans, who are very recent settlers, and are under the direction of a clergy born and educated abroad. The German Catholics, many of whom are labourers and mechanics, escape observation on account of their position and language, but the Irish are held in general contempt, and are reckoned as morally and intellectually an inferior race. Criminal statistics place them in a very unfavourable light. They have certainly managed to make themselves felt and feared, ever since the Fenians were allowed openly and with impunity to preach political murder; and the Tammany Ring in New York has revealed to what extent, thanks to the American Municipal Constitution, even one of the world's capitals can be robbed by a determined band of swindlers. It is hardly to be expected that, by a common feeling of patriotism and habits of social intercourse, the Catholic portion of the population will ever be brought to unite with the great Protestant masses in mutual toleration and esteem; for the conviction prevails everywhere that a believing Catholic must necessarily, at least at heart, be an opponent of the Constitution and of the judicial principles of the Union, since these are at variance with the teaching of his Church.

Protestant theology in America can point to no leader or master whose name is recognised as an authority by the nation. This fact is due to the diversity of denominations or sects, which are, almost without exception, of European origin, and continue to own some sort of allegiance to the land of their birth, be it England, or Holland, or any other country. Translations of German theological works are so numerous and in such demand that American works of the same kind take an inferior position and are little known to Europe.

A people wholly addicted to politics like the Americans need, at least for their leaders, historical training. Many,

[7] 6,378,858 members, with 6,366 ecclesiastics, according to the official report of the Catholic Calendar of 1881.

indeed, may possess some amount of historical information, but this is far from implying the historical culture necessary to enable the genuine statesman to form a correct judgment of current events, the history of the future.

America is rich in one department of history, that of biography, and in this she follows the example of the mother-country, for in England the number of biographies published is greater than anywhere else in Europe. But the two countries differ in this respect, that England produces many more autobiographies. The reason may well lie in the great contrast, made evident in so many ways, between the aristocratic and democratic tone of mind. On the other side of the ocean men are much afraid of running counter to the prevailing idea of universal equality, if by thrusting their personality into notice they put themselves upon a pedestal. But the number of lives of famous or quasi-famous American statesmen, politicians or authors written by friends, relations, or admirers, or frequently by the wife of the hero, is simply endless. Twelve biographies of Washington have already appeared, and others are still forthcoming. The same may be said of lives of Jefferson and Franklin. Persons whose position in society is so insignificant that their reputation has never extended beyond the limits of a country town, find partial and admiring biographers.

As a contribution to literary history, the excellent work of Ticknor on Spanish Literature still stands alone. It must be frankly acknowledged that no small credit is due to Americans for their histories of Spain and of Spanish America, as the above-mentioned works of Prescott, as well as those of Irving and Gayarré, show. The thought of a 'manifest destiny,' and the hope that the Spanish-speaking portion of America will one day become a part of the Great Union, turn intellectual effort in this direction.

That the history of England is unrepresented in American literature by works of independent research is natural.

VIII PART TAKEN BY NORTH AMERICA IN LITERATURE 289

Within the last forty or fifty years the mother-country has produced a number of most excellent works on her own history. Transatlantic historians cannot come into competition with authors like Lingard, Macaulay, Freeman, Froude, and Green. The politico-religious point of view, moreover, from which the American looks at the past history of England, is sufficiently represented by competent writers in the old country.

German history would seem to possess no attractions for Americans, as they are satisfied with a translation of the work of Wolfgang Menzel. Four editions of Ranke's 'History of the Popes' have been published. The first part of his 'Universal History' has also been translated, but the rest of his works are only accessible to the scanty number of German readers.

It is more surprising that Roman history should as yet have found no adequate exponent, since of all histories that of Rome is the most instructive to the politician, and it might be supposed that a people amongst whom politicians are legion would be eager to welcome a work on that subject.

Yet Americans are behind no other nation in the diligent and careful elaboration of their own history. The works of Bancroft and of Francis Parkman are as brilliant as they are scholarly and trustworthy. Bancroft's great history is a national monument, κατ' ἐξοχήν; the patriotic sentiment which it breathes seldom oversteps the proper bounds.

The most noticeable American work on the history of civilisation is that of Amos Dean, who left it incomplete at his death in 1868, although seven volumes had already appeared. The author is the type of a 'self-made man,' as the phrase there goes, *i.e.* of a man who owes everything to his own exertions. He had no knowledge either of the classics or of modern languages, and could consequently only make use of English books. For a considerable time he carried on business as a lawyer, and afterwards he became professor of jurisprudence, and wrote a series of legal works, which have been much praised; amongst them a handbook of medical jurisprudence. His work on civilisation was to have been, he hoped, his *monumentum ære perennius*, but his system of compilation and the arrangement of his materials show that he lacked the primary qualifications of an historian.

John William Draper, professor of chemistry and physiology in New York, wrote a history of the intellectual development of Europe, which has been thought worth translating into German. In America itself the book has been somewhat neglected, but not so in Europe, where his master, Buckle, has found not a few followers. Draper, following the bent of his professional studies, carries natural laws into the history of mankind, and develops a system of physical fatalism, which in the end makes all original research or enquiry into particulars superfluous, as it is a matter of indifference whether ten or ten thousand examples are brought forward to prove a law which acts from physical necessity.

Of works on the history of Greek philosophy we have only to notice a book by Professor B. F. Cocker of Michigan,[8] who maintains, on very insufficient grounds, that the Greek system and theories were the precursors and pioneers of Christianity.

Oriental studies in connexion with the history of religions are at present receiving great attention in Europe. Important discoveries inviting further investigation have been made; but Transatlantic scholars show little energy on the subject, and do not even seem inclined to profit by results already obtained. One work, however, deserves to be named, coming from the pen of a very prolific and liberal-minded author, the Unitarian, James Freeman Clarke,[9] who has thought out and introduced, if not a new

---

[8] *Christianity and Greek Philosophy.* New York, 1870.

[9] *Ten Great Religions: an Essay in Comparative Theology.* Boston, 1871.

religion, at least a peculiar form of worship. Clarke in his book draws a comparison between ten different religions and Christianity.

Legal science is the study which most attracts the youth of America, because it forms the best preparation and recommendation for taking an active part in politics, and opens the surest way to office and a salary. Law schools exist in considerable numbers, but the system of teaching and study is more practical than theoretical, and includes a smaller number of departments than in Germany. Roman law, which with us takes so important a place, is entirely disregarded; elementary works are thought sufficient, and of these I have noted only six. Any knowledge of canon law is thought superfluous, owing to the complete severance of Church and State. Protestant ecclesiastical law does not exist. German law or general constitutional history never came under consideration. The subjects for instruction are therefore limited to English common law and to American statute law, in which, owing to the numberless yearly additions made to it, everything depends upon a good memory.

America has a national economy peculiar to itself. It has produced a school of which the founder and master was Matthew Carey, who died in 1839. His most important work was translated into German and was published in Munich.[1] He was a bookseller of Irish extraction. Irish hatred of England, and American optimism form the motives and foundation of his system. His optimism rests upon the possibility, which he magnified into a general law, of the most unlimited geographical development ever conceived even by Transatlantic imagination. In spite of his many inaccuracies, he is held in considerable repute as an apologist for the system of high protective duties still maintained by the Republican party.

---

[1] [The work translated was not that of Matthew Carey, but of his son, Henry Charles.]

The sphere of poetry is much more restricted in America than amongst European nations. In the first place, poetical tradition is wanting. There are no old popular songs; the Puritans did not bring with them the rich treasury of English song, and their descendants were of too rigid a temper to create popular poetry for themselves. For the same reason there is no original dramatic literature. Comedy, as well as the more serious dramas, lacks the necessary materials. Life is too dry and uniform to be represented on the stage by mirthful scenes and comical entanglements, whilst the youthful nation lacks the historical material for serious plots.

Bret Harte, the favourite poet of the day, whom Freiligrath has introduced into Germany, is a poetical autobiographer of singular power and truthfulness; the theme of his verses is the narrative of his own experience amongst the Californian gold-diggers. Next to him in popularity comes Mark Twain, whose real name is Samuel Langhorne Clemens. Once a boatman on the Mississippi, he is now a merry scoffer at human folly, or what appears to him as such, and the most versatile amongst the writers of his country. In mastery of language, however, they are both far behind their predecessor, Edgar Allan Poe, who, after an adventurous life full of vicissitudes, and far from blameless, died in hospital at the age of forty, 1849. Bret Harte is the American Dickens; and it may be presumed, from the beautiful poetical ode composed upon the death of the latter in 1870, that he regarded Dickens as his master and model. Nature and life in California are depicted in his stories and sketches with poetic truth and beauty, placing before us in a few touches a vivid picture of colonial life on the border-line between barbarism and rising civilisation.

In discussing the literature of a people, works of fiction must not be left out. They are more in demand among all classes of the nation than any other books, and in the number published during the past fifty years America is at least on a level with England, France, or Germany. She has even invented new varieties of fiction which have rapidly made their way in the old world; so much so that even in England, formerly the classic ground of good novels, the American novel is now preferred. Germans seem to have come to the same opinion, for they reprint American novels both in the original and in translations. Personally I am acquainted with only one, 'Democracy,' and I confess that I found in it much desired information on that subject.

Youthful as American literature still is, it has as yet survived, we cannot say got over, two very prevalent diseases, which have been imported into Europe, where they have proved extraordinarily infectious.

One of these diseases originated in the brain of an elderly lady.[2]

. . . .

Whether the disease just mentioned be of a purely literary character or not, the other, Spiritualism, which has created a literature of its own, is certainly a moral malady of a very malignant type, and is one of the most extraordinary phenomena in the history of widespread popular delusions. It was reckoned in 1865 that over two millions in America had accepted the teaching of spiritualism, that is to say, of the spiritualist prophets Edmonds and Davis.

A word, in conclusion, on the subject of language. English is at present the spoken and written language of ninety millions of people; it is the common language of two nations of which each is a world-power. Each, despite a diversity of interests, is physically and intellectually bound to the other. They must, therefore, in the future continue to possess the same literature, and with it a common store of ideas and theories. To the Anglo-Saxon race, rather than to the German or the Slav, is assigned in the coming age the intellectual supremacy that in ancient

[2] [Some remarks upon the originator of the Shakespeare-Bacon theory, Miss Delia Bacon, were here intended to follow, but were omitted both in the lecture when delivered, and in Döllinger's MS.]

times belonged to the Greeks and afterwards to the Romans. The Germans will have their share in this primacy, and assuredly it will not be a small one; but they will have it indirectly merely through the medium of the English language. The German language can never become universal, because it is so difficult to acquire. It is right and needful that we should distinctly and betimes acknowledge this to be the case.

INDEX

ADENULF

Adenulf Papareschi, 184
Ado of Vienna, 151
Adoptionist controversy, 110-119
Adrian, Pope, 96, 101-104, 116
Aeneas Silvius, 176, 177
Aetius, 81, 133
Akbar, Emperor, 54, 67
Alberich, 156
Albrecht, King, 169
Alcuin, 120, 132
America and England, 272
America, North, and religious freedom, 246-248
American Literature, 269-294; beginnings of, 270; Milton's influence, 270; newspapers, 271, 283; Jonathan Edwards, 271; Franklin, 272; *Edinburgh Review*, 1828, 273; Emerson, 273; state of, 1845, 275; England's influence on, 275-278, 279; fetters on, 283; democracy of, 284-286; recent, 286-293; diseases of, 293
Anagni, events at, 181-201; eye-witnesses cited, 181, 182; other chroniclers, 194-201; Dante on the, 188
Andrea, Valentine, 11
Angilbert, son-in-law and confidant of Charlemagne, 116, 119, 120, 123, 124
Appendix on the Knights Templars, 219; on religious freedom, 251
Aquinas, Thomas, 252
Arians, the, 234
Arnold of Brescia, 158
—— — Lisieux, 158
Artaxerxes Mnemon, 64
Augustine pleads for religious coercion, 233
Austria, universities of, 19

CHANNING

B

Bab, a founder of religion, 70
Bacon, Roger, on law, 2
Balbo, Count Cesare, on Dante, 36
Baldus, school of, 6
Bancroft, historian, 289
Bartolus, school of, 6
Belgian universities, 30
Berlin, University of, 18
Bernard Guidonis, 167
— of Parma, 164
Berzelius, 31
Beza and religious coercion, 237
Biography of Charles, 152
Blackie, Professor, on Scotch universities, 27
Bohemia and religious strife, 240
Bologna, School of Law at, 1
Boniface VIII. at Anagni, 182-192; at Rome, 192
Bonizo of Sutri, 315-155
Bonn, University of, 19
Bossi, Donato, 177
Brand, Sebastian, 7
Breslau, university of, 19
Bret Harte, 292
Broglie, Duc de, on the French Revolution, 255, 256
Buddha, 56
Byzantium, 75, 112

C

Calvin, founder of a religion, 69; and religious coercion, 237
Capito and toleration, 237
Carey, Matthew, 291
Cassiodorus, 79, 81
Channing, W. E., 274

CHARLES

Charles the Great and the Patriciate, 94, 96, 104, 113; donation to the Pope, 103; owner of Rome, 105; crowned Emperor, 105, 126, 132; events leading thereto, 106 *seqq.*; views as to Papal authority, 109; and the Byzantine Court, 112; and Synods, 110, 115; in Rome, A.D. 801, 147; death of, 814, 149. *See* Coronation, Irene, Leo III.
Christianity and Islam, 251
Christians, early, why persecuted, 229
Chroniclers, mediæval, on the coronation of Charles, 150-180; on the events at Anagni, 181-201
Chrysostom on religious freedom, 233
Church of the Reformation. 253
Clarke, James Freeman, 290
Clemens, S. L., 'Mark Twain,' 292
Clement V., Pope, and the Knights Templars, 210-217
Cocker, Professor B. F., 290
Codex Carolinus, 99
Coercion, early religious, 231-236
Collège de France, 24
Cologne, Annals of, 150
Comte a founder of religion, 71
Confucius, 55
Conring, Hermann, 12
Constans II. and Rome, 88
Constantine and religious liberty, 230 son of Irene, 115, 117, 175
Cooper, Fenimore, 274
Coronation of Charles the Great, 105, 106, 123; Roman and Frankish views thereon, 127-132, 139; Greek sentiments, 134-136
Counter-Reformation, the, 237
Cromwell and religion, 65
Crusades, the, and religious coercion, 235
Curtisan, a, on the events at Anagni, 181, 182, 185, 186, 190, 192
Czech universities, 29

D

Dahlmann on Denmark, 35
Danish universities, 30
Dante, on study in Italy, 2; German and Italian works on, 36; on the coronation of Charles, 162; on the events at Anagni, 188
Dean, Amos, 289
Decretal of Innocent III., 164

GEILER

Decretals, the, 2
Detmar of Lübeck, 199
Dietrich of Niem, 176
Diocletian, persecution by, 230
Donation of Constantine, 101
Draper, John William, 290
Dubois, Peter, 169
Dukes, Roman, 93
Dumont and the art of government, 262
Dutch universities, 30

E

Edict of Nantes, the, 253
Education in German universities, 20
Edwards, Jonathan, 271
Eginhard and Charlemagne, 118, 120, 125, 132
Ekkehard of Aurach, 156
Emerson on American intellect, 273
England and religious freedom, 243-245
English universities, 25
Era, the new, 81
Este, Chronicle of, 196

F

Faculties and sciences, duty of, 22
Ferreto of Vicenza, 192, 198
Fichte, 16-18
Formulæ, Book of, 90
Franklin, Benjamin, 272
Freedom, history of religious, 229-250; present state of, 248-250; appendix to, 251-254
French Revolution, the, 255; benefits of, 256; illusive glory of, 256; literature of, 257-263; was it avoidable, 263; the cause of, 265, 268; false views on behalf of, 265; the court and, 266; Paris and, 266; uniqueness of, 267; the Church and, 268
Fulda, Annals of, 150

G

Galerius grants toleration, 230
Galileo, 11
Gallienus legalises Christianity, 230
Geijer, 31
Geiler of Kaisersberg, 7

INDEX

GEOGRAPHY

Geography, German, 48
German universities, 5 *seqq.*; fourfold purpose of, 37
Gervase of Tilbury, 160
Gifts, allocation to nations of, 31; specially German, 31
Gladstone on Huber, 34
Gneist on English Law, &c., 35
Goethe and the French Revolution, 264; on the historic sense, 38
Gottfried of Viterbo, 159
Göttingen from 1734, 14
Gregorovius on Boniface VIII., 183, 195
— on Charles the Great, 118, 122
Grimm, Hermann, and the French Revolution, 261
Grimm, Jacob, 39
Gymnasien, 20, 25

H

Haen, de, 19
Halle from 1690 to 1730, 14, 18
Haller, 21
Hameln, Chronicle of, 178
Heathenism persecuted, 230; restored, 231; extinct, 231
Hegel's philosophy, 42
Hegel on Italy, 35
Heinrich of Hervord, 174
Helinand, 156
Heliogabalus and religion, 64
Henry VIII. as founder of religion, 64
Historic sense, the, 34-37; heroes of, 38; application of, 39-44
History in Germany, universal, 43
Honorius of Autun, 151
Huber's *Geschichte der englischen Universitäten*, 34
Hugo of Flavigny, 156
Hugo, science of law, 39
Hugo, Victor, on the French Revolution, 260
Humanists, the, 9
Humboldt, A. von, 38
Humboldt, W. von, 18

I

Imperium Romanum, 82, 85, 90, 144, 145
Inquisition, the, 235, 252; in France, 209; in Italy, 242
Inventions in N. America, 279

VOL. II.

LIBER

Irene, Empress, 114, 117, 133
Irving, Henry, 70
— Washington, 274, 288
Istorie Pistolesi, 196
Italian universities, 28
Italy and religious strife, 242

J

Jena and 'Natural Philosophy,' 16
Johannes Diaconus, 123
John of Viktring, 199
John of Yprès, 175
Joseph, Emperor, and toleration, 238
Julian and heathenism, 231
Justinian, 84-86

K

Kant, 16
Kneeling in homage, 142
Knightly orders and toleration, the, 235
Knights Templars, the, 202-228; guilt of the, 202; recent authorities—German, 203, 205; French, 204; Italian, 204; English, 205; American, foot-note, 205; seized, 213; tortured, 213; and the Pope's instructions, 215; articles of accusation against, 216-218; observations on the trial of, 225-228. *See* Order
Königsberg and Kant, 16

L

Lamartine and the French Revolution, 257, 259
Lambert of Hersfeld, 156
Language, the English, 293; the French, in Germany, 14; Latin *v.* German, 12
Lappenberg, 35
Law, study of, 2; Dante and Roger Bacon on, 2; Roman and German, 5
Laws against heretics, 251
Leibnitz, 14, 21
Leo, Emperor, 77-79
Leo of Orvieto, 164
Leo III., Pope, 105-109, 118, 122-129, 128, 142, 146, 149. *See* Coronation
Liber Pontificalis, 107, 122, 138, 150, 153, 251

X

L

Linnæus, 31
Literature, history of, 44
Lombards, the, 87; kingdom of, 87; conversion of, 87; residence of, 88; and the Popes, 90, 91; and the Italian people, 96-98; subdued, 98, 102
Lorsch, annals of, 107, 156
Ludwig, Emperor, 148
Luther, 68; and religious freedom, 236

M

Magnus of Reichersperg, 152
Malmesbury Chronicle, 175
Malvezzi of Brescia, 163
Mansi, Chronicle at, 192
Marbach, Annals of, 152
Marianus, the Monk, 156
Martin, Henri, on the French Revolution, 260
— of Fulda, 174
— the Minorite, 173
Martinus Polonus, 163, 167
Medicine, Germans on, 41
Meisterlin of Nürnberg, 178
Melanchthon and religious coercion, 237
Mignet on the French Revolution, 257, 259
Missionaries of the Middle Ages, 251
Modesty, academic, 23
Mohammedanism, origin and progress of, 57
Moissac, chronicle of, 107
Molay, Jacques de, Grand Master of the Knights Templars, 214; accusations against, 214; confession of, 214; retractation of, 214
Monk of St. Gall, the, 150
Motto, Döllinger's, 49

N

Naples, University of, 1
Napoleon a Mahdi, 65; and universities, 24
Netherlands, the, and religious freedom, 245, 246
Nicholas of Cusa, 7, 178
Niebuhr, 38
Nogaret and the events at Anagni, 181 seqq.; and the Knights Templars, 207
Normal year, the, 238
Numa Pompilius, 63

O

Odoacer, 77-82
Order of Knights Templars, the: foundation and rule of, 219; constitution of, 220; admission into and withdrawal from, 221; rule of life of, 221; ranks of, 222; alleged wealth of, 223. *See* Knights Templars
Orderic Vitalis, 160
Orestes, the patrician, 79
Orvieto, the chronicler of, on the events at Anagni, 182, 186-188, 190-193
Ostrogothic kingdom, the, 82; fall of, 83
Otto of Freising, 157

P

Padua, school of law at, 1
Papal chair, 685-752, the, 89; and the house of Arnulf, 98 seqq.
Paris, high school of, 3
Parkman, Francis, 289
Parma, annals of, 197; chronicle of, 192
Patriciate, the Roman, 92-96
Paulinus of Aquileia, 110
Peace of 1555, religious, 237
Persecutions, effect of the, 239
Peter of Andlau, 7, 179
Philip the Fair and Boniface VIII., 182 seqq.; and the Knights Templars, 206 seqq.
Philo, 61
Philology, German, 42, 43
Philosophy, German, 42
Pilgrim Fathers, the, 270
Pipin, King, and the Patriciate, 94, 95; and the Papal chair, 99-102
Pipin the chronicler, 198
Plotinus, 61
Poland and religious strife, 241
Polish universities, 29
Political science, German, 41
Popes, the, and the Greek emperors, 91
Prague, University of, 5
Prescott, W., historian, 274, 288
Priscillian, first heretic beheaded on German soil, 232
Procopius, 82, 84
Prophetic office, the, 57
Prussia, regeneration of, 17
Prutz, Hans, on the Templars, 203

INDEX

P

Publicists, the, on the transference of the empire, 170-173

R

Radulf de Diceto, 161
Rainulf of Supino at Anagni, 185
Rambaldi of Imola, 176
Ranke, History of France by, 35 ; on the Templars, 203
Ravenna and Rome, 88
Reformation, the, and religious freedom, 236
Reil, 18
Religion, universality of, 51; and morality, 51; origin of, 51, 55; new developments of, 71
Religions, founders of, 50-72; the *term* defined and limited, 52 ; impulsive periods, 54 ; requisites for the, 56 ; Akbar, 54 ; Artaxerxes Mnemon, 64; Bab, 70 ; Buddha, 56 ; Calvin, 69 ; Comte, 71 ; Confucius, 55 ; Cromwell, 65 ; Heliogabalus, 64; Henry VIII., 64 ; Irving, 70 ; Luther, 58 ; Mohammed, 57 ; Napoleon, 65 ; Numa Pompilius, 63 ; Saint-Simon, 70 ; Swedenborg, 60 ; Zoroaster, 56
Respublica Romana, 89, 90, 92, 102
Restitution, in the Papal sense, 100
Revolution. *See* French, &c.
Richard of Poitiers, 161
Ricimer, 77, 78
Ricobald of Ferrara, 163
Ristoro Castaldo, 179
Ritter, Karl, 39
Roger de Hoveden, 161
Rolewink, 176
Roman conception of religion, 229
Rome, old and new, 73-77; and Ravenna, 88
Romuald of Salerno, 159
Romulus Augustulus, 79, 81
Roscher on political science, 41
Rudolf of Habsburg, 168
Ruinart, chronicle of, 81
Russian universities, 30

S

Saint-Simon, a founder of religion, 70
Salerno, medical school at, 1
Savigny, 18, 35, 39
Scaliger, 21

Schack, Von, 35
Schäffner, 35
Schelling, 16
Schisms, religious, 67
Schleiermacher, 18
Schools, high and special, 1 *seqq.*
Sciarra Colonna at Anagni, 185
Scotch universities, 27
Ségur on the French Church, 268
Senate, the Roman, 75-77, 83
Servetus, the burning of, 237
Shakespeare, commentaries on, 35
Sicard of Cremona, 159
Sieges of old Rome, A.D., 75
Siena, chronicler of, 196
Siffrid of Meissen, 173
Sigebert of Gembloux, 156
Simeon of Durham, 196
Society, U.S. America, 278-282 ; negroes, 285 ; immigrants, 285 ; marriage, 285
Spangenberg, 14
Spanish Netherlands, the, 254
Spanish universities, 29
Speier, Annals of, 174
Spittler's history, 15
Sprengel, Kurt, 41
Staël, Madame de, on the French Revolution, 255
Stein, 35
Stilicho, 76
Stoll, 19
Strasburg, Annals of, 157
Students, address to, 46
Studium Generale, 3
Style, allocation of, 34
Swedenborg, a founder of religion, 60, 62
Swedish universities, 30
Swiss universities, 30
Synods and coercion, 234 ; of Nicea and Frankfort, 110

T

Tae-ping rebellion, the, 63
Taine on the French Revolution, 256, 261, 262
Terreur, La, 258, 259, 262
Tertullian on religious freedom, 232
Theodoric the Ostrogoth, 82-85
Theodosius I., and heathenism, 231; establishes Christianity, 231 ; denounces heresy, 231
Theology, importance of, 39, 47-49
Thierry, Amadée, on the French Revolution, 259

www.ingramcontent.com/pod-product-compliance
Lightning Source LLC
Chambersburg PA
CBHW022057230426
43672CB00008B/1202